Critical Criminological Perspectives

Series editors:

Professor Reece Walters: Faculty of Law, Queensland University of Technology, Australia

Dr. Deborah Drake: Department of Social Policy and Criminology, The Open University, UK

The Palgrave *Critical Criminological Perspectives* book series aims to showcase the importance of critical criminological thinking when examining problems of crime, social harm and criminal and social justice. Critical perspectives have been instrumental in creating new research agendas and areas of criminological interest. By challenging state defined concepts of crime and rejecting positive analyses of criminality, critical criminological approaches continually push the boundaries and scope of criminology, creating new areas of focus and developing new ways of thinking about, and responding to, issues of social concern at local, national and global levels. Recent years have witnessed a flourishing of critical criminological narratives and this series seeks to capture the original and innovative ways that these discourses are engaging with contemporary issues of crime and justice.

Titles include:

Kerry Carrington, Matthew Ball, Erin O'Brien and Juan Tauri
CRIME, JUSTICE AND SOCIAL DEMOCRACY
International Perspectives

Claire Cohen
MALE RAPE IS A FEMINIST ISSUE
Feminism, Governmentality and Male Rape

Marianne Colbran
MEDIA REPRESENTATIONS OF POLICE AND CRIME
Shaping the Police Television Drama

Pamela Davies, Peter Francis and Tanya Wyatt (*editors*)
INVISIBLE CRIMES AND SOCIAL HARMS

Melissa Dearey
MAKING SENSE OF EVIL
An Interdisciplinary Approach

Michael Dellwing
THE DEATH AND RESURRECTION OF DEVIANCE
Current Ideas and Research

Deborah Drake
PRISONS, PUNISHMENT AND THE PURSUIT OF SECURITY

Margaret Malloch and William Munro (*editors*)
CRIME, CRITIQUE AND UTOPIA

Erin O'Brien, Sharon Hayes and Belinda Carpenter
THE POLITICS OF SEX TRAFFICKING
A Moral Geography

Maggie O'Neill and Lizzie Seal (*editors*)
TRANSGRESSIVE IMAGINATIONS
Crime, Deviance and Culture

Diane Westerhuis, Reece Walters and Tanya Wyatt (*editors*)
EMERGING ISSUES IN GREEN CRIMINOLOGY
Exploring Power, Justice and Harm

Tanya Wyatt
WILDLIFE TRAFFICKING
A Deconstruction of the Crime, the Victims, and the Offenders

---

Critical Criminological Perspectives
Series Standing Order ISBN 9780–230–36045–7 hardback
(*outside North America only*)

You can receive future titles in this series as they are published by placing a standing order. Please contact your bookseller or, in case of difficulty, write to us at the address below with your name and address, the title of the series and the ISBN quoted above.

Customer Services Department, Macmillan Distribution Ltd, Houndmills, Basingstoke, Hampshire RG21 6XS, England

Invisible Crimes and Social Harms

Edited by

Pamela Davies
*Teaching Fellow and Programme Director of Criminology,
Northumbria University, UK*

Peter Francis
*Professor of Learning and Teaching and Pro-Vice Chancellor,
Northumbria University, UK*

and

Tanya Wyatt
Principal Lecturer in Criminology, Northumbria University, UK

Editorial matter and selection © Pamela Davies, Peter Francis and Tanya Wyatt 2014
Individual chapters © Respective authors 2014
Foreword © Nigel South 2014

All rights reserved. No reproduction, copy or transmission of this publication may be made without written permission.

No portion of this publication may be reproduced, copied or transmitted save with written permission or in accordance with the provisions of the Copyright, Designs and Patents Act 1988, or under the terms of any licence permitting limited copying issued by the Copyright Licensing Agency, Saffron House, 6–10 Kirby Street, London EC1N 8TS.

Any person who does any unauthorized act in relation to this publication may be liable to criminal prosecution and civil claims for damages.

The authors have asserted their rights to be identified as the authors of this work in accordance with the Copyright, Designs and Patents Act 1988.

First published 2014 by
PALGRAVE MACMILLAN

Palgrave Macmillan in the UK is an imprint of Macmillan Publishers Limited, registered in England, company number 785998, of Houndmills, Basingstoke, Hampshire RG21 6XS.

Palgrave Macmillan in the US is a division of St Martin's Press LLC, 175 Fifth Avenue, New York, NY 10010.

Palgrave Macmillan is the global academic imprint of the above companies and has companies and representatives throughout the world.

Palgrave® and Macmillan® are registered trademarks in the United States, the United Kingdom, Europe and other countries

ISBN: 978–1–137–34781–7

This book is printed on paper suitable for recycling and made from fully managed and sustained forest sources. Logging, pulping and manufacturing processes are expected to conform to the environmental regulations of the country of origin.

A catalogue record for this book is available from the British Library.

A catalog record for this book is available from the Library of Congress.

Contents

Foreword
Nigel South   vii

Acknowledgements   ix

Notes on Contributors   x

1   Taking Invisible Crimes and Social Harms Seriously   1
Pamela Davies, Peter Francis and Tanya Wyatt

2   Gender First: The Secret to Revealing Sexual Crimes and Victimisations   26
Pamela Davies

3   Politics, Power and the Media: The Visibility of Environmental and Eco Terrorism   44
Hayley Watson and Tanya Wyatt

4   The Visual Acuity of Climate Change   61
Avi Brisman

5   'Honour' Crimes   81
Alexandra Hall

6   Elder Abuse   102
Matthew Hall

7   Selling Sex Invisibly: Solicitation as an Invisible Crime   123
Mary Laing

8   Air Pollution and Invisible Violence   142
Reece Walters

9   Invisible Pillaging: The Hidden Harm of Corporate Biopiracy   161
Tanya Wyatt

10   War and Normative Visibility: Interactions in the Nomos   178
Wayne Morrison

11   Health and Safety 'Crimes' in Britain: The Great Disappearing Act   199
Steve Tombs

| 12 | Regulating Fraud Revisited
Michael Levi | 221 |
| 13 | Invisible Crime, Social Harm and the Radical Criminological Tradition
Peter Francis, Pamela Davies and Tanya Wyatt | 244 |

Index   257

Foreword

Seeing the invisible

In his poem 'When Evil-Doing Comes Like Falling Rain', written in 1935, the German playwright and poet Bertolt Brecht wrote a prescient warning about the horrors that were to come in Nazi Germany. Brecht was drawing attention to what happens when citizens choose to ignore crimes and injustices and when states and societies find it expedient or agreeable to make them invisible:

> When crimes begin to pile up they become invisible. When sufferings become unendurable the cries are no longer heard.

A similar concern is at the heart of Stan Cohen's (2001) magnificent exposure of our many and varied *States of Denial*. Brecht and Cohen both write to appeal to us to open our eyes and see, and to acknowledge the hidden crimes, horrors and indignities inflicted by humans on others. Cohen's work explored themes of truth and deception: the distortion of the former and the ways in which we produce the latter individually and collectively. Cohen examined our personal and political motives for wishing to avoid encounters with uncomfortable realities and how we therefore adopt strategies and vocabularies of avoidance and evasion. This state of being in which we 'know but do not act' is commonplace in our everyday lives: we cannot personally bring world peace or save the starving of the world; we live in media-saturated societies with in-depth news stories available 24/7 but cannot live comfortably with constant exposure to misery and calls on our compassion; and we suffer disillusionment with politicians and turn to cynicism and comedy as therapy (this latter condition being caught in the old Soviet joke that Cohen quotes: a comrade explains why she needs to visit both an optician and an ear specialist, 'What I see, I do not hear; what I hear, I do not see'). More recently, *Inventing Peace* by Wenders and Zournazi (2013) raises similar questions about how we can look around us at the world yet not see it as it is, beset by wars, injustice, suffering and violence. Two accompanying Web films are entitled *Invisible Crimes* and *War in Peace*.

In this collection, a very welcome sequel to an earlier volume, the editors and contributors focus their attention on the important project of revealing and analysing cases of injustice, victimisation, crimes and social harms that are generally hidden from view. Their aim is to provide a critical perspective and contribute to 'making visible the invisible'.

These are particularly dangerous and corrosive crimes and harms because they have profoundly damaging effects and impacts yet are often under-reported, under-regulated, under-controlled and under-investigated. These are not necessarily crimes of war or abuses of human rights though in the entanglement of global politics and economics they may not be far from connecting to such events. They may be old or new: environmental pollution and destruction is an old but worsening problem while cybercrimes are more recent. They may be behaviours that damage and diminish individuals personally or communities locally, they may destroy working lives and workplaces or natural resources and heritage but they all represent lack of care, sympathy, empathy and respect.

It is important to emphasise just how easy it is for the victims of these invisible crimes to be overlooked and forgotten. In part this happens for obvious reasons given that offenders seek to hide their actions and the injuries caused but it is also particularly the case when these victims are already socially invisible, marginalised or forgotten – the elderly, sex workers, and ethnic minority women would be examples.

The discussions here consider the limits of 'public' knowledge, limitations of political engagement and insufficiency of regulatory response. They expose various 'spaces' of invisibility – the body, home, urban street, environment, corporate suite, state and virtual world – and examine reasons for the invisibility of crimes and harms. These crimes and social harms are doubly significant, for while they contribute to real inequality and injustice, all too often they remain disguised, hidden and are even cloaked by our own willingness to turn away and ignore them. The editors and contributors must be congratulated for shining some light into these dark corners.

Professor Nigel South
Department of Sociology
University of Essex

References

Brecht, B. (1935) 'When Evil-Doing Comes Like Falling Rain', from John Willett and Ralph Manheim (eds) (1979) *Poems (1913–1956)/Bertolt Brecht*. London: Methuen.
Wenders, W. and Zournazi, M. (2013) *Inventing Peace: A Dialogue on Perception*. London: I.B. Tauris.

Acknowledgements

This book is the first the three of us have written together and it has proved to be a particularly enjoyable collective endeavour.

We have been fortunate to work with a number of close and supportive colleagues who have shared our thinking, ideals and values. We would like to take this opportunity to thank each and every one of them for their contribution to this book. We have been great admirers of their work for many years and it is a delight to be able to bring together a collection of our work with theirs and to have it published in such a prestigious series. We are particularly grateful to Professor Reece Walters and Dr Deborah Drake, series editors of the 'Critical Criminological Perspectives Series', whose support for the project has been unquestioning.

We would also like to extend our thanks to Harriet Barker, Editor of the Scholarly and Reference Division of Palgrave Macmillan. She has remained supportive at all times and has worked wonders to ensure the timely production of the book following submission of the manuscript.

Finally, we would like to acknowledge the late Victor Jupp, whose passing in 2012 was a premature end to a long and productive career at Northumbria. We dedicate this book to the memory of Victor.

Notes on Contributors

Avi Brisman is Assistant Professor in the School of Justice Studies at Eastern Kentucky University in Richmond, Kentucky. His writing has appeared in such journals as *Contemporary Justice Review; Crime; Law and Social Change; Crime Media Culture; Critical Criminology; Journal of Contemporary Criminal Justice; Journal of Qualitative Criminal Justice and Criminology; Journal of Theoretical and Philosophical Criminology; Race and Justice; Theoretical Criminology;* and *Western Criminology Review*, among others. He is co-editor, with Nigel South, of the *Routledge International Handbook of Green Criminology* (2013), co-editor, with Nigel South and Rob White, of *Environmental Crime and Social Conflict: Contemporary and Emerging Issues* (2014), and co-author, with Nigel South, of *Green Cultural Criminology: Constructions of Environmental Harm, Consumerism, and Resistance to Ecocide* (2014).

Pamela Davies is Teaching Fellow and Programme Director of Criminology at Northumbria University. Pam teaches criminological theory, gender, crime and justice, and crimes of the powerful. She has research interests around gender, harm and victimisation and has conducted research on female offending and on support for those affected by serious abuse. Pam has co-edited a number of texts, including *Doing Criminological Research*, 3rd edition (with Peter Francis) and *Victims, Crime and Society*, 2nd edition (with Peter Francis and Chris Greer). Her most recent publication comments on green crime and victimisation and the tensions between social and environmental justice.

Peter Francis is Professor of Learning and Teaching and Pro-Vice Chancellor (Learning and Teaching) at Northumbria University. Peter teaches criminological theory. His most recent publications include *Victims, Crime and Society*, 2nd edition (with Pamela Davies and Chris Greer) and *Doing Criminological Research*, 3rd edition (with Pamela Davies). He is currently writing a textbook on contemporary criminological theory.

Alexandra Hall is a doctoral candidate at Northumbria University and Research Associate in the Social Futures Institute and Centre for Realist Criminology, Teesside University. Alex is in the final stages of her PhD research, which explores honour, respect and status among a British-Pakistani diaspora in the context of global neo-liberalism. She is also involved in research projects on cybercrime and counterfeit pharmaceuticals and on the financing of organised crime. Her work combines an interest in criminology, international political economy, political theory and cultural studies.

Matthew Hall is Professor of Law and Criminal Justice and Director of Research, School of Law, University of Lincoln. Matthew's key areas of interest include victims of crime and their interactions with criminal justice systems (on which he is the author of two monographs) and the study of environmental crime and green criminology (on which he has published a monograph specifically focused on environmental victimisation). He is also interested in gender issues related to crime and criminal justice as well as the law/policy/science nexus. More recently Matthew has published on the areas of elder abuse and elder victimisation as well as species justice.

Mary Laing is Senior Lecturer in Criminology at Northumbria University. Her research explores the criminalisation of sex and sexualities, with a specific focus on the sex industry. Recent projects have included an exploration of licensed adult work in Canada, and a participatory research study with sex workers in Newcastle upon Tyne (UK). She has eight years of' experience as a volunteer outreach worker delivering services to male and female sex workers. Mary is the joint academic board representative for the UK Network of Sex Work Projects and has publications in *Sexualities*, *Geoforum* and the *Journal of Law and Society*.

Michael Levi has been Professor of Criminology at Cardiff University School of Social Sciences since 1991. He has been conducting international research on the control of white-collar and organised crime, corruption and money laundering/financing of terrorism for over 40 years, and has published widely on these subjects as well as editing major journals. He is President, US National White-Collar Crime Research Consortium and has been appointed to several international committees on economic and organised crime. In 2013 he was given the Distinguished Scholar Award by the International Association for the Study of Organised Crime. His recent books include *The Phantom Capitalists*, *Regulating Fraud*, and *Drugs and Money*.

Wayne Morrison is Professor of Law and Director of the External Programmes in Law at Queen Mary College, University of London. His most recent publications are *Cultural Criminology Unleashed and the New Punitiveness* (co-edited) and a history of criminological theory in a global and colonial context *Criminology, Civilisation and the New World Order*.

Steve Tombs is Professor of Criminology at the Open University. He has published widely on the incidence, nature and regulation of corporate crime and harm, and in particular the regulation and 'management' of health and safety at work. He is a founding member of the Centre for Corporate Accountability.

Reece Walters is Professor and Assistant Dean, Research for the Faculty of Law at Queensland University of Technology in Australia. He researches in the area of eco crime and environmental justice, state violence and corporate crime. His current research focuses on green criminology and crimes against the 'essentials of life', namely food, air and water. He is the author of *Deviant Knowledge: Criminology, Politics and Policy* (2003) and *Eco Crime and Genetically Modified Food* (2011). He is currently completing two more books: *Dissenting Criminology, Narratives of the Critical Voice* and *Global Kitchens and Superhighways: Harm and the Political Economy of Food*.

Hayley Watson is an associate partner of Trilateral, a research and consultancy group she joined in 2012. Her main area of expertise includes the role of technology and social media in relation to security. Prior to joining Trilateral, Hayley worked as a lecturer in sociology at Canterbury Christ Church University (2011–2012), as well as an assistant lecturer at the University of Kent (2007–2011). She has also worked as a research associate at the University of Kent, on a previous EC-funded FP7 project called 'CPSI: Changing Perceptions of Security and Interventions' (2008–2010). She has published peer-reviewed journal articles on citizen journalism in relation to security.

Tanya Wyatt is Principal Lecturer in Criminology at Northumbria University. She teaches criminological theory, green crime and crimes of the powerful. Tanya's publications are featured in *Crime, Law and Social Change*, *Contemporary Justice Review* and the *Asian Journal of Criminology* among others. Her book, *Wildlife Trafficking: A Deconstruction of the Crime, Victims and Offenders*, was nominated for the 2014 British Society of Criminology's Book Prize. Her other works include an edited collection with Reece Walters and Diane Solomon Westerhuis, *Emerging Issues in Green Criminology: Exploring Power, Justice and Harm*, and with Nigel South and Piers Beirne, a special issue on green criminology for the *International Journal of Crime, Justice and Social Democracy*.

1
Taking Invisible Crimes and Social Harms Seriously

Pamela Davies, Peter Francis and Tanya Wyatt

Background, context and approach

In 1999, Jupp et al. mapped the contours of what they termed invisible crime and victimisation and considered the commonalities associated with this range of acts, events and experiences. They suggested that there are seven interacting and overlapping features that help make harms or crimes more or less invisible. These features are no knowledge, no statistics, no theory, no research, no control, no politics and no panic! The purpose of the book, entitled *Invisible Crimes, Their Victims and Their Regulation* (Davies et al. 1999), was fourfold. First, to explain why it was possible for particular types of crime, harm and injustice that clearly incurred suffering and victimisation to remain hidden and neglected, and therefore unregulated and uncontrolled. Second, to explore the occurrence, nature and impact of these 'invisible crimes' by bringing together the work of scholars undertaking innovative and challenging research in this area. In doing so, the book focused on white-collar crime, workplace crime – including health and safety crimes, illicit drug use, fraud and cybercrimes, and to an extent the book also mapped out a research agenda for this area. A third ambition was to demonstrate that a criminology informed by feminist, radical and critical traditions should continually refresh and reassess its ambitions by refocusing the 'criminological telescope' beyond what is typically encountered within the mainstream with a view to inform and intervene in the name of social justice. A final aim of the book was to support students' exploration of the social construction of crime, as well as the dark figure of crime, with a view to broaden and deepen their criminological imagination (Mills 1958; Young 2011). Overarching these was a shared belief in the importance of a progressive social democratic criminology intent on exploring fertile ground, developing new ways of thinking informed by a range of research methodologies, written from within a broadly radical and critical paradigm, and with the intention of working towards a better and just society.

Whilst much in the world and within the field of criminology has changed in the 15 years since the original conception of neglected crimes and victimisations was formulated and *Invisible Crimes* was published by Macmillan, this new book provides evidence that invisible crimes continue to persist and that much criminological and victimological scholarship continues to neglect them. It also, however, provides evidence of a growing and rich array of progressive research and scholarship on hidden crime and victimisation, of ways of theorising about them and of the available and possible opportunities to respond to them. The rationale of this current book is partly to provide a contemporary review of this research and scholarship by collating and exploring the work of researchers who have inspired our own thinking in this area. A further aim of the book is to contribute to a critical tradition of questioning and challenging commonly held beliefs and ways of thinking about crime, harm, victimisation, regulation and crime control.

In compiling this current collection, our main inspirations mirror the original formulation of the seven features, that is, feminist, radical and critical traditions of criminology (see Hudson 2010; Taylor et al. 1973; 2013). Indeed, an important golden thread running throughout the book is of the rich contribution the radical tradition within criminology has made to exposing, critiquing, re-interpreting and uncovering particular crimes and social harms (Dorling et al. 2008; Hillyard and Tombs 2008). The modern feminism of the 1960s, the precursor to feminist activism in the 1970s and the opening of women's refuges over the following decade, made visible what had previously been hidden (Pahl et al. 2004) in terms of men's violence against women and children in the home. The notion of relative invisibility has been more recently used in conjunction with the comparison of 'crime on the streets', or conventional crime as compared with crime 'behind closed doors' (Walklate 2007), such as domestic violence in the home and other less than transparent locations of crime and victimisation which, like domestic abuse, also carry gendered risks to victimisation (Davies 2008). Similarly, in the four or so decades following the 1970s and 1980s, radical left realism, radical victimology and critical criminology can all be credited with exposing social harms, non-typical/ideal victims, and human rights issues, and analysing the role of the capitalist state, the law and their impact. Recently, the work of Matthews (2009; 2010; 2014) and Currie (2007; 2010), writing in the shadow of debates about the role a public criminology (Loader and Sparks 2006) should play, has reconfirmed for us the importance of a radical criminological agenda that is theoretically aware, research informed and politically engaged, one that is able to connect the intellectual with the search for social justice and social policy.

The inclusion of *social harm* in the current book's title and exploration of topics within it provides a second golden thread and provides a clear acknowledgement that there continues to be definitional issues about what constitutes crime, and our foregrounding of 'harm' in the title emphasises more forcefully that crime is a social construct (Dorling et al. 2005, 2008; Hillyard et al. 2004). Who is constructing that definition plays a large part in not only whether a social harm is labelled as a crime, but also the degree to which that crime or social harm is visible. As Jupp et al. (1999) argued previously, some criminal acts are not visible to even the most careful observer. The inclusion of social harm in the book's title is also in acknowledgement of the impact a wide range of acts can have on individuals, communities and populations. Uncovering crime, realising that it is a criminal act and defining it as such continues to depend on a variety of factors. By and large, there must be witnesses, detection and recognised victims. Crime and social harm take place at the intersections between the meeting of perpetrators, victims, the state and the public at particular times and places (Lea, 2002). It is this dynamic that allows crimes and harms to have different *degrees of invisibility* that stem from the interplay of this range of factors which overlap and interact to decrease or increase the level of visibility.

A third and final golden thread running throughout the book is a concern for equality, diversity and social justice (see Davies and Francis forthcoming). This was another core concern of the original book, and one that remains foregrounded in this current volume. We concur with Currie (2010: 114) when he states that crime '… affects some people, in some kinds of places, far more than others', and that there is a real, acknowledged unequal distribution of the risk of harm that must be addressed by any progressive radical criminology. In each of the chapters that follow, injustice, suffering and harm are central themes, themes the lived reality of which impacts disproportionately on some rather than others, and often on those who are already the most marginalised and vulnerable in society.

Together with a new co-editor in lieu of the late Victor Jupp, and inspired by Wyatt's own brand of radical green criminology (see Wyatt

2012), we believe it is timely to revisit the main themes and arguments of the original book, develop and expand upon them since, as we have begun to map out more extensively below, invisible crimes and harms continue to cause considerable and enduring suffering, injury and injustice in our society. We especially draw from the first chapter of the original book which was entitled 'The Features of Invisible Crimes'. In mapping the contours of invisibility, Jupp et al. (1999) outlined the seven 'headline' features to categorise and characterise the nature, form, type and range of invisible crimes and victimisations with a view to providing an analysis of issues regarding their control and regulation.

The rest of this chapter offers a discussion of the continuing relevance of the original formulation of the features of invisibility thesis through an overview of three contemporary cases and a discussion of the alignment of the seven features to a range of typologies before outlining the structure and content of the various contributions to this volume.

The contours of invisible crimes and social harms

In *Invisible Crimes, Their Victims and Their Regulation*, Jupp et al. (1999: 5) articulate the seven headline features as follows:

> The degree of invisibility is dependent upon a number of factors, often, but not always, specific to particular acts or events. For our purposes here, we detail a number of characteristic features against which degrees of invisibility can be judged. These include: *no knowledge* (there is little individual or public knowledge that the crime has been committed); *no statistics* (official statistics fail to record or classify the crime); *no theory* (criminologists and others neglect to explain the crime, its existence and its causes); *no research* (such crimes are not the object of social research, either in terms of their causes or their control); *no control* (there are no formal or systematic mechanisms for the control of such crimes); *no politics* (such crimes do not appear as a significant part of the public political agenda); and finally, *no panic*! (such crimes are not constituted as moral panics and their perpetrators are not portrayed as folk devils).

These seven features (see Box 1.1 for a detailed illustration of each of the seven features), Jupp et al. suggested, provide a useful means of categorising and characterising a wide range of acts and events which remain invisible in everyday life. Moreover, when combined, they went on to suggest, such features constitute a framework or template with which to assess relative invisibility. Each feature (no knowledge, no statistics, no theory, no research, no control, no politics and no panic!) can be viewed as independent of one another but there is also the potential for mutual reinforcement; we further develop the mechanism of this process in the following section and in the chapters that follow. The relative invisibility of particular acts, events and, we now argue, experiences, their subsequent recognition and identification as a crime or harm, and their identification by criminological research and inquiry or not, depends on which features in the template are present, to what degree or magnitude they are expressed, the power of mutual reinforcement where features interact to increase the degree of invisibility and the ability of criminology to penetrate, uncover and challenge. We suggest that these features have lasting resonance and are as applicable today as when they were developed 15 years ago.

Box 1.1 The Seven Features of Invisibility

Feature	Summary description	Consequence of:
1 No Knowledge	There is little individual or public knowledge that the crime or social harm has been committed	Offenders actively hide their antisocial activities Lack of awareness of the criminal or social problem Normalisation problem associated with acts and events being taken for granted and/or defined as normal Problem of ideology in which particular acts and events are framed in particular ways Collusion problem in which individuals knowingly collude in their own harm and victimisation
2 No Statistics	Official statistics (including those collected by the police and through the survey method approach) fail to record or classify the crime	Inadequacies of official statistics to uncover crime and social harm because of: Definitional limitations of what is to be included Breadth and scope of survey-based methodology Administrative problems of sampling the population Under-reporting Under-recording Misclassification

Continued

Feature	Summary description	Consequence of:
3 No Theory	Criminologists and others neglect to explain the crime, its existence and its causes	Pre-eminence of administrative and scientific criminologies emphasis on what works and pseudoscientific approaches
		Liberal criminologies focus on conventional or mainstream crime and criminal justice
		Conceptual and definitional problems associated with what constitutes crime and harm
		Breadth of acts and events mean that discipline of criminology is unable to adequately capture all
4 No research	Such crimes and social harms are not the object of social research, either in terms of their causes or their control	Mutually reinforcing effects of no knowledge, no statistics and no theory
		Failure of theory to frame and identify social problems worthy of criminological research
		Limited access and resources as a result of the power of gatekeepers
		Problems to do with the politics and ethics of research
5 No control	There are no formal or systematic mechanisms for the control of such crimes	Lack of knowledge that crime and harm has occurred, particularly beyond official legal definitions (e.g., financial sector)
		Blurring of the boundaries between the legitimate and illegitimate makes detection and recording difficult
		Policing priorities and the predominance of 'street' over 'suite' crimes and 'visible' rather than 'invisible' victims
		Inadequacies in the response to cross-border, transnational and virtual crimes and harms
6 No politics	Such crimes do not appear as a significant part of the public political agenda	Political agenda remains focused on crimes as defined by the law and crime victimisation
		Politics of law and order and the tenacity of the electorate

Continued

Feature	Summary description	Consequence of:
7 No panic	Such crimes are not constituted as moral panics and their perpetrators are not portrayed as folk devils	Media commitment to those crimes defined by law and constructed through politics of law and order Few folk devils and media reaction Lack of public reaction and media outrage Media focus on one-off 'scandals' and 'incidents' rather than sustained outrage based upon cumulative events

Through the various chapters in this book we (re-)establish the application of this template and spark (re-)examination of invisible crimes, social harms and victimisations. In this reconstruction and re-presentation of the key features of invisibility, we expand our analysis to examine why these features are present: is it because of deliberate action or passive omission? We also more directly explore the commonalities and differences between invisible crimes and harms and in doing so have constructed typologies that reflect the diverse range of suffering and injustices that are discussed. To illustrate the usefulness of the seven features, we briefly apply them to three contemporary examples below.

Writing from an emerging radical tradition, Pearce (1976) explored invisible crimes or harms as 'crimes of the powerful'. Flowing from a radicalism informed by Marxist philosophy and critical social commentary and often drawing on the work of Quinney (1972) and Elias (1985), there is now critical scholarship, research, knowledge and theoretical insight around a range of activities and experiences that constitute crimes and victimisations behind closed workplace, institution and corporate doors. Some researchers have pursued white-collar and financial crimes: frauds, illegal share deals and mergers/takeovers, and tax evasions (Croall 2003, 2007b; Levi 2008, 2013); crimes against consumers: mis-selling of pensions and endowment policies, illegal sales and marketing (Croall 2007a; Spalek 1999, 2001, 2004, 2007); corporate crimes: crimes against employees, violations of employment and wage laws, occupational health and safety crimes (Pearce and Tombs 2003, 2012; Tombs

2000; Tombs and Whyte 2003, 2007, 2008); environmental crimes: illegal emissions to air, water and land, hazardous waste dumping and illegal manufacturing processes (Bisschop 2012; Pearce and Tombs 2012; Ruggiero and South 2010). However, many acts of crime and experiences of social harm, including many of the aforementioned, continue to remain relatively hidden from view.

For example, corporate and international crime scholarship has unmasked a range of different dimensions to industrial harms and case studies have revealed chemical, automobile, pharmaceutical, cosmetic and construction industry hazards. Yet, Snider (2000: 3), commenting upon the sociology of corporate crime at the turn of this century, argues that the brand of state regulation known as corporate crime has basically disappeared and been argued into obsolescence 'through neo-liberal knowledge claims advanced through specific discourses by powerful elites'. This is evident in such incidents as the Libor Scandal. Libor, the London Interbank Offered Rate, is a key interest rate within the global financial system. Yet, when it was fully uncovered in 2012 that Barclays had been manipulating this rate and their own rankings within the system for at least seven years, they were fined £290 million (BBC News 2013). Three individuals were arrested and other banks were investigated for rate manipulation as well, but what became apparent was that this activity is a widespread practice that was allowed to continue though it was suspected that Barclays and other institutions were involved in unethical and potentially criminal practices. Such rate manipulation gave the false impression that the economy before the recession was in a better state than it was and thus contributed to the collapse by misrepresenting the financial viability of banks and the robustness of the economy. This is one of several instances in the last decade of financial institutions engaged in malfeasance. They are then barely held accountable for the harms that they cause. Efforts to alter the regulation governing their actions are blocked by powerful lobbyists that protect the corporations and the interests of the wealthy.

The above example highlights that despite a growing body of research and scholarship on financial crime and its regulation, malpractice, suffering and a culture of denial remains, much of it opaque. A similar illustrative point can be drawn from a review of interpersonal crimes of violence and abuse. Once again, informed by and influenced heavily by the pioneering radical and feminist work of the 1970s and 1980s, there is now a wealth of research on the nature, extent and impact of interpersonal violence and abuse at home, in public, in organisations and institutions among adults, against women and children (see, for example, the edited volume by Brown and Walklate 2012). Nevertheless, there continues to be much that remains hidden, such as the nature of human trafficking, same-sex abuse and, for the purpose of the current section, sexual abuse carried out in institutions and organisations. This is evident in the case of allegations of sexual abuse against the late television presenter and entertainer Jimmy Savile. The joint report by Gray and Watt (2013) for the Metropolitan Police and the National Society for the Prevention of Cruelty to Children (NSPCC) into these allegations notes that 'It is now clear that Savile was hiding in plain sight and using his celebrity status and fund-raising activity to gain uncontrolled access to vulnerable people across six decades' and that 'For a variety of reasons the vast majority of his victims did not feel they could speak out' (Gray and Watt 2013: 6). The report acknowledges that perpetrators are reliant upon victims and witnesses of abuse not speaking out and the partnership inquiry into scoping the claims adopted an approach that was aimed at empowering people to overcome their reluctance to speak out. One of the report's concluding remarks is that 'sexual abuse, whether in street gangs, through trafficking or within families and institutions, often involves the use of powerful coercion, intimidation and manipulation to exploit the vulnerable' (Gray and Watt 2013: 24). The Savile case and its continuing legacy played out as a moral crusade (Furedi 2013) and highlights in particular that a lack of evidence manifests in a variety of ways and has significant impact for the visibility of crimes and harms. Victims being unable to speak out prevented knowledge of the crime from being communicated and when victims did talk about their experiences, those they confided in acted as gatekeepers. Their reports were effectively silenced via a combination of six key 'silencing agents' (Jordan 2012). Furthermore, whilst legislation and organisational procedures exist(ed) to address sexual abuse, these measures were circumvented and manipulated by powerful actors hiding the harms they had caused. 'Historical abuse' entered the lexicon of crime and victimisation in twenty-first century Britain.

A key element of the Savile case is denial – from the organisations and institutions that employed Savile, and from those whose responsibility was to identify, apprehend and expose his wrongdoing. Additionally, victim denial can also be identified. In simple terms the case is one in which it appears that there is both a history and a politics of denial resulting ultimately in the denial of justice for the victims involved, a theme which lies also at the heart of our final example – the case of the Hillsborough football disaster of 1989.

On 15 April 1989, 96 people lost their lives at Leppings Lane, Hillsborough, home to Sheffield Wednesday Football Club in the north of England, who were amongst the 50,000 fans there to watch an FA Cup semi-final between Liverpool and Nottingham Forest. At some time around 3 p.m. on that Saturday afternoon, Britain's worst football disaster had started to happen. The Hillsborough Independent Panel report describes it thus:

> the small area in which the crush occurred comprised two pens. Fans had entered down a tunnel under the West Stand into the central pens 3 and 4. Each pen was segregated by lateral fences and a high, overhanging fence between the terrace and the perimeter track around the pitch. There was a small locked gate at the front of each pen.
>
> The crush became unbearable and fans collapsed underfoot. To the front of pen 3 a safety barrier broke, creating a pile of people struggling for breath. Despite CCTV cameras transmitting images of distress in the crowd to the Ground Control Room and to the Police Control Box, and the presence of officers on duty on the perimeter track, it was a while before the seriousness of what was happening was realised and rescue attempts were made.
>
> As the match was stopped and fans were pulled from the terrace through the narrow gates onto the pitch, the enormity of the tragedy became evident. Fans tore down advertising hoardings and used them to carry the dead and dying the full length of the pitch to the stadium gymnasium.
>
> Ninety-six women, men and children died as a consequence of the crush, while hundreds more were injured and thousands traumatised. In the immediate aftermath there was a rush to judgment concerning the cause of the disaster and culpability. In a climate of allegation and counter-allegation, the Government appointed Lord Justice Taylor to lead a judicial inquiry.
>
> What followed, over an 11-year period, were various different modes and levels of scrutiny, including Lord Justice Taylor's Interim and Final Reports, civil litigation, criminal and disciplinary investigations, the inquests into the deaths of the victims, judicial reviews, a judicial scrutiny of new evidence conducted by Lord Justice Stuart-Smith, and the private prosecution of the two most senior police officers in command on the day. (Hillsborough: The Report of the Independent Panel Review 2012: 1)

Writing some 25 years later, the truth about Hillsborough is only now starting to be told, in large part due to the work of the Hillsborough Family Support Group, an independent campaigning group seeking justice for those who died on that Saturday afternoon and their families. Despite the wide-scale presence of the media at the event, crucial questions remained unanswered about what actually happened, why, and who was responsible. Indeed, the victims' families were profoundly concerned that following unsubstantiated allegations made by senior police officers and politicians and reported widely in the press, it had become widely assumed that Liverpool fans' behaviour had contributed to, if not caused, the disaster. Drawing upon the evidence that came to light about the events on that day, most notably from the waiving of the 30-year rule withholding public records, from the pioneering research carried out by Scraton et al. (1995) and Scraton (1999; 2007) as well as new evidence drawn from a review of supporting contributions, the Review uncovered how and why 'truths' were constructed through a combination of organisational, institutional, political, and media factors. The final report demonstrates how 'institutionalised injustices' and 'systemic biases' left the families of the Hillsborough victims mourning long after the events of the day. It examines the way in which politics and media influenced the reporting and subsequent police and political response. It highlights how calls for the truth were examined, and the way in which 'myths' became the popular perception of what happened.

In different historical and political contexts and locations, these three examples highlight the continuing relevance of the seven features of invisibility described above. All three examples highlight the way in which corporations, institutions and organisations are all variably able to reconstruct a reality of their choosing, of the way in which media reporting can be manipulated and framed, of the way in which victims and human suffering can be ignored, and of the way in which the actions of perpetrators are obscured, denied or ignored. Often such crimes are connected to the function and operation of the market economy, like the Libor case, following Snider's predictions. In some instances there are historical, cultural, legal and/or political differences in terms of how crime, threats, risks, harms and victimisations are categorised and classified, as in the Savile and Hillsborough examples. Often the crimes are a consequence of the actions of organisations, as in the case of Hillsborough; in other instances they are committed by private individuals, such as in the case of Savile. In many cases it is both. As our examples highlight, in some instances an organisation or institution masks the crime, in other instances the state itself is the perpetrator of such harms.

For some there is an obvious transparency and physical location attached to the act or event (Hillsborough), albeit 'behind closed doors' (Libor), whereas others represent elusive examples of criminal activity and victimisation in closed (Savile), or non-transparent locations. Sometimes victims acknowledge their victimisation privately, informally and even tentatively to statutory agencies as evidenced in the Savile case. In some instances, victims publicly highlight their victimisation (Hillsborough), but in some representations victims are depicted as inviting, precipitating, participating or even being 'predatory' in their victimisation (again Hillsborough). Sometimes victims may be seen as colluding or they may be normalising their predicament; frequently they cannot, or simply do not, know about it, in which case the invisibility relates to 'problems of knowing' (Tombs 1999). In all cases justice is denied to the victims and their families (Scraton 2007).

It is with these further observed elements of complexity of invisible crimes and harms in mind and within the contemporary context of economic recessions and global depressions that we expand upon the seven features of invisibility. This is accomplished through postulating that within invisible crimes there are typological underpinnings which provide distinctions within the range of these hidden harms. The next section will present our proposal for typologies of invisible crimes and harms.

The typologies of invisible crimes and social harms

All invisible crimes and social harms are not the same. While the seven features of invisibility are founded upon the societal factors that create and expand the hidden nature of a crime or harm, there are typological differences seen within, and stemming from, the relationship of those invisible crimes and harms with the various bodies of power within society that control the seven features. These power structures can actively make crimes and harms invisible or at least opaque by suppressing one or many of the seven features. Equally, they can make crimes and harms more visible by opening one or more of the seven features, an example being that of the Hillsborough disaster with the waiving of the 30-year public disclosure rule. Structural power is at the heart of this contemporary analysis. These invisible crimes and harms can be broken down into categories that, as will be explored, share common underpinnings. The categories of invisible crimes and social harms can be conceptualised as the body, the home, the street, the environment, the suite, the virtual and the state. These categories each have commonalities (as well as differences) and the nature, degree and extent of invisibility is underpinned by different levels and sources of power: the moral and ethical; the institutional and organisational; the systemic. They are also, as we go on to show, influenced by the socio-legal, the historical, the political and the spatial/global contexts.

Invisible crimes and harms that stem from moral and ethical underpinnings are diverse in nature, but predominantly are prevalent in crimes and harms pertaining to the body and within the home. Violence and abuse against sex workers, men and women, and intimate partner violence provide evidence for this. The hegemonic morality that stigmatises sex work means that when sex workers are victimised their access to help and support can be limited if available at all. The moral underpinnings of society at large that define selling the body as immoral and 'dirty' drive the crimes perpetrated against sex workers into the dark, thus making the sex workers invisible victims of invisible crimes. In a similar vein, domestic violence between same-sex partners has historically been invisible to the criminal justice system. This has persisted even though heterosexual interpersonal violence and abuse, while still invisible to some degree, has been witness to more progress in terms of victims' services and the criminal justice system's response. It can be argued that the invisibility of violence between same-sex partners also stems from the hegemonic morality that has traditionally viewed same-sex relationships as immoral. Morality and ethics and the ownership and control of them are the underpinnings of why some harms and crimes remain invisible though they cause suffering and injury. They enable victims to be 'othered' and therefore outside of the gaze of the criminal justice system.

Morality and ethics may be powers that make individual instances of victimisation invisible, whilst institutional and organisational powers are capable of hiding crimes and harms that are pervasive and have the scope to victimise large numbers of people. The categories for exploration here are the street, the environment and the suite. The street is a way of conceptualising those hidden crimes and harms that take place in the public sphere. Whilst happening in plain sight, powerful entities are able to make these activities and injuries invisible regardless. An ongoing example of this would be the racial discrimination practiced by some police agencies. The disproportionate stopping and searching of ethnic minorities is an event that takes place in the public sphere with the potential for witnesses. Even with exposure of racial discrimination at an institutional level by the Macpherson Report, current stop-and-search data still indicates a disproportionate amount of ethnic minorities are targeted in some areas. The breakdown by ethnicity, for instance, for the stop and searches conducted by the Metropolitan Police in 2010–2011 was 52 per cent for ethnic minorities compared to 13 per cent in other areas of the United Kingdom; this is only partly explained by the higher numbers of ethnic minorities in those police jurisdictions (Home Office 2012). Yet, as a powerful institution, the police are rarely questioned and until recently mechanisms for accountability have remained weak. This was seen until recently in the common practice that investigations into police misconduct were carried out by fellow officers. The 'thin blue line' was rarely crossed to uncover racist, sexist or abusive officers. Moreover, the covert practices of the police that remain within the public sphere, but out of sight, appear to receive even less accountability and opportunity for redress. For example, the recent report into possible corruption and the role of undercover policing in the Stephen Lawrence case (Ellison 2014) identified the lack of transparency of undercover policing, particularly by the Special Demonstration Squad (SDS), at the time of the police investigation into the death of the teenager Stephen Lawrence, and the failure of the inquiry to locate written police reports that should have been available. As in the example of the Hillsborough disaster, this provides further evidence of the power of an institution to keep the harms that it perpetrates hidden and even to continue to try to hide them again after they have been exposed.

The environment is a further category where entrenched hidden crime and harm are underpinned by institutional and organisational power. For instance, though pollution harms millions of people and can be viewed as quite pervasive – air pollution from cars and planes, soil pollution from fertilisers, water pollution from industrial factories and so on – it remains largely invisible. The processes by which environmental pollution occurs as well as its scale and extent remain hidden through the power of corporations to not only hide environmental harms and violations, but also because of the associated power structures that keep environmental harm from being criminalised. By manipulating the legal system to adopt regimes of voluntary compliance and self-regulation, polluting industries such as pharmaceutical companies and chemical manufacturers avoid the oversight and punishment of the criminal justice system. With low risk of detection of environmental harms and weak punishments if infractions are uncovered, institutional practices that degrade the environment as a way of cutting costs become entrenched and part of 'business as usual'.

Corporations often hide this aspect of business by 'green washing' their company image. Oil companies, despite continual spills and polluting incidents, market themselves as champions of alternative energy research. Soft drink companies that manufacture some of the highest levels of plastic on the planet brag that their bottles are mostly from recycled plastic. This focus on other good practices turns scrutiny away from the environmental damage being caused. Who the typical victims of environmental pollution are also aids the corporations in keeping the harm and victimisation hidden. The environment itself as a victim is certainly invisible to a majority of people due to victim status only being open to humans. Yet victims of such harm are also hidden as they are often people of marginalised groups within societies and indeed within marginalised communities (Davies 2014). As Lynch and Stretesky (2003) have found, ethnic minorities, the lower classes and women are more likely to live near environmental pollution. Their lack of voice, political and economic power leads to their victimisation in terms of environmental health as well as economic and political oppression (Lynch and Stretesky 2003). This is further exacerbated by the claims about the work of undercover policing practices in attempting to destabilise and devalue those individuals and groups that attempt to question through challenge and protest organisations and institutions. The environment then, as a category, has multiple hidden victims stemming from hidden crimes and harms made so by institutional power.

Other crimes committed in the suites – corporate crimes – are also underpinned by organisational and institutional practices that enable them to remain hidden. The previously mentioned Hillsborough disaster and the Libor scandal provide two good examples. In the Hillsborough disaster, evidence of attempts to devalue the claims of the victims' families through the use of media campaigns and the doctoring of evidence further indicates organisational and institutional power dynamics that can work against making visible the invisible. With regard to the Libor scandal, institutional practices that were legal and acceptable, yet setting the stage for wide-scale harm, were routinely practiced by several banks within the financial sector. Complicated, secretive regulatory regimes contribute to corporations' ability to keep the harms that they are causing hidden. The complexity of the legislation and of the workings of the system in essence makes it invisible to outsiders who are unable to penetrate and fully comprehend the processes governing the system. Organisational practices in these cases also attempt to divert attention from wrongdoing by marketing corporate social responsibility schemes to investors and the public. As stated above, the power of corporate legal departments and the political influence that they hold squash changes that might make them more accountable and limit the harm that they are responsible for.

Whereas not every person may come into contact with an institution or organisation that is criminogenic, there is another layer of society that is even more pervasive and holds the potential for even more serious victimisation and ultimately has the most power to keep the crimes and harms that they cause invisible. The categories that shed light onto these systemic power structures are the virtual and the state. With the adoption of technology as a key aspect of the lives of a majority of people in the world and as a defining feature of the modern era, crimes and social harms hidden within the virtual space are systemic in nature. In the case of personal identity much of this is tied to the cyber-structure that now provides the framework for people's personal, social, economic and consumptive interactions. Even within this space that is not a physical location, crimes and harms take place creating hidden victims. There are instances of identity theft, where people have their names, bank accounts and individual identity numbers like Social Security numbers or National Insurance numbers stolen and used by offenders. People are bullied and threatened. In this virtual space there are even more challenges to uncovering social harm and injustice. Without a physical crime scene and only web addresses or mobile phone locations to document a series of events, proving victimisation or understanding that a person is a victim becomes problematic. With technology's ubiquitous nature, such invisible and hidden victimisations can be pervasive and systemic.

It could be argued that one of the largest perpetrators of invisible crimes and harms is the state. For instance, the victims of state-sanctioned violence are both civilians where the conflict is occurring and the very soldiers (representatives of the state) who are instigating the violence. Yet violence and harm initiated by governments under the label of 'war' remains largely but not entirely outside of criminological inquiry and outside of the sphere of the legal system. The social and political construction of war that enables the extensive harm caused by the state to be defined as heroic or patriotic, thus making it invisible, is done by the state itself. The powerful state re-labels acts that in other contexts would be criminal and glorifies and encourages them within battle (Cohen 2000). This power also enables the state to hide the victimisation that takes place through its control of information and definitions, for instance, calling anyone within certain militarised zones enemy combatants. Victimisation within the context of war is deeply hidden. This could be civilian deaths, but also soldiers who are victims of assault perpetrated by other soldiers, the victimisation caused by the psychological and emotional harm of serving in combat, or the lack of treatment and services for returned soldiers after the conflict has ended. All of these harms can be made to disappear by a powerful state that controls most if not all of the seven features of invisibility. Nearly every person on the planet then could potentially become a victim of crimes of the state. As the current scandal of the widespread hidden collection of private telephone calls and emails of the public by Western government security services demonstrates, virtual and state power can combine to cause thousands of violations of privacy to citizens of multiple countries. Yet it continues because of the influence of an elite few who control the discourse on security and thus engrain the nearly invisible violations of people's right to privacy.

As mentioned at the beginning of this section, woven into this fabric of typologies is that there is a socio-legal, historico-cultural, political and global context to all crimes and harms. This again relates to actors involved and the power dynamics that enable individuals, institutions or the state to maintain the invisibility of crimes and harms and or create the conditions that will hide them.

The socio-legal context refers to the means through which perpetrators of invisible crimes and harms and their supporters are able to actively manipulate the seven features of invisibility as well as the legislative system that defines crimes. Control and influence over the media plays a large part in creating knowledge of these incidents. Similarly, power of official agencies that track crimes and harms, such as the police and regulatory agencies like the Environment Agency for instance, means power over statistics and thus effectively research. Control over what is researched and ultimately what is theorised about stems from power over funding agencies and the money that goes to support research activity. It is in the interest of some perpetrators of invisible crimes to deny access to sources that would aid in uncovering their crimes. The interconnected nature of the features means that with control over knowledge and so forth this also leads to control over politics and panic. Uncovering knowledge alongside discovering the various knowledges then is key to shedding light on hidden harms.

It could be argued that the perpetrators of invisible crimes and harms have inherited the power that enables them to remain hidden from scrutiny. As stated above, whilst there are new invisible crimes it seems that those perpetrating them are part of the hegemonic social structures that have already been criminogenic. Bankers and celebrities can be seen as such perpetrators. Institutions and organisations are two others. Corporations and states are others again. This indicates that there is an historical context to invisible crimes as well. The power dynamics enabling them to take place and remain hidden may have a long precedence and make them particularly resilient to challenge and questioning.

Intertwined with the social-legal, historical and cultural contexts are the political, economic and global aspects of invisible crimes and harms. No politics is one of the features of invisibility, but the political context also refers to the fact that crime is a political issue and that the definition of crime, harm and injustice and the functioning of the criminal justice system are highly politicised. The criminal justice system is used as a means of imposing political philosophies and deriving legitimacy for that philosophy (Findlay et al. 2013). This is accomplished because the pervasive all-encompassing nature of the criminal justice system serves to integrate and institutionalise norms and values, particularly around crime and harm (Findlay et al. 2013). So if the criminal justice system does not recognise killing in war as murder, for instance, then the societal narrative repeats this belief and the harm and injustice remains invisible partly because of this political context.

Given societal changes over the last 30 years or so, associated with the transition to late modernity, it is perhaps also inevitable that discussion must focus explicitly on the interconnected role played by free market economics, neo-liberalism, globalisation and a market society (Reiner 2006, 2007, 2012a, 2012b; Taylor 1997) in creating the conditions for crime, social harm and their relative invisibility. Indeed, the macro global and economic contexts within which invisible crimes occur, and their impact on local opportunities and relationships, form a key strand running throughout the chapters within this book. For some invisible crimes and social harms the perpetration is often cross-border and inter- (and intra-) state. Rules, regulations and controls differ markedly across jurisdictions, as does the legislative, regulatory and criminal framework around them. It is again important that the global, international and comparative aspects of invisible crime are taken into account. The increasingly globalised world, associated with a reframing of the boundaries of nation states, and a reframing of the dynamic interplay between capital, finance, big business and the state means that any understanding of invisible crime and social harm must take greater account of the global reality in which social problems have intensified, the risks of exposure intensified, and the opportunities for political, economic and criminal justice responses have been weakened. As many of the contributors highlight, global neo-liberal state and economic projects and policies have invariably impacted on the nature, extent and impact of acts, events and incidents, of how they have been defined as crime or have remained hidden, neglected and/or denied, and on the way in which the administration of the state and its agencies have responded. Certainly each of the contributors highlight how a changing conception of the nature of the world and the connections and interconnections that lie within it have and do impact on the way in which crime is conceptualised, understood and responded to, or not.

Invisible crimes and social harms: their nature, type and control

The continuing invisibility of much crime and victimisation, in the United Kingdom and overseas, and the lack of adequate response to them, is, as has been described above, a central organising tenet of this book, as is the way in which some crimes/social harms and/or victims/injustices become visible or invisible over time and place. The 'headline' features, which have been used to categorise and characterise invisible crimes, emerge at different points in subsequent chapters. Additionally, the socio-legal, historico-cultural, political and global contexts explored above are interwoven throughout as we see them as inseparable from an examination as to what is invisible and why it is hidden.

The remainder of this book consists of 13 original chapters that brings together the golden threads identified in this chapter and explores the parameters of a research agenda for the future. Writing from a broadly critical social science perspective, the various contributions examine particular invisible crimes, social harms and injustices that take place within the global world. Each chapter explores one or more aspects of the 'spaces' of invisibility – the body, home, street, environment, suite and state – through various examples and case studies. We decided to commission chapters on the basis that each contribution would examine their specialist topic area in the context of the spaces of invisibility. The illustrative case studies, within the context of our explanatory framework, therefore explore in depth the complexity of the persistence and existence of invisible crimes and harms, and the broader reasons for their invisibility, as well as the various regulatory issues at individual, institutional and structural levels.

In Chapter 2, Pamela Davies investigates the historically structured underpinnings to sexual abuse and violent crimes and victimisations.

She argues for a 'gender-first' approach to unlocking the secrets to such gendered crimes. Following this historical and inequality context, the global and cultural factors that contribute to invisibility are examined in Chapter 3. In that chapter, Wyatt and Watson explore the role politics, power and the media play in shaping and defining, uncovering or covering suffering and injustice through an exploration of two forms of terrorism – environmental and eco. In Chapter 4, Avi Brisman, in an innovative examination of climate change, considers the role that globalisation and mass consumer culture play in the perception of the crime, as well as a cultural construction of the harm of climate change (or lack thereof).

In Chapter 5, Alex Hall's discussion is based on an analysis of the concept of izzat, which occupies the centre of the distinct honour–shame complex that plays an important reproductive role in specific South Asian cultural groups. Feminist and cultural criminology inspired debates are explored, as are relations between the body and the family, all of which are located in the broader criminological field of violence against women. Exploration then turns in Chapter 6 to the typology of 'the home' where Matthew Hall draws upon a case study of older people, crime and victimisation. This chapter argues that despite a growing acknowledgement of the wide range of social harms inflicted upon older people in the home, there continues to be much about the nature, type and extent of these risks and abuses that we do not know, and much therefore that we do not respond to. He offers a broader theoretical assessment of why old age, crime and victimisation have been conceptualised and mediatised in the way that it has, which leads to an examination of the factors responsible for ensuring the continuing invisibility of much crime and victimisation within mainstream criminological, media and political discourse and practice.

'The street' is our categorisation of the typology of invisible crimes and harms taking place in public spaces. In Chapter 7 Mary Laing explores the regulation of male sex work, and argues that, despite there being a considerable male sex industry existing in England and Wales, men are noticeably absent in policy, policing and service-led contexts. This continued invisibility has a material impact on the male sex workers and on the practitioners dedicated to providing services for sex workers across the UK. In Chapter 8, Reece Walters explores the nature and types of environmental pollution, the processes by which these pollutions occur, as well as the scale and extent of such harms and risks. He not only theorises how the environment itself can be viewed as a hidden victim, but he also proposes crimes and harms against the environment as invisible forms of violence. Whilst environmental pollution is often perpetrated by corporations, corporations are also plundering the knowledge of indigenous peoples in isolated parts of the world. In Chapter 9 Tanya Wyatt uses two case studies to demonstrate the invisible victimisation of indigenous groups when multinational corporations use their powerful Western legal system to patent stolen knowledge.

From the suite typology and the institutional and organisational level of power, Chapter 10 moves to the systemic level of power described earlier and the state typology of invisible crimes and harms. This chapter explores the social and political construction of war that enables the extensive harm caused by the state to be redefined as heroic or patriotic, thus making it invisible. Within the discussion, Wayne Morrison considers not only the injured and killed civilians as invisible victims, but also examines the soldiers as hidden victims of the state. Chapters 11 and 12 take as their departure point the regulation and enforcement measures pertaining to invisible crimes and harms or the lack thereof. The regulation and enforcement of occupational health and safety in British workplaces – and thus the visibility or otherwise of health and safety crimes – is the focus of Steve Tombs in Chapter 11. After providing an overview of health and safety crimes and a thorough examination of the trends since the turn of the century, he addresses an apparent anomaly in the general shift towards decriminalisation: the introduction, in 2008, of a new criminal offence of corporate manslaughter. This may or may not have an impact upon the visibility of these crimes and harms in the future. Chapter 12 by Mike Levi focuses on a case study of the economic crime of fraud and issues surrounding finance and regulation. Whilst the chapter selects a number of illustrative and case study examples, it does so in the context of a variety of recent developments. The latter includes financial deregulation, the financialisation of the new economy and other associated factors, including the continued revelation of financial crimes in recessional climates across the globe. As the chapter explores the ubiquity and diversity of these activities and experiences, it simultaneously demonstrates their systemic nature.

The final chapter of the book by Peter Francis, Pamela Davies and Tanya Wyatt brings together what we see as the ten thematic points that offer some way of making visible the invisible in relation to crime and social harm. We offer insight into why we view this task as one for the radical/critical criminological tradition, and make reference to what the next steps might look like. In doing so the chapter highlights the consequences for the discipline of criminology itself, the importance of interdisciplinary research to making visible the invisible, the interconnectedness of theory, method and intervention, and the potential for political change and policy transformation in the search for social justice.

References

BBC News (2013) 'Timeline: Libor-fixing Scandal', *BBC News Business*. Available at: http://www.bbc.co.uk/news/business-18671255. Accessed 19 February 2013.
Bisschop, L. (2012) 'Is It All Going to Waste? Illegal Transports of E-waste in a European Trade Hub', *Crime, Law and Social Change*, 58(3): 221–249.
Brown, J.M. and Walklate, S.L. (eds) (2012) *Handbook on Sexual Violence*. Abingdon: Routledge.
Cohen, S. (2000) *States of Denial: Knowing about Atrocities and Suffering*. London: Wiley
Croall, H. (2003) 'Combatting Financial Crime: Regulatory versus Crime Control Approaches', *Journal of Financial Crime*, 11: 144–155.
—— (2007a) 'Food Crime', in P. Beirne and N. South (eds), *Issues in Green Criminology*. Cullompton: Willan, 206–229.
—— (2007b) 'Victims of White-Collar and Corporate Crime', in P. Davies, P. Francis and C. Greer (eds), *Victims, Crime and Society*. London: Sage.
Currie, E. (2007) 'Against Marginality: Arguments for a Public Criminology', *Theoretical Criminology*, 11(2): 175–190
—— (2010) 'Plain Left Realism: An Appreciation of Some Thoughts for the Future', *Crime, Law and Social Change*, 54: 111–124
Davies, P. (2008) 'Looking Out a Broken Old Window: Community Safety, Gendered Crimes and Victimisations', *Crime Prevention and Community Safety: An International Journal*, 10(4): 207–225.
—— (2014) 'Green Crime and Victimization: Tensions between Social and Environmental Justice', *Theoretical Criminology*, 18(3): 300–316. doi:10.1177/1362480614522286.
Davies, P. and Francis, P. (eds) (forthcoming) *Doing Criminological Research*. 3rd edn. London: Sage.
Davies, P., Francis, P. and Jupp, V. (eds) (1999) *Invisible Crimes: Their Victims and Their Regulation*. Basingstoke: Palgrave Macmillan.
Dorling, D., Gordon, D., Hillyard, P., Pantazis, C., Pemberton, S. and Tombs, S. (2008) *Criminal Obsessions: Why Harm Matters More Than Crime*, 2nd edn. London: Centre for Crime and Justice Studies.
Dorling, D., Gordon, D., Hillyard, P., Pantazis, C. and Tombs, S. (2005) *Criminal Obsessions: Why Harm Matters More Than Crime*. London: Centre for Crime and Justice Studies.
Elias, N. (1985) *The Loneliness of Dying*. London: Continuum.
Ellison, M. (2014) *The Stephen Lawrence Independent Review*. London: House of Commons.
Findlay, M., Kuo, L.B. and Wei, L.S. (2013) *International and Comparative Criminal Justice: A Critical Introduction*. London: Routledge.

Furedi, F. (2013) *Moral Crusades in an Age of Mistrust: The Jimmy Savile Scandal.* London: Palgrave-MacMillan.

Gray, D. and Watt, P. (2013) *Giving Victims a Voice: Joint Report into Sexual Allegations Made against Jimmy Savile.* London: MPS/NSPCC.

Hillsborough Independent Panel (2012) *Hillsborough: The Report of the Hillsborough Independent Panel.* Available at: http://hillsborough.independent.gov.uk/repository/report/HIP_report.pdf. Accessed 27 April 2014.

Hillyard, P., Pantazis, C., Tombs, S., Gordon, D. (eds) (2004) *Beyond Criminology: Taking Harms Seriously.* London: Pluto.

Hillyard, P. and Tombs, S. (2008) 'Beyond Criminology', in D. Dorling, D. Gordon, P. Hillyard, C. Pantazis, S. Pemberton and S. Tombs (eds), *Criminal Obsessions: Why Harm Matters More Than Crime.* 2nd edn. London: Centre for Crime and Justice Studies, 6–23.

Home Office (2012) 'Stop and Searches'. Available at: http://www.homeoffice.gov.uk/publications/science-research-statistics/research-statistics/police-research/police-powers-procedures-201011/stops-searches-1011. Accessed 25 February 2013.

Hudson, B. (2010) 'Critical Reflection as Research Methodology', in P. Davies, P. Francis and V. Jupp (eds), *Doing Criminological Research.* 2nd edn. London: Sage.

Jordan, J. (2012) 'Silencing Rape, Silencing Women', in J.M. Brown and S.L. Walklate (eds), *Handbook on Sexual Violence.* Abingdon: Routledge.

Jupp, V., Davies, P. and Francis, P. (1999) 'Features of Invisibility', in P. Davies, P. Francis, and V. Jupp (eds), *Invisible Crimes: Their Victims and Their Regulation.* Basingstoke: Macmillan Press.

Lea, J. (2002) *Crime and Modernity: Continuities in Left Realist Criminology.* London: Sage

Levi, M. (2008) *The Phantom Capitalists: The Organisation and Control of Long-firm Fraud.* 2nd edn. Aldershot: Gower.

—— (2013) *Regulating Fraud: White-Collar Crime and the Criminal Process.* London: Routledge.

Loader, I. and Sparks, R. (2006) *Public Criminology.* London: Routledge.

Lynch, M. and Stretesky, P. (2003) 'The Meaning of Green: Contrasting Criminological Perspectives', *Theoretical Criminology*, 7(2): 217–238.

Matthews, R. (2009) 'Beyond "So What?" Criminology: Rediscovering Realism', *Theoretical Criminology*, 13: 341.

—— (2010) 'Realist Criminology Revisited', in E. McLaughlin and T. Newburn (eds), *The SAGE Handbook of Criminological Theory.* London: Sage.

—— (2014) *Realist Criminology.* Basingstoke: Palgrave Macmillan .

Mills, C.W. (1958) *The Sociological Imagination.* London: Kogan-Page.

Pahl, J., Hasanbegovic, C. and Yu, M.-K. (2004) 'Globalisation and Family Violence', in V. George and R. Page (eds), *Global Social Problems and Global Social Policy.* Cambridge: Polity Press.

Pearce, F. (1976) *Crimes of the Powerful: Marxism, Crime and Deviance.* London: Pluto.

Pearce, F. and Tombs, S. (2003) 'Multinational Corporations, Power and "Crime"', in C. Sumner (ed.), *The Blackwell Companion to Criminology.* Oxford: Blackwell, 359–376.

—— (2012) *Bhopal: Flowers at the Altar of Profit and Power*. North Somercotes: Crimetalk Books.
Quinney, R. (1972) 'Who Is the Victim?', *Criminology*, 10(3): 314–323.
Reiner, R. (2006) 'Neo-liberalism, Crime and Criminal Justice', *Renewal: A Journal of Labour Politics*, 14 (3): 10–22.
—— (2007) *Law and Order: An Honest Citizen's Guide to Crime and Control*. London: Polity Press.
—— (2012a) 'What's Left?: The Prospects for Social Democratic Criminology', *Crime, Media, Culture*, 8(2): 135–150.
—— (2012b) 'Casino Capital's Crimes: Political Economy, Crime and Criminal Justice', in M. Maguire, R. Morgan, and R. Reiner (eds), *The Oxford Handbook of Criminology*. 5th edn. Oxford: Oxford University Press, 301–335.
Ruggiero, V. and South, N. (2010) 'Green Criminology and Dirty Collar Crime', *Critical Criminology*, 18: 251–262.
Scraton, P. (1999) *Hillsborough: The Truth*. Edinburgh: Mainstream.
—— (2007) *Power, Conflict and Criminalisation*. London: Taylor and Francis.
Scraton, P., Jemphrey, A. and Coleman, S. (1995) *No Last Rights: The Denial of Justice and the Promotion of Myth in the Aftermath of the Hillsborough Disaster*. Liverpool: Liverpool City Council.
Spalek, B. (1999) 'Exploring Victimisation: A Study Looking at the Impact of the Maxwell Scandal upon the Maxwell Pensioners', *International Review of Victimology*, 6: 213–230.
—— (2001) 'White Collar Crime and Secondary Victimisation: An Analysis of the Effects of the Closure of BCCI', *The Howard Journal of Criminal Justice*, 40(2): 166–179.
—— (2004) 'Policing Financial Crime: The FSA and the Myth of the Duped Investor', in R. Hopkins-Burke (ed.), *Hard Cop/Soft Cop: Dilemmas and Debates in Contemporary Policing*. Cullompton: Willan, 163–174.
—— (2007) *Farepack Victims Speak Out: An Exploration of the Harms Caused by Farepack*. London: Centre for Crime and Justice Studies/Unison.
Snider, D. (2000) 'The Sociology of Corporate Crime: An Obituary. (Or, Whose Knowledge Claims Have Legs?)', *Theoretical Criminology*, 4(2): 169–206.
Taylor, I. (1997) 'The Political Economy of Crime', in M. Maguire, R. Morgan, and R. Reiner (eds), *The Oxford Handbook of Criminology*, 2nd edn. Oxford: Oxford University Press.
Taylor, I., Walton, P. and Young, J. (1973; 2013) *The New Criminology*. London: Routledge
Tombs, S. (1999) 'Health and Safety Crimes: (In)visibility and the Problems of "Knowing"' in P. Davies, P. Francis and V. Jupp (eds), *Invisible Crimes: Their Victims and Their Regulation*. Basingstoke: Macmillan Press.
—— (2000) 'Official Statistics and Hidden Crime: Researching Safety Crimes', in V. Jupp, P. Davies and P. Francis (eds), *Doing Criminological Research*. London: Sage, 64–68.
Tombs, S. and Whyte, D. (eds) (2003) *Unmasking the Crimes of the Powerful: Scrutinizing States and Corporations*. New York: Peter Lang.
—— (2007) *Safety Crimes*. Cullompton: Willan.
—— (2008) *A Crisis of Enforcement: The Decriminalisation of Death and Injury at Work*. London: Centre for Crime and Justice Studies.

Walklate, S. (2007) *Imagining the Victim of Crime*. Maidenhead: Open University Press.
Wyatt, T. (2012) *Wildlife Trafficking: A Deconstruction of the Crime, Victims and Offenders*. Basingstoke: Palgrave Macmillan.
Young, J. (2011) *The Criminological Imagination*. London: Willan.

2
Gender First: The Secret to Revealing Sexual Crimes and Victimisations

Pamela Davies

Introduction

This chapter examines the secrets to revealing sex crimes and victimisations. It does so in the context of broader social-structural and cultural silencing factors in the United Kingdom in the twentieth and twenty-first centuries. Drawing on gendered theorising, the chapter illustrates how a predatory sexual paedophile was able to hide in plain sight and not be exposed for decades.

> It is now clear that Savile was hiding in plain sight and using his celebrity status and fund-raising activity to gain uncontrolled access to vulnerable people across six decades. For a variety of reasons the vast majority of his victims did not feel they could speak out and it's apparent that some of the small number who did had their accounts dismissed by those in authority including parents or carers. (Gray and Watt 2013: 6)

Why is it that it took over half a century to expose the UK television celebrity and charity fundraiser Jimmy Savile as a serial sex offender? The quote above, taken from the joint report by Gray and Watt (2013) for the Metropolitan Police (MPS) and the National Society for the Prevention of Cruelty to Children (NSPCC) into sexual allegations made against Jimmy Savile, uses several telling phrases: 'hiding in plain sight', 'vulnerable people' and 'accounts dismissed'. The short title of the report is 'Giving Victims a Voice' and the report acknowledges that perpetrators are reliant upon victims and witnesses of abuse not speaking out and the listed reasons for this were: fear of not being believed or taken seriously; shame being brought on one's self or the family; a perception that they were responsible; a lack of trust in statutory agencies and feeling the justice system would be ineffective in prosecuting the offender; a fear of getting themselves or the perpetrator into trouble; a perception that the abusive behaviour was 'normal'; the perpetrator used threats and coercion to silence them (Gray and Watt 2013: 20).

The vast majority of Savile's victims did not speak out. Even for those who did attempt to report their experiences when they happened, the factors that prevented their voices being heard were so institutionalised that the risk of exposure was minimal. The Savile scandal is useful for illustrating a combination of features that ensure that the real levels – past and present – of sexual abuse and violence in the United Kingdom are unknown and experiences of such victimisations are rendered invisible. Through a gendered and critical perspective, this chapter explores why and how Savile's crimes and victimisations were hidden for so long. The chapter foregrounds gender as omnirelevant to understanding sexual abuse and victimisation. The relevance of this case study analysis sheds light on the relative invisibility of sexual violence and abuse in society more generally. By surrounding this scandal with insights from gendered theorising the chapter illustrates hierarchies of knowledge about sexual abuse. Using the Jimmy Savile scandal as a springboard, the chapter examines various gatekeepers to knowledge and visibility-limiting features that ensure the threshold of risk to exposure – even for a high-profile celebrity like Savile – was always low. It underscores that, despite almost a quarter of a century of feminist thinking and its impact on exposing the gendered nature of much interpersonal violence and abuse, and, despite the higher levels of sexual and physical violence being reported today than 20 years ago, under-reporting, under-recording and attrition rates remain stubbornly problematic. The remainder of the chapter is organised under three areas for discussion. First, I justify why gender matters in respect to the exposing of sexual abuse. Second, the relevance of vulnerability is discussed, and, third, gendered and critical insights are called upon to show how a very visible personality was able to hide his sexually predatory behaviour.

Hidden sexual abuse: gender matters

The intersectionalities of class–race–age–gender or multiple inequalities (Daly 1993) variously combine 'as intersecting, interlocking and contingent' (Daly 1997: 33). Class–race–age–gender can be extended to encompass other social divisions such as sexuality and (dis)ability. In the context of examining predatory paedophile behaviour and sexual abuse and violence more generally, this chapter argues for the prioritisation of gender over and above other social divisions. The remainder of this chapter explains why accountability to gender is essential to expose such hidden crimes, and to make such victimisations more visible, it justifies why 'Gender First'.

Following observations about the absence of women in criminology (Heidensohn 1968; Smart 1976), the feminist critique in the 1970s and 1980s drew attention to gender blindness and subsequently the gendered nature of many interpersonal crimes of violence. In the case of such crimes that take place in the home, there is much evidence of a very distinct gender bias whereby men are predominantly violently abusive to women. According to the 2010–2011 BCS, 7 per cent of women and 5 per cent of men were estimated to have experienced domestic abuse in the last year, equivalent to an estimated 1.2 million female and 800,000 male victims. Furthermore, around 6 per cent of women and 4 per cent of men had experienced partner abuse in the last year, equivalent to around 900,000 female and 600,000 male victims (Smith et al. 2012). Thus one in four women will be a victim of domestic violence in their lifetime and, on average, 35 assaults happen before the police are called.

Nowadays violent and sexual crimes constitute a major category of crime and a range of crime types fall within this classification, including robbery, sexual offences, domestic violence and offences involving weapons. Headline figures for sexual assault and violence are reported upon every year and this includes information on injuries sustained and weapons used in violent incidents. In 2010 Flatley provided a detailed risk-factor analysis of incidents of sexual assault and violence, a year that evidenced increases in recorded sexual crimes. In addition, experimental statistics are now also published on the number of violent crimes experienced by children aged 10 to 15. In 2010–2011, 576000 violent incidents of this nature were estimated, accounting for two-thirds of all crimes experienced by this age group, with 77 per cent of these resulting in injury to the victim (Chaplin et al. 2011). Others have reported on the gendered nature of domestic homicide where victims are predominantly women and men the perpetrators. This is true of all forms of homicide, especially domestic homicide including child homicide (see Stern 2010). According to Home Office data for England and Wales, female victims were more likely to be killed by someone they knew. Over three-quarters (78%) of female victims knew the main suspect, compared with 57 per cent of male victims. In most of these cases, female victims were killed by a current or ex-partner (47%) while male victims were most likely to be killed by a friend or acquaintance (42%) (Smith et al. 2012).

There is then, in the twenty-first century, enhanced knowledge of the various types of sexual abuse and violent interpersonal crimes that take place in a variety of different public and private locations, as compared with six decades ago when Savile reportedly began offending. In the 1950s there was less of a focus on victimisation and public concern was about the immorality of sexual offending. The tenor of that debate culminated in the Wolfenden Committee and the Report of the Departmental Committee on Homosexual Offences and Prostitution of 1957. Over the last 30 to 40 years much feminist-inspired work has ensured that: victims are more confident about reporting sexual violence and abuse; victims are treated more sensitively; such violence is regarded as serious, is recorded as such and is prosecuted more zealously through the criminal courts.

Knowledge about the nature and extent of such crimes in the twenty-first century however remains extensively contested and, as explored below, despite much greater knowledge and less tolerance of domestic violence, there is still evidence of insensitive response to reporters and to treatment of victims. The nature and scale of sexual violence is then especially difficult to ascertain and several have explored the meaning and implications of measuring it (see, for example, Walby et al. 2012). Though there appears to be increased reporting and official recording, as noted above, which show gendered risks, there are nuances to the gender patterns as well as gaps and omissions in knowledge. In terms of gendered nuances, while the vast majority of domestic sexual and violent abuse is male to female, there are pockets of same-sex intimate partner violence and evidence of women perpetrating violence on their male partners. This only reinforces the importance of a gendered analysis that takes account of gender difference. Some women's subjection to domestic and sexual abuse is multiplied by factors of race, class and age. Where gender is not prioritised women's disproportionate levels of victimisation are rendered invisible. For example, Penhale (2013) concludes that the term 'elder abuse' hides the fact that it is older *women* who are far more often the victims of such abuse compared to older men. Official knowledge has omissions with regard to adults and 10- to 15-year-olds' experiences, and the gulf between self-reported experiences and official reporting remains wide for sexual abuse and violence where victims and offenders tend to be acquainted. This under-reporting, under-recording and under-counting of such crimes diminish their visibility in spite of their serious nature.

In focusing on the Jimmy Savile case, we move beyond crimes of sexual abuse and violence that take place in the hidden confines of the domestic setting. Nevertheless, the salience of gender remains crucial. The first page of this chapter drew attention to three telling phrases: 'hiding in plain sight', 'vulnerable people' and 'accounts dismissed'. It also highlighted, with reference to a quote from the joint MPS/NSPCC report into sexual allegations made against Jimmy Savile, some key explanations for non-reporting, under-recording and under-counting and some reasons for victims' invisibility. The reasons for victims and witnesses not speaking out are well known to those who are familiar with the findings from the various British Crime Surveys (BCS, now the Crime Survey for England and Wales). The BCS has been conducted regularly across the United Kingdom since 1983, and findings have been published citing these very same reasons for not reporting over the last three decades. There is plenty of knowledge about why people do not speak out about their experiences of harm generally and why women in particular do not speak out about their experiences of sexual abuse and violence. There are many factors that would be conducive to encouraging a 'speaking-out' culture. These include being confident that the disclosure will be believed and that the report will be taken seriously, that the reporter or their family will not be made to feel ashamed, responsible or blamed. Faith and trust in statutory agencies will only flourish in a culture that endorses and upholds such 'speaking out'. In terms of disclosing and reporting sexual violence and abuse in the Savile scenario, 'the self' appears to be the primary 'silencing agent' (Jordan 2012), the buffer to knowledge.

Speaking out and 'deaf ears'

In the minority of cases when Savile's victims acknowledged their victimisation, and tried to disclose it to those in authority, there were a number of factors that prevented victims from confiding in anyone with any confidence about their experiences. The vast majority of Savile's victims did not speak out. However, 'it's apparent that some of the small number who did had their accounts dismissed by those in authority including parents or carers' (Gray and Watt 2013: 6).

There are a number of contributory factors that conspire against victims' voices being heard and to accounts dismissed. These factors relate to the bigger social-structural and cultural picture relating to inter-personal abuse and sexual violence. If 'the self' is overcome as a primary silencing agent – a gatekeeping barrier to exposing such crimes and victimisations – there are, according to Jordan (2012) no fewer than five more key authorities or 'silencing agents', including those emanating from police responses, court and trail processes, formal and informal supports, researchers and academics, and the media (Jordan 2012: 254). The reaction and type of response the disclosure produces from friends, family, partners, police (and, in the case of Savile, health, education, social service professionals, BBC, other media and politicians) or others in authority is a critical moment in the life of a complaint. Some of these critical moments are discussed further below. However, rather than blaming the problem of non-exposure on the victim, compounding factors at play include social-structural and culturally constructed and pervasive rape myths.

The legal heritage of the crime of rape, even in nations appearing to have progressive legal reforms, see rape myths getting smuggled into the process through entrenched attitudes by agents in the system, namely, police, judges and even the public (McGregor 2012: 87).

Croall (2011) identifies six 'rape myths' that include: women really want and enjoy rape; women provoke rape; it only happens to certain kinds of women; women lie about it; rape can be prevented; rapists are sex fiends. Jones (2012: 196) lists five similar assumptions and myths around sexual violence: sexual violence is rare; false allegations of rape are common; rape victims should put up a fight and show signs of struggle and a victim will sustain genital injuries; most rapes are committed by strangers; stranger rape is more traumatic than rape by a known person.

As Brown and Walklate have recently reminded us, there are patterns to the big picture relating to sexual violence and these include:

> underreporting, attrition of cases as they drop out at key stages of the criminal justice process, disbelieving of complaints and giving men's explanations greater credence than those of women complainants. (Brown and Walklate 2012: 3)

This bigger picture is hugely significant with respect to the Savile inquiry where under-reporting and disbelief were major features. As noted above, the extent and nature of the under-counting of such victimisations and invisibility of those suffering is universally agreed to be significant. Brown and Walklate (2012) flag additional factors that contribute to the problems of measuring sexual violence. Attrition is particularly significant. The process of attrition or 'drop out' in rape cases is stubbornly problematic (see Daly and Bouhours 2010). Rape cases reported to the police can drop out and result in attrition at any one of three stages: at police involvement and investigation; during CPS involvement; or at court (Hester 2013). In Hester's research into adult rape cases and the criminal justice system in the Northeast of England three-quarters of the cases dropped out at the police stage, with many of these involving very vulnerable victims such as those with extensive mental health problems (Hester 2013).

For Savile's victims, fear, shame and self-blame are underpinned by rape myths, silencing agents and authorities all ensuring poor reporting and recording and significant levels of attrition as attempts to disclose and speak out fell on deaf ears.

Vulnerable victims and witnesses

For women, and vulnerable women in particular, rape myths are immensely worrisome, fear-inducing and problematic at a number of levels. Rape myths feed and fuel the practice of 'victim blaming' – arguably the biggest barrier to meaningful reforms in the criminal justice system. Victim blaming can manifest itself in a number of different ways and connects directly to the drop-out rate, as discussed above, of rape, sexual and interpersonal violence cases from the criminal justice system. The practice of victim blaming is especially problematic with respect to vulnerable victims/witnesses.

Vulnerable witnesses are defined by section 16 of the Youth Justice and Criminal Evidence Act 1999 as all child witnesses (under 18), and any witness whose quality of evidence is likely to be diminished because they: are suffering from a mental disorder; have a significant impairment of intelligence and social functioning; have a physical disability or are suffering from a physical disorder. Those experiencing specific types of harm, such as serious sexual abuse or physical violence, can also be deemed vulnerable. An application can be made for special measures that help vulnerable and intimidated witnesses and these can include screens, live links, video-recorded interviews, provision of evidence in private and other provisions.

Vulnerability, however, is a poorly understood and interpreted concept in the context of the criminal justice system. Though there is little academic research on the 'justice gap' for vulnerable victims there is some evidence that the approaches taken by police and prosecutors result in a lack of protection for the vulnerable. In support of this are disproportionate numbers of complaints of victimisation from those deemed vulnerable that are no-crimed, dismissed or sifted out. Complaints have a short life and are effectively rendered invisible to the criminal justice system. Additionally, critics have argued that the politicisation of the victim (Miers 1978; Walklate 2007a; Williams 1999) and concerns about different parties' 'rights' in the courtroom have resulted in complainants being put on trial as non-credible victim–witnesses.

As noted above, all child victim–witnesses are deemed vulnerable. A recent Inquiry into Child Sexual Exploitation, supported by the NSPCC, suggested that an excess of 2,409 children in England are abused every year and a further 16,500 are at high risk of sexual exploitation (Beckett et al. 2012). Few of these children will gain access to criminal justice and their cases are unlikely to progress through it. Victims and victimisations remain hidden. Vulnerability is an 'intrinsic attribute of children' (Furedi 2013: 42) yet vulnerability is a multidimensional concept and being vulnerable due to being youthful can coexist with emotional, socio-economic and undiagnosed psychological vulnerabilities. This is partially supported through gender-based evidence linked to female offenders (Corston 2007; Stern 2010). Where children are supported to report acts committed against them there is evidence of them being responded to as offenders and they run the risk of being criminalised. Where children and young people do engage with the criminal justice system as victims, there is evidence of secondary victimisation and practices that discredit them, turning child victims into offenders. Vulnerable children and young people are therefore re-represented as offenders and out-of-control troublesome, often promiscuous, or lately even 'predatory' (see Toynbee 2013), youth.

Children's charities work hard to alter the perception of such extremely vulnerable children as offenders and refer to a 'perception and reality gap' (see Crawley et al. 2004). Muncie (2009) and Brown (2005) have similarly drawn attention to these problematic and inaccurate cultural and mediated representations of children as more 'sinning than sinned against'. In the area of child sexual exploitation there are attitudinal and perceptional problems where tensions produce scepticism and queries over whether or not the young person is a passive 'innocent' victim (Pearce 2009). Thus there are perceptions and reality gaps to add to the rape myths discussed earlier. In summary, there is a mismatch between perceptions and the reality of those who are vulnerable and who experience sexual abuse. This mismatch is presented here as a justice gap for victims who are vulnerable due to the nature of the abuse and exploitation and due to their gender and age profile.

Returning to the notion of silencing agents and gatekeepers to knowledge, in the context of sexual violence and rape of female adults, as noted above, Hester (2013) concludes that to varying degrees the police adopt a victim-focused approach with an emphasis on believing victims from when they report and supporting them to remain in the criminal justice system. So the police are a key authority and the police response is another critical moment in the life of a complaint. The police can be a key silencing agent, or the police can respond sensitively and treat the complaint seriously, and the nature of this response may lead to a longer exposure of the complaint. In contrast to the positive conclusions regarding the victim-focused police response, Hester (2013) concluded that CPS has a focus on victims at the centre of its decision-making:

> The CPS may be characterised as having an approach with 'focus on victims', where what matters and appears central to decisions about taking a case forward is: the credibility of the victim (consistency of account and with other witnesses, i.e. victim believable); corroboration (through penetration); and that it is in the public interest that the perpetrator is convicted (behaviour is part of a pattern). (Hester 2013)

The CPS represents another critical moment in the life of a complaint where accounts can be dismissed. The CPS sifting stage is another gatekeeper to knowledge and a sexual crime and abuse visibility-limiting opportunity. Hester's research refers exclusively to vulnerable adults, yet children and young people who have experienced sexual violence, exploitation and/or physical abuse, have mental health problems or learning difficulties (often as a result of institutionalisation) comprise an extremely vulnerable victim group who are denied access to the criminal justice system or fail to progress through it without being re-victimised. Although the police have increasingly adopted a victim-focused approach and the CPS now claim they adopt a merits-based approach, focusing on the overall case, ignoring myths and stereotypes rather than dwelling exclusively on the credibility of the victim, there is little evidence of vulnerable victims proceeding confidently and with satisfactory outcomes, through the criminal justice system.

Keir Starmer QC, Director of Public Prosecutions before he stepped down in October 2013, has spoken about the need to establish a collective response and national consensus about the way forward in prosecuting sexual abuse and violence. Starmer's observations of unfolding events in 2012–2013, draw on evidence from panel reviews and, in the case of the Savile allegations, the Levitt Report (2013). In both instances policy changes and cultural shifts over time are revealed as key to establishing a more equal approach to doing and achieving justice in the future. It is worth focusing on two prosecutorial examples that Starmer makes observations upon as they illustrate several justice issues for young and vulnerable victims and problems surrounding the criminal justice response to sexual offending more generally. The first concerns a CPS decision not to proceed with a prosecution. In May 2012 a conviction was secured in Rochdale where defendants were found guilty of serious serial sexual abuse. However, this was achieved only on re-examination of an earlier 2009 decision by the CPS not to proceed. The second concerns a proposition to sift out weak cases of child sexual assault by way of a higher evidential test threshold, as dealt with by a Home Affairs Committee in 2003. In relation to the first example and the CPS decision not to proceed, changes in policy relating to the review of previous decisions led to a prosecutorial re-examination. Commenting on the review of the 2012 Operation Span case in Rochdale Starmer observes that the approach to credibility was flawed:

> it was clear that if the yardsticks traditionally used by prosecutors for evaluating the credibility and reliability of victims in other cases were used without adaptation in cases of child sexual exploitation, the outcome could potentially be a category of vulnerable victims left unprotected by the law. (Starmer 2013: 2)

In this case many of the victims are vulnerable precisely because they are young and their credibility and reliability was tested by asking questions about current or previous features of their character (distrustful of authority, slow to report, use alcohol, use drugs, return to the perpetrator, dishonest, self-harm) that make them vulnerable in the first place.

In relation to the second example, as Starmer points out, by 2013 the sifting in relation to cases of child sexual assault would appear to have been overzealous. There is a delicate balance between an overzealous approach to investigating and prosecuting in cases where the only witness is the victim and an overly cautious approach to complainants and their accounts. An overly cautious approach is seen in the use of higher evidential tests for vulnerable victims and for cases of intimate abuse and violence and the sifting out of allegedly weaker potential cases. Such prosecutorial approaches allow for the dismissal of accounts from vulnerable victim–witnesses. In relation to the Savile case, the Levitt report to the DPP (2013) concluded:

i. I have seen nothing to suggest that the decisions not to prosecute were consciously influenced by any improper motive on the part of either police or prosecutors.

ii. That having been said, I have reservations about the way in which the prosecutor reached his decision.
iii. On the face of it, the allegations made were both serious and credible; the prosecutor should have recognised this and sought to 'build' a prosecution. In particular, there were aspects of what he was told by the police as to the reasons that the victims did not want to give evidence which should have caused him to ask further questions. Instead, he appears to have treated the obstacles as fatal to the prospects of a prosecution taking place.
iv. Looked at objectively, there was nothing to suggest that the alleged victims had colluded in their accounts, nor that they were in any way inherently less reliable than, say, a victim of a burglary or a road traffic accident. Despite this, the police treated them and the accounts they gave with a degree of caution which was neither justified nor required.
v. Most of the victims continue to speak warmly of the individual officers with whom they had contact. However each of those to whom I have spoken has said that had she been given more information by the police at the time of the investigation, and in particular had she been told that she was not the only woman to have complained, she probably would have been prepared to give evidence.
vi. Having spoken to the victims I have been driven to conclude that had the police and prosecutors taken a different approach a prosecution might have been possible.

Levitt (2013), as noted in (ii) above, had 'reservations about the way in which the prosecutor reached his decision'. These examples illustrate the serious impact prosecutorial decision-making has on the visibility of serious sexual violence and intimate abuse in the courts. They also illustrate an impact on justice for the vulnerable and point towards injustices and a justice gap for vulnerable and intimidated victims who warrant special measures. Both of the examples above demonstrate that the qualities that render the already vulnerable, vulnerable, are then turned into measures used to test their status as real victims. The examples show how police and prosecution decision-making resulted historically in social exclusion from justice. Vulnerable victims will often fail to come to the attention of any caring profession or social control agency, including the police. They are silenced and denied access to the law. In the already reduced likelihood of these vulnerable people gaining access to the law and criminal justice system, the qualities that render them vulnerable are again used to test their credibility and reliability as worthy and 'good' victims and witnesses. Special measures are used as a sop to achieving best evidence rather than an aid to establishing equal justice for all. Some are left 'stranded victims' isolated from any effective process of remedying the wrongs they experience (Clements 2005). The justice gap is widened as victims are treated with a degree of caution that is not generally justified and sexual-offence victims are subjected to a different and more rigorous set of credibility, reliability and evidential tests than those applied to other victims. A combination of socio-structural and cultural mutually reinforced factors conspires to diminish the visibility of these serious types of harm and hides a plethora of injustices for some of the most vulnerable.

Hiding in plain sight

> Why was Savile not noticed and stopped by the police, health, education or social service professionals, people at the BBC or other media, parents or carers, politicians or even 'society' in general? (Starmer 2013)

The earlier discussions go some way to understanding why Savile's predatory offending was not noticed and stopped. However, unlike interpersonal violence and abuse in the home, Savile was a very prominent and public figure who abused in public institutions such as schools, hospitals and the British Broadcasting Corporation (BBC). How did Savile 'hide in plain sight'? The MPS/NSPCC report connects this with Savile's celebrity status and fund-raising activities which gave him uncontrolled access to vulnerable people across six decades. Savile's celebrity status and fund-raising activities stopped the authorities – the police, health, education or social service professionals, people at the BBC or other media, parents or carers, politicians or even 'society' in general – from seeing Savile the predatory paedophile.

At the start of this chapter I made it clear that, in the context of predatory paedophile behaviour and sexual abuse and violence more generally, gender matters and should be prioritised and foregrounded if such crimes and victimisations are to be exposed and made more routinely visible. Gender is arrived at through a process of ongoing methodical and situated accomplishments (Lorber 1994; Simpson and Elis 1995; West and Fenstermaker 1995; West and Zimmerman 1987). The arguments in support of 'Gender First' are now elaborated upon drawing upon gender-accomplishment theorising. The discussion explores the combination of institutionalised social-structural and cultural factors that help reveal why, even when victims spoke out, their voices were not heard and justice failed to be achieved during Savile's lifetime. The discussion of Savile as perpetrator hiding in plain sight is approached through the lens of crime and structured masculinity.

Performing sexual abuse in plain sight: crime as structured and institutionalised masculinity

For structural criminology, power relationships are a central part of crime and victimisation (Hagan 1988), essential to understanding the actions of the perpetrator and the reactions of the victim and others to the offending. From a structural criminologist's perspective, Savile had instrumental and symbolic power at his disposal. His actions were based on a form of power that, when imposed upon the vulnerable – for the most part young women and girls – would ensure that even the most seriously abusive of behaviour would render his victims speechless and the reactions of others would be to dismiss and ignore.

Messerschmidt's analysis directly links structured action and gendered crime. Under his (1993) formulation, crime is a form of structured/situated action/accomplishment, a resource for accomplishing or 'doing-gender' (West and Zimmerman 1987). Gender is omnirelevant and this formulation makes sense of what crimes men and boys do, how they do them and why they do them. If crime is used as a resource for 'doing-gender', crime by men is a means of accomplishing masculinity (Messerschmidt 1994, 1995). In respect to young men he suggests crime offers 'lads' and men a 'daring opposition masculinity' (Messerschmidt 1994: 97). Men and boys achieve masculinity through the doing of violent crimes and property crime. Several contributors to this influential body of work demonstrate (see Newburn and Stanko 1994; Messerschmidt 1993; Daly 1997; Joe-Laidler and Hunt 2001; Miller 1998) that there are variations in the application of 'doing-gender' and different masculinities.

Under the theoretical construction of how men do gender through violence there is an underlying group dynamic to the doing of masculinity. According to Connell (1987), the ways in which men express their masculinity in contemporary society is connected to the powerful position held by the presumption of normative heterosexuality. Normative heterosexuality defines the structure and the form of manhood that any individual man is constrained to live up to. For Connell (1995) hegemonic masculinity is a culturally idealised form of masculinity, an ascendancy of a certain form of masculinity that promotes particular expressions of masculinity. There is a wide range of settings in which the job of enacting masculine gender is done, including the home and the workplace. The group dynamic that ensures the job is achieved is embedded in authorities such as the police, health, education, social service professions, the BBC, politicians and so on. In any specific time (Savile's six decades) and place (Savile's workplace – the BBC and charity venues including hospitals and schools), hegemonic masculinity was 'culturally honored, glorified, and extolled at the symbolic level' (Messerschmidt 1997: 9). In this particular example his 'victims' were 'put in their place' as non-victims and men were confirmed as men. Normative heterosexuality conditioned and perpetuated workplace activities and practices promoting coercive behaviours and sexually violent and abusive practices. The responses of those in authority result in them being the gatekeepers to knowledge of sexual violence and abuse. Harms and victimisations are occluded, rendering those experiencing them invisible and inciting further masculine violence and abuse.

Denial of victimhood

Sexual abuse analysed as structured and institutionalised masculinity illuminates how Savile was able to perform sexual abuse in plain sight and in public places over six decades. Savile's personal instrumental and symbolic power meshed with the institutionalised presumptions of normative hegemonic heterosexuality embedded in the major institutions where he worked. These pervasive ideologies meant that, though his secrets were well known to many, they were also well kept. Hegemonic agencies and personnel within them colluded in the abuse by failing to acknowledge the crimes and victimisations. Many victims were not aware or did not fully appreciate that they were victims; others may have normalised their experience. Most of his victims did not know one another, but taken together the inquiry concluded that their accounts 'paint a compelling picture of widespread sexual abuse by a predatory sex offender' (Gray and Watt 2013: 4). It was not until all of the separate accounts were collated and the similar evidences were brought together that the repeat offending became evident and diffuse and multiple victims were identified.

Victims were denied their victimhood. This analysis illustrates the complex dynamics of victimisation and victim–offender relationships. The traditional and positivist victimological concepts of victim precipitation, victim proneness, victim culpability, victim provocation and the notion of victim blaming (see Miers 1978; Walklate 2007b) are all relevant to this analysis and are part of the secret to revealing sexual crimes and interpersonal violences well into the twenty-first century.

Revelations of sexual crimes and victimisations

Though there have been enormous changes in terms of moving the victim more centre stage in matters of criminal justice of the last 40 years or so, and academic and activist knowledges have had their role to play in effecting these changes, there remain serious flaws and gaps in our knowledge about some very serious types of crimes and the victimisations and harms they incur. The cultural shift that acknowledges the victim of crime may partially explain why, following the Jimmy Savile inquiry and other inquiries, commissions and investigations on institutional and serial sexual abuse, allegations of indecent assault in the latter half of the twentieth century are now being heard and taken seriously, why historical abuse has now entered mediated accounts and become more commonplace vocabulary. The Savile revelations only became widely visible after his death. Other abuses die a death during the criminal justice process and complaints are dismissed, sifted out or drop out. A better appreciation and understanding of the gendered nature of vulnerability may be the key to unlock some of these injustices, to prevent dismissal of accounts and to achieve a collective response and national consensus. Victims need the confidence to come forward; they currently feel let down by a systemic failure of criminal justice and other responsible agencies and authorities. The culture of intimidation and the preferred practices of protecting the reputations of institutions through cover-ups, whether in schools or the BBC, demand an overhaul of systems that are not working. Complaints and their victims are rendered invisible.

Conclusion

This chapter has used the Jimmy Savile scandal – where the key reasons as to why victims did not speak out were fear, shame, others' perceptions, trust and self-blame – as a touchstone for understanding the wider socio-structural and cultural features that render child sexual abuse, and gendered crimes and harms more generally, relatively invisible. It has insisted on the salience of gender to unlocking the secrets of sexual crimes and victimisations. In doing so it has exposed a justice gap that contemporarily exists for already vulnerable victims and witnesses. This gap emerges as child sexual abuse and exploitation investigations are hampered by failures to believe victims and by further failures, including insensitive handling and interviewing of victims, failure to take detailed statements and to seek out corroborating evidence, incomplete or truncated investigations and sifted-out prosecutions. The analysis of the Savile scandal has been approached through the lens of crime as structured masculinity. The extreme visibility of Savile as celebrity paradoxically served to protect him from being exposed as a prolific predatory paedophile. The chapter has suggested there are gatekeepers to knowledge and critical moments that limit visibility and hierarchies of knowledge about sexual abuse and interpersonal violence. Thus, in broader terms, the chapter has emphasised the gendered nature of violence and sexual abuse and illustrates how gender matters in this context, yet other inequalities combine to render some victims even more vulnerable and exempt from justice than others. They may experience problems accessing legal remedies and the criminal justice system and/or they may experience a problem with the law itself. They are left stranded. The law and the criminal justice system can be seen and experienced as inaccessible, unattractive or irrelevant, even victimising.

References

Beckett, H. with Brodie, I., Factor, F., Melrose, M., Pearce, J., Pitts, J., Shuker, L. and Warrington, C. (2012) *Research into Gang-Associated Sexual Exploitation and Sexual Violence*. Interim Report University of Bedfordshire.
Brown, J.M. and Walklate, S.L. (eds) (2012) *Handbook on Sexual Violence*. Abingdon: Routledge.
Brown, S. (2005) *Understanding Youth and Crime: Listening to Youth?* Maidenhead: Open University Press.
Chaplin, R., Flatley, J. and Smith, K. (2011) *Crime in England and Wales 2010/11*. London: Home Office Statistical Bulletin 10/11.
Clements, L. (2005) 'Winners and Losers', *Journal of Law and Society*, 32(1): 34–50.
Connell, R.W. (1987) *Gender and Power*. Cambridge: Polity.
—— (1995) *Masculinities*. Cambridge: Polity.
Corston, J. (2007) *Corston Report*. London: Home Office.
Crawley, M., Roberts, P. and Shepherd, W. (2004) *Taking Stock: Children and Young Peoples at Risk of or Involved in Abuse through Prostitution within Stockton-on-Tees*. (SECOS Project). Ilford: Barnardo's.
Croall, H. (2011) *Crime and Society in Britain*. 2nd edn. Harlow: Pearson.
Daly, K. (1993) 'Class-Race-Gender: Sloganeering in Search of Meaning', *Social Justice*, 20(1–2): 56–71.
—— (1997) 'Different Ways of Conceptualising Sex/Gender in Feminist Theory and Their Implications for Criminology', *Theoretical Criminology*, 1(1): 25–51.
Daly, K. and Bouhours, B. (2010) 'Rape and Attrition in the Legal Process: A Comparative Analysis of Five Countries', *Crime and Justice: An Annual Review of Research*, 39: 565–650. Chicago: University of Chicago Press.
Flatley, J., Kershaw, C., Smith, K., Chaplin, R. and Moon, D. (2010) *Crime in England and Wales 2009/10*. London: Home Office Statistical Bulletin 12/10.

Furedi, F. (2013) *Moral Crusades in an Age of Mistrust: The Jimmy Savile Scandal.* London: Palgrave-MacMillan.
Gray, D. and Watt, P. (2013). *Giving Victims a Voice: Joint Report into Sexual Allegations Made against Jimmy Savile.* London: MPS/NSPCC.
Hagan, J. (1988) *Structural Criminology.* Cambridge: Polity Press.
Heidensohn, F. (1968) 'The Deviance of Women: A Critique and an Enquiry', *British Journal of Sociology*, 19: 160–175.
Hester, M. (2013) *From Report to Court: Rape Cases and the Criminal Justice System in the North East. Executive Summary.* Bristol: University of Bristol in association with the Northern Rock Foundation.
Home Office (1990) *The Victims Charter: A Statement of Rights for Victims of Crime.* London: Home Office.
Joe-Laidler, K. and Hunt, G. (2001) 'Accomplishing Femininity among the Girls in the Gang', *British Journal of Criminology*, 41: 656–678.
Jones, H. (2012) 'On Sociological Perspectives', in J.M. Brown and S.L. Walklate (eds), *Handbook on Sexual Violence.* Abingdon: Routledge, 181–202.
Jordan, J. (2012) 'Silencing Rape, Silencing Women', in J.M. Brown and S.L. Walklate (eds), *Handbook on Sexual Violence.* Abingdon: Routledge.
Levitt, A. (2013) *In the Matter of the Late Jimmy Savile: Report to the Director of Public Prosecutions.* London: Crown Prosecution Service.
Lorber, J. (1994) *Paradoxes of Gender.* Yale: Yale University Press.
McGregor, J. (2012) 'The Legal Heritage of the Crime of Rape', in J.M. Brown and S.L. Walklate (eds), *Handbook on Sexual Violence.* Abingdon: Routledge, 69–89.
Messerschmidt, J.W. (1993) *Masculinities and Crime: Critique and Reconceptualisation of Theory.* Lanham, MD: Rowman and Littlefield.
—— (1994) 'Schooling, Masculinities and Youth Crime by White Boys', in T. Newburn and E. Stanko (eds), *Just Boys Doing Business?* London: Routledge, 81–89.
—— (1995) 'From Patriarchy to Gender: Feminist Theory, Criminology and the Challenge of Diversity', in N. Hahn Rafter and F. Heidensohn (eds), *International Feminist Perspectives in Criminology: Engendering a Discipline.* Philadelphia: Open University Press.
—— (1997) *Crime as Structured Action.* London: Sage.
Miers, D. (1978) *Responses to Victimisation.* Abingdon: Professional Books.
Miller, J. (1998) 'Up It Up: Gender and the Accomplishment of Street Robbery', *Criminology*, 36(1): 37–65.
Muncie, J. (2009) *Youth Crime.* 3rd edn. London: Sage.
Newburn, T. and Stanko, E. (eds) (1994) *'Just Boys Doing Business': Men, Masculinities and Crime.* London: Routledge.
Pearce, J.J. (2009) Young People and Sexual Exploitation 'It's Not Hidden, You Just Aren't Looking'. London: Routledge.
Penhale, B. (2013) 'Older Women, Domestic Violence, and Elder Abuse: A Review of Commonalities, Differences, and Shared Approaches', *Journal of Elder Abuse & Neglect*, 15(3–4): 163–183.
Simpson, S.S. and Elis, L. (1995) 'Doing Gender: Sorting Out the Class and Crime Conundrum', *Criminology*, (33): 47–81.
Smart, C. (1976) *Women, Crime and Criminology: A Feminist Critique.* London: Routledge and Kegan Paul.

Smith, K., Osborne, S., Lau, I. and Britton, A. (eds) (2012) *Homicides, Firearm Offences and Intimate Violence 2010/11*. London: Home Office Statistical Bulletin 10/12.

Starmer, K. (2013) *The Criminal Justice Response to Child Sexual Abuse: Time for a National Consensus*. London: Crown Prosecution Service.

Stern, V. (2010) *The Stern Review: A Report by Baroness Stern CBE of an Independent Review into how Rape Complaints Are Handled by Public Authorities in England and Wales*. London: Home Office.

Toynbee, P. (2013) 'Misogyny Runs So Deep in This Society, It Is Even Used against Abused Children', *The Guardian*, 7 August.

Walby, S., Armstrong, J. and Strid, S. (2012) 'Developing Measures of Multiple Forms of Sexual Violence and Their Contested Treatment in the Criminal Justice System', in J.M. Brown and S.L. Walklate (eds), *Handbook on Sexual Violence*. Abingdon: Routledge, 90–113.

Walklate, S.L. (2007a) *Imagining the Victim of Crime*. Maidenhead: Open University Press.

—— (2007b) 'Men, Victims and Crime', in P. Davies, P. Francis and C. Greer (eds), *Victims, Crime and Society*. London: Sage.

West, C. and Fenstermaker, S. (1995) 'Doing Difference', *Gender and Society*, 9(1): 8–37.

West, C. and Zimmerman, D.H. (1987) 'Going Gender', *Gender and Society*, 1(2): 125–151.

Williams, B. (1999) *Working with Victims of Crime: Policies, Politics and Practice*. London: Jessica Kingsley.

3
Politics, Power and the Media: The Visibility of Environmental and Eco-Terrorism

Hayley Watson and Tanya Wyatt

We are often told by politicians and the media that we live in an increasingly dangerous world, with many threats facing us. There is also an assumption that we face a far greater number of risks/threats than we have ever faced in the past (Beck 1999; Furedi 2002) in part due to our increased interconnectedness (Aas 2013). Whether that is true is debatable and possibly the result of more visibility and awareness of threats through better reporting rather than actual danger. These threats are crimes and harms that take on many forms, from random violence on the street to natural disasters exacerbated by climate change, but none may be more fear-inducing than terrorism. As proposed in the Introduction to this volume, there are a variety of features that make crime and harm, such as terrorism, visible or invisible, exposed or hidden. Whereas Chapter 2 details some historico-structural-cultural aspects that impact upon the existence and resilience of invisibility, this chapter investigates the role of politics, power and the media in shaping and defining, uncovering or covering, suffering and injustice through an exploration of two particular kinds of terrorism – environmental and eco.

Terrorism is now of course a widely utilised and recognised term. Following the terrorist attacks in the United States on 11 September 2001, terrorism became a topic that continues to attract great attention within political agendas and in the media. This is not confined to Al Qaeda and Islamic extremists, but new threats that have been labelled 'terrorism' by politicians, government agencies and media empires as is the case analysed in this chapter with environmental and eco-terrorism. The chapter will begin by offering definitions of environmental and eco-terrorism in order to establish an understanding of what these activities include. Then, the methodology for our analysis of the news media coverage of environmental and eco-terrorism will be detailed. This is followed by illustrations and analysis from the news media that evidences the political construction and manipulation of these terms. In so doing, we also explore the power dynamics in play to make visible these so-called terrorists. This will be followed by counter-arguments against labelling these actors as terrorists and the proposal that by keeping the 'terrorists' in the spotlight other harms by power entities are kept invisible.

What are environmental and eco-terrorism?

The Federal Bureau of Investigation has tagged environmental and eco-terrorism at different times as one of the fastest growing domestic terrorist threats facing Western society or the Uniteds States's 'biggest domestic threat' (Fox News 2008; *Orange County Weekly* 2005). At the same time, fear of what is also called 'environmental terrorism', but encompassing very different actions, has become part of the wider discourse surrounding 'terrorism'. But what are 'ecoterrorism' and 'environmental terrorism'? Do they really constitute acts of terror?

Much academic literature has paid attention to the difficulties in defining the concept of terrorism. Due to space constraints, it is not possible here to fully explore this debate. For the purpose of this chapter, a definition originating from an academic consensus of terrorism in 1988 by over 90 terrorism experts is used. Recently, this definition has been revised and has been written up by media and terrorism expert Alex Schmid (2008):

> Terrorism refers on the one hand to a doctrine about the presumed effectiveness of a special form or tactic of fear-generating, coercive political violence and, on the other hand, to a conspiratorial practice of calculated, demonstrative, direct violent action without legal or moral restraints, performed for its propagandistic and psychological effects on various audiences and conflict parties.

For an attack to be an act of terrorism, it must have two elements: the belief that the fear-inducing or coercive violent act will be effective, and that this unrestrained violent action is undertaken for its effect on certain audiences and opponents, which are not necessarily those targeted by the action.

This conceptual foundation can now be expanded to the forms of terrorism under scrutiny here. In academic terms, Chalecki (2002: 48) has come to define environmental terrorism and eco-terrorism thus:

> Environmental terrorism can be defined as the unlawful use of force against in situ environmental resources so as to deprive populations of their benefit(s) and/or destroy other property.... The professed aim of eco-terrorists is to slow or halt exploitation of natural resources and to bring public attention to environmental issues such as unsustainable logging or wildlife habitat loss through development.

As outlined by Chalecki, the term eco-terrorism was first brought to public attention by the radical environmental group Earth First!, which formed in 1980. Chalecki (2002) argues that the 'modern' successor of carrying out eco-terrorism is the Environmental Liberation Front, otherwise known as ELF, which developed in England in 1993. Chalecki points to action by ELF, such as the burning down of a ski lodge in Colorado in 1998; she also refers to acts in January 2001 in which new homes in London Island were burnt in protest of human's unceasing encroachment on nature (Chalecki 2002). By completing a news media search on LexisNexis database, it is possible to trace the term eco-terrorism back to an article written in September 1989 for the Canadian *The Globe and Mail*; the article refers to a letter written warning of spikes being placed on trees by the Temagami Wilderness Society to stop a lumber company from cutting them down. The article shows how the president of the lumber company identifies this action as 'eco-terrorism' (*The Globe and Mail* 1989).

In contrast to these examples of eco-terrorism, environmental terrorism involves acts that are intent on using the environment to harm people and targets natural resources. Chalecki (2002) argues that groups such as Earth First! and ELF do not target natural resources. Again, by completing a LexisNexis newspaper search, the term environmental terrorism can be traced back to a July 1985 article written for the *San Diego Union-Tribune*; the term is used in conjunction with a discussion over the survival of a Californian bird, Bell's Vireo, from extinction; action to prevent this would have caused various industrial projects to be put aside. People in charge of the projects accused Fish and Wildlife officials of environmental terrorism (Lamb 1985).

Whereas the initial definition of eco-terrorism found in *The Globe and Mail* (1989) corresponds to Chalecki's definition, the first incident recorded by the news media of so-called environmental terrorism (1985) does not have the same meaning as proposed by Chalecki, nor does its meaning fall within eco-terrorism. Environmental terrorism seems to have first been used as a label to describe legal actions to protect species by conservationists and officials that came into conflict with development and industrial projects. This usage begins to uncover the manipulation of stigmatising labels by powerful entities to weaken those in opposition to their expanding business projects. In protecting the environment, there is no doctrine or practice that qualifies as terrorism according to Schmid (2008). In this initial 1985 usage, it is clear that the term has been used to attempt to discredit those blocking industrial development. This represents an evolution in its meaning.

The mid- to late 1980s are a pivotal time period in environmental movements and their relationship to political structures. This is evident by the campaigning efforts of multiple non-governmental organisations, but in particular Greenpeace. In 1985, the Greenpeace vessel *Rainbow Warrior* was docked in Auckland, New Zealand preparing to peacefully protest against French nuclear testing on a nearby island (Greenpeace 2014). French secret service agents bombed the vessel, killing one crew member. Only two of the agents went to trial and though they were sentenced to ten and seven years, they were released after two years (Greenpeace 2014). Within this historic context then, the emerging visibility of environmental and eco-terrorism can be seen. The evolution of the usage of the terms is now explored through investigation of the news media coverage.

The power of the news media and the visibility of environmental and eco-terrorism

Traditionally speaking, from a sociological perspective, the social constructionist approach to the media suggests that the news media can be seen to play a significant role in influencing the public agenda in society (Chibnall 1977; Jewkes 2004). Arguably, by influencing the public agenda, the media also influences the visibility and therefore the invisibility of crimes and harms. For example, they tell us what security issues, such as the threat of environmental or eco-terrorism, are important and worthy of public attention. The more important and worthy threats are deemed (Chibnall 1977; Greer 2005; Jewkes 2004), the more coverage they receive and thus the greater their visibility. Thus, with the stance that the media influence public opinion of security issues and the related visibility, it is necessary to consider how exactly the news media sets the public and potentially political agenda.

The creation of news is, put simply, the construction of information surrounding a piece of news that allows for the development of knowledge of an event, such as a case of environmental or eco-terrorism. For Berger and Luckmann (1966) the development of knowledge is a construction process. The news media then are key instruments that tell individuals what to think about and how to perceive something (McNair 1998). Thus, the public's understanding of the threat posed by environmental and eco-terrorists is largely a result of the way in which the terrorists (and their actions) are presented to the public via word of the news media. Similarly, Best (2008) believes that issues are presented to the public by the news media in such a way that promotes them as presenting a threat to society; they are 'social problems'.

In 1922 Lippmann (2008: 28) argued that individuals are presented with a number of 'pictures' that influence people's knowledge of the occurrence of an event. Pictures are very rarely developed from direct experience of an event, but instead are a result of pictures that are given to people. In Western society, these 'pictures' originate (more often than not) from the news media; in this sense, reality is created by an outside force. Similarly, Schudson (2003: 2) suggests that the news media, in particular, journalists, not only 'report reality', but, in addition, they 'create it'. News then is not simply a 'mirror of reality', rather it is what Schudson (2003: 33) refers to as a 'representation of the world', meaning that it is a depiction of reality that is selected and constructed by human beings.

Relevant to the way in which news is constructed is the sociological process: agenda setting. McCombs and Shaw (1972: 176) argue that the news media are responsible for setting the agenda for what the public should think about and deem important:

> In choosing and displaying news, editors, newsroom staff, and broadcasters play an important part in shaping political reality. Readers learn not only about a given issue, but also how much importance to attach to that issue from the amount of information in a news story and its position.

The link to an issue's (in)visibility and the construction of that image is clear. Agenda-setting theory argues that the news media have a direct influence on their audience via their choice of what news items they decide are newsworthy and the resulting amount of space and prominence those newsworthy items are given (Chibnall 1977; Jewkes 2004). Via this agenda-setting process, the news media are able to control and construct the content of the news. In setting the news agenda, the news media are then able to place pressure on the public in influencing the public's choice of what the most important matters of news are in society. As argued by Hall (1978: 62), 'Concentrated media attention confers the status of high public concern on issues which are highlighted; these generally become understood by everyone as the "pressing issues of the day". This is part of the media's "agenda setting function".' As politicians rely on public opinion for votes and elections, these pressing issues become features of political agendas and campaigns. What has been made visible by the media can then be amplified if incorporated in the political sphere.

In order to identify the presence of agenda setting within the media, it is necessary to consider the use of what McCombs (2006: 2) refers to as salience cues:

> Newspapers communicate a host of cues about the relative salience of the topics on their daily agenda. The lead story on page 1, front page versus inside page, the size of the headline, and event, the length of a story all communicate the salience of topics on the news agenda.

The physical visibility then – the placement, the size, the colour of the piece – affects the social and political visibility of threats, crimes and harms. The media has significant power in determining what is hidden and how it is perceived. This power sits in the hands of fewer and fewer people as news corporations are consolidated. There are a small number of people who control media empires, which gives them substantial influence over public opinion and the political agenda. This is further exacerbated by the constant presence of the news in people's lives via the vast range of mobile digital technologies and the up-to-the-minute reporting of news via the Web and social media.

Politics

The ways in which the news media construct an issue are, as has been identified, extremely important to how the issue is received and perceived by the public. However, it is important to understand that it is not simply the news media that are responsible for setting the news agenda, for they are influenced by a range of outside sources, one of which is the government. Altheide (2003, 2006) suggests that when reporting acts of terror, the news media, in conjunction with authorities, have cast 'fear' as the contemporary predominant discourse of 'being' for individuals. Jewkes (2004) argues that one of the criteria for newsworthiness is 'risk' and the idea of a lasting danger to society.

Fear of terrorism or the risk from it, then, are said to take a step forward from being a 'considered' reaction to being a state of 'normality' for individuals (Altheide 2003; Jewkes 2004). Through popular culture and news this social construction of 'fear' becomes a reality in what Altheide describes as a 'Politics of Fear'. In this sense, the news media shape public perceptions of threats to security with vulnerability as the predominant state of being, a preconception of a weak society unable to cope with security threats facing it. In considering the relationship between terrorism and the news media, this perception of 'fear' as a 'normal' state of mind is important as it takes on one of the central goals of terrorism; to incite fear into a mass audience. This 'discourse' of fear shapes the production of news and can therefore greatly affect the representation of the threat of terrorism by the news media.

Altheide (2006: 6) argues that it is not simply that fear is a bad thing, but, what is of utmost importance, is how 'fear is promoted and exploited by leaders for their own survival and policies rather than that of their audiences'. Conceptualised another way, fear or the risk of terrorism can be seen as a political diversion, a distraction from wider problems (Jewkes 2004). Thus we see for the purpose of this chapter, from a methodological point of view, it is necessary to examine the complex nature and portrayal of terrorism coverage by the news media and what the effects of this media dramatisation of security have upon society. For example, are other issues, such as violent protests, seen in London in 2011, labelled terrorism as a dramatic attempt to force individuals to consider this 'action' to be a threat to society? For this reason it is essential to determine whether the discourse used to discuss the actions of those involved in these incidents are simply cases of environmental protest or are actually acts of 'terror'.

Methodology

The chosen form of methodology for understanding the news media's portrayal of environmental and eco-terrorism was qualitative media analysis (QMA).[1] This method stems from the work of the American sociology professor David Altheide (1996), who specialises in conducting an alternative form of content analysis to media text. QMA is a form of document analysis, and consists of a mixture of content analysis with participant observation allowing for a form of ethnographic content analysis. Altheide (1996: 2) states that the purpose of QMA is to: 'Blend the traditional notion of objective content analysis with participant observation to form ethnographic content analysis, or how a researcher interacts with documentary materials so that specific statements can be placed in the proper context for analysis'.

Put simply, it allows for an understanding to be developed regarding the meaning behind text by taking one step further than solely looking at the number of times a term occurs (as with traditional content analysis). As such, QMA allows for the exploration of meaning within context. Crucially, for the present analysis, it is necessary to understand the context that the terms environmental and eco-terrorism occur in; only then will it be possible to determine how the news media discuss events labelled as such, which would in turn allow for analysis as to whether these acts constitute the label of 'terrorism'.

QMA includes a number of steps that 'should' be followed. Accordingly, this research began by pursuing 'a specific problem to be investigated', in this case, what is meant by the terms environmental and eco-terrorism and whether or not events labelled this way should in fact be labelled as 'terrorism' (Altheide 1996: 23). The second step of QMA is to 'become familiar with the process and context of the information source.... Explore possible sources (perhaps documents) of information' (Altheide 1996: 24). For this it was necessary to consider how would we know about environmental and eco-terrorism? The obvious answer is the news media. For this reason it was decided to use newspapers for investigative purposes.

Using the online newspaper archive database tool, LexisNexis, a search was conducted of almost nine years of all US newspapers between the dates of 1 January 2001 and 16 November 2009. By entering the terms 'eco-terrorism' and 'environmental terrorism' into the database under the search definitions of US National Newspapers (excluding news wires), the following sample was established: under the heading of 'ecoterrorism' a total of 389 articles were identified, 325 of which were relevant to the analysis. Under the search term 'environmental terrorism', 114 articles were identified, 112 of which were relevant. When determining 'relevant' articles to examine, we chose to exclude articles that consisted of letters to the editor of the newspaper, book reviews, movie reviews and reference to any television programme instead, we chose to focus solely on news media articles written in response to an emerging news story.

Following the identification and collection of data, the integral aspects of research began. First it was necessary to develop a protocol for coding. All articles were initially read and the use or uses of 'eco' and/or 'environmental' terrorism transferred into a Microsoft Excel spreadsheet. The usage patterns were then re-read and analysed and it was determined that throughout both data sets there were four distinct categories into which the articles fell. Category A contained articles that used the terms to mean actions taken against an individual, company and so forth. because of a perceived harm to the environment caused by that entity. Category B contained articles that used 'eco' and/or 'environmental' terrorism to mean actions that directly harm the environment, such as killing of endangered wildlife or mountaintop removal mining. Some articles used the terms, but from the context it was not possible to understand what the meaning was and these fell into Category C. Finally, Category D, where both terms were also used to mean actions that used the environment as a tool or target to inflict injury on humans and/or damage their settlements, such as when Saddam Hussein drained the marshes of southern Iraq.

Knowing the news media influences the public perception of environmental and eco-terrorism, which then contributes to the agenda setting by officials and governments, we examined our data. The content of news media articles covering the two topics was explored in two stages. First, we broke down the data set by the number of articles in each of these categories. Second, we examined in greater detail how the terms were employed. Once the depictions were clearer, it then became possible to further examine if they actually merit the label of 'terrorism'.

The news media and the interpretation of terrorism

The 437 articles were broken down into four distinctive categories (Table 3.1).

Table 3.1 Number of US newspaper articles from 1 January 2001 to 16 November 2009*

Terrorism Term	Categories				Total
	A	B	C	D	
Eco	301	6	15	3	325
Environmental	79	14	4	15	112
Total	380	20	19	18	437
Percentage of Total	87%	4.5%	4.4%	4.1%	

Note: *Category A: actions taken against an individual, company and so forth. because of a perceived harm to the environment caused by that entity. Category B: actions that directly harm the environment, such as killing of endangered wildlife or mountaintop removal mining. Category C: meaning not able to be determined from the context. Category D: actions that used the environment as a tool or target to inflict injury on humans and/or damage their settlements.

In 380 (87%) of the total articles either term is used as the label for actions taken against those perceived to be hurting the environment, Category A. In 20 (4.5%) of those articles both terms appear together and are used interchangeably. The actions that are being described vary in their target, but consistently lack injury or death to people. These incidents range from vandalism, such as tree spiking and graffiti, to property destruction, such as arson of SUVs and the destruction of genetically modified crops.

There are three particular examples that highlight this usage. For instance, the *University Wire* on 17 February 2005 contained this story: 'so-called "eco-terrorists" set fire to housing developments, lumber companies, restaurants, car dealerships and even university buildings. Just last week, seven planted firebombs scorched an apartment complex under construction in Sutter Creek, Calif[ornia]'. Other incidents of eco-terrorism involved defending animals, such as setting free laboratory animals or minks kept on fur farms and ramming ships hunting whales. On 13 December 2001, *The Topeka Capitol-Journal* of Kansas reported that both the Earth Liberation Front and the Animal Liberation Front have admitted 'starting a fire at a primate research laboratory in New Mexico, setting loose mink from an Iowa fur farm and setting off a firebomb in a federal corral for its wild horses project.' Additionally, *The Philadelphia Inquirer* reported on 7 February 2004, 'Also troubling is the animal-rights faction forming around board member Paul Watson, founder of the radical Sea Shepherd Conservation Society. Why is he bad news? This "pirate" rams and sinks ships to save whales.' This was by far the largest category.

Category B consisted of actions that were actually hurting the environment. These 20 articles detailed the killing of endangered species, military bombings and the accompanying destruction, mountaintop mine removal where the peaks are blown off mountains to gain access to coal, and the purposeful introduction of invasive species that then kill the native wildlife and spread throughout the ecosystem. A specific example is that on 19 May 2006 *The Register Guard* reported, 'Dressed in a navy blue T-shirt and blue jeans, Churchill also touched on eco-terrorists, a term he says was invented by the U.S. intelligence community. "Taking the tops of mountains in Appalachia, that's eco-terrorism," he said, which was met by rousing applause.' So whereas to some those claiming to defend the environment are 'eco' or 'environmental' terrorists, to others it is those that actively destroy the environment who are terrorists.

Category C contains articles for which it was impossible from the context of the terms to be able to determine their meaning. This occurred in 19 (4.4%) of the total articles, more often in the case of eco-terrorism. For example, in *The Seattle Post-Intelligencer* on 22 April 2004:

> Hayes recently sat down in his office inside a converted Capitol Hill carriage house to reflect, hitting surprisingly disparate themes, including crumbling schools, the need for environmentalists to connect with working-class citizens, how eco-terrorism is 'dumb' and why the Chinese are hot on Buicks.

Finally, Category D, the smallest group with 18 articles (4.1% of the total number of articles), consisted of news stories that detailed actions where destruction of the environment was used to harm people. This blurb from *The Dallas Morning News* just following 11 September 2001 describes the varied environmental terrorist threats:

> No one knew whether the violence of the hijackings and attacks would be followed by a wave of environmental terrorism: black-market plutonium from the former Soviet Union or home-grown anthrax spread from the sky. An airliner crashing into a nuclear reactor. Poison in the water. Invisible death gripping the public.

Environmental terrorism was used to describe actions by former Iraqi dictator Saddam Hussein before the second war in Iraq: 'As the Gulf War raged on, a huge oil slick began to form in the Persian Gulf on this date in 1991 as Iraqi forces sabotaged Kuwaiti oil terminals. The United States called it an "act of environmental terrorism"' (Rosenthal 1991). Interestingly, during the same time frame, the term 'Environmental Protest' appeared in 1,076 articles, suggesting that perhaps these acts of 'eco' and 'environmental' terrorism may be considered under a host of names, rather than simply a terrorist threat.

As seen within the categorisation of the terms, there appears to be much confusion, on part of the news media, over which term to use and what precisely that term implies. For instance, under Category B it is not clear who the label 'eco-terrorist' or 'environmental terrorist' actually applied to. Are the perpetrators of the resistance/protest the terrorists, or is it those who are causing damage to the environment? Confusion over the use of the terms causes great problems in understanding what constitutes eco or environmental terrorism. The status of knowledge of these acts is therefore incomplete or, put differently, not entirely accurate. The slippage of the use of terms is confused on the part of the news media and potentially creates confusion for the public as to what their appropriate response should be. If eco-terrorism, for instance, is the greatest terrorist threat facing the United States, then is it not of central importance for the government, alongside the media, to clearly explain the threat? If the news media does not have internal consistency of what eco and environmental terrorism means, how is the public to understand the threat, other than being told that they are vulnerable to yet another harm. Such inconsistencies with what constitutes acts of eco and environmental terrorism causes public distrust in the news media and possibly the agenda set by the government tied to the media coverage. It also leads us to question whether those acts are in fact acts of terrorism, or is this a case of wrongful labelling and scaremongering on the part of the media?

A great 'threat' or inaccurate reporting? An analysis of environmental and eco-terrorism

Category A, which contains actions against individuals or corporations that are judged by the perpetrator to be harming the environment, does not constitute the label of terrorism as it is compiled by Schmid (2008) from 90 terrorism experts. There is a doctrine behind the eco-terrorism in Category A, which is to target objects that symbolise the degradation and exploitation of the environment or animals. This also corresponds to Chalecki's (2002) definition of eco-terrorism as trying to draw public attention to the powerful entities that are responsible for environmental degradation in an attempt to stop them. What is missing from Category A though is the practice portion of the criteria. These actions have a very specific target audience. The perpetrators of these activities, while committing acts that can be viewed as violence – vandalism and arson – do not commit violence directly aimed at people. In fact, as stated in several of the media accounts of eco-terrorism, no human life has ever been lost in these incidents. Several of these organisations also advocate for non-violence to people in their activities (Loadenthal 2013).

For example, the *University Wire* reported in October 2006 that while anti-abortion protestors have not been called terrorists, activist organisations such as the Earth Liberation Front and Animal Liberation Front are labelled as terrorists. They have 'over time, caused $110 million in property damage, nobody has ever been killed, and most vandalism has been designed to avoid hurting anyone'. A particular group of people are the focus of these actions, rather than multiple audiences, and there is no threat of bodily harm, only the threat of the destruction of property. Based upon the analysis of the incidents reported, we are then led to conclude that so called eco-terrorism, and the less often used environmental terrorism, has been mislabelled in a world characterised by increasing risk, fear and an atmosphere of vulnerability. The reasons for this will be returned to.

Category B includes those incidents where the environment was harmed directly. This, too, is not terrorism. In this case both the doctrine and practice are lacking. There is no specific target for these actions; the destruction of the environment is a side effect for other profit-making or legally sanctioned activities. For instance, the *State News Service* on 15 June 2009 reported that a Special Committee of the US Congress addressing the question of statehood for the territory of Puerto Rico characterised the nuclear testing that had taken place on the island 'acts of environmental terrorism'. Furthermore, such military or corporate actions do not have a propagandist or psychological intent aimed at inducing fear in a specific audience, so Category B also lacks the practice portion of a terrorist act.

Category C, as mentioned, are those articles where the usage of 'eco' or 'environmental' terrorism is unclear, so it is not possible to analyse if these constitute terrorism or not. For Category D, as is evident from the descriptions of both real and hypothetical instances of environmental terrorism, there is both the element of doctrine – the perpetrators choose this act as a special way of instilling fear or carrying out political violence – and practice – the act is one of direct violence that has psychological effects across an array of audiences. The previous quote from *The Dallas Morning News* demonstrates both of the aspects of this type of terrorism. The doctrine is seen in the widespread fear brought on by such tactics as anthrax from the air or poison in the water. The practice is evident in that the entire public is subjected to this 'invisible death' and not just a single targeted group. This also is in agreement with Chalecki's (2002) definition of environmental terrorism, where damaging the environment itself is used as a means to injure people. Presumably this could be used as a tactic to instil fear in a range of audiences as with conventional terrorism.

From this analysis, we have determined that categories A and B are in fact not terrorism, while Category D actions should indeed be included in the terrorism discourse. Nevertheless, eco-terrorism, as is evident by the articles in the US news media, is newsworthy with its political, criminal and possibly 'celebrity' aspects. If the news media are a key source of information for the public and influential to the political agenda, the misuse or manipulation of the word 'terrorism' – in general and specifically, in both the eco-terrorism and environmental terrorism contexts – has serious implications. The mislabelling then of eco-terrorism, and sometimes environmental terrorism when used as in Category A, as terrorism solidifies the misperception of the actions undertaken by these groups throughout society. It removes the potency of the word terrorism (Sumner and Weidman 2013). From a public point of view, with the news media placing eco-terrorism on its news agenda which is then publicised and 'fed' to audiences for consumption, unless the audience is critical, this mislabelling has the potential to add to a growing sense of fear and risk regarding security. Additionally, this misperception can lead to increased penalties for those who carry out eco-terrorism and the unnecessary allocation of time and resources to a threat that is not as severe as is portrayed by the label of terrorism.

In terms of the political agenda, the manipulation by corporations and the reporting of such in the media of protest actions to protect the environment as eco-terrorism serves two purposes. First, it protects the interests of the ruling class by silencing the opposition and maintaining the status quo of the priority of economic growth. The media empires and transnational corporations keep their power while the challengers are labelled as the criminals and terrorists. As Joose (2012) found in his research into the social construction of the eco-terrorist threat in *The New York Times*, media coverage has prevented the ideology of groups such as ELF from being publicised. The state is a key element in this as they generate the 'threat' as well as the juridical and law enforcement response (Loadenthal 2013).

Second, it renders invisible the crimes and harms of those doing the mislabelling. By the media focusing on the illegalities of the so-called eco-terrorists, the injustices caused by the powerful entities remain hidden and unexposed. This supports Jewkes (2004) idea of political diversion. For example, vandalism that has destroyed genetically modified test crops is focused upon and targeted by the news media for the destruction that has been caused. The companies doing the genetic modification, though, which have falsified reports as to the safety of these crops and in some instances smuggled genetically modified crops into countries where they are banned (Ramos 2013), are portrayed as the victims. The environmental and social injuries that they are continually engaged in are kept in the shadows due in part to the manipulation of labels and visibility by the media. Similarly, these harmful institutional practices are absent from political agendas as politicians cannot risk alienating campaign donors by exposing the invisible crimes and harms.

Conclusion

As terrorism has become more prominent in the news, different types of terrorism have also received media attention. Two of these are 'environmental terrorism' and 'eco-terrorism'. This chapter has reported results of a qualitative media analysis of articles in the US national newspapers featuring these two terms, where it was found that the news media usage of such terms is sometimes undefined, inaccurate or confusing.

Our analysis resulted in four categories of usage for environmental and eco-terrorism. In one category, C, the terms were unable to be defined because there was no contextual reference to draw a meaning from. Environmental terrorism is a term that appears to be dynamic in its usage and has yet to be used in a singular, clear way though scholars have introduced a distinct usage where the destruction of the environment is used as tool to harm people (Chalecki 2002). The phrase environmental terrorism was used interchangeably with eco-terrorism in categories A, B and D to mean destructive acts that target the property of people who harm the environment, exploitation of the environment and terrorist acts that use the environment to harm people. We support the use of environmental terrorism to describe the latter. Eco-terrorism, on the other hand, has a clear meaning that is rarely used out of context, but which we find to be inaccurate since the incidents being described do not truly constitute terrorism. Calling something terrorism that actually does not involve the level of violence and instilling of fear associated with terrorism, creates a climate of fear and false belief surrounding a threat that poses less of a danger to life and property than is widely believed.

This mislabelling creates excessive stigma and possibly punishments to those labelled as supposed 'eco-terrorists' and also devalues the word terrorism. We propose the use of 'eco-vandalism' or 'eco-destruction' to capture what these incidents actually entail, or support the use of 'eco-tage' as argued by Sumner and Weidman (2013). 'Eco-tage' combines the concern for the environment of the actors as well as the 'sabotage' of the development or industrial projects that are being destroyed. Finally, Category B, which contained incidents that directly harmed the environment, is also not terrorism but straightforward environmental exploitation. As such a powerful medium in society, the news media plays a central role in determining newsworthiness and in placing 'issues' on the public and political agendas via the process of agenda setting. Once on the public agenda, the news media can then directly influence public perceptions and understanding of matters, including inducing fear around the threat of risks such as terrorism. Thus it is important both for the media to label all incidents, not just terrorism, correctly, as detailed above, and to not use distinctive terms interchangeably, which can cause confusion and lead to misunderstanding and increased fear by the public.

Most importantly though, manipulation of the terrorist label focuses attention on groups that, while they are causing harm to property, are potentially not as dangerous as those attaching the label. Media empires, politicians and corporations that are able to control the discourse around threats in general – environmental and eco-terrorism were used here as an illustration – are able to render their own crimes and harms invisible. The political–media power nexus enables suffering and injury to stay unexposed, undiscovered and unchallenged.

Note

1. Qualitative media analysis has been used in a range of other studies, including a study on the construction of fear and victimisation in the news by Altheide et al. (2001) and a study on differences in news coverage of how Vietnamese youth crime differs from Hispanic and Black youth crime (Eyres and Altheide 1999).

References

Aas, K.F. (2013) *Globalization and Crime (Key Approaches to Criminology)*. 2nd edn. London: Sage.
Altheide, D.L. (1996) *Qualitative Media Analysis*. California: Sage.
—— (2003) 'Notes towards a Politics of Fear', *Journal of Crime, Conflict and the Media*, 1: 37–54.
—— (2006) *Terrorism and the Politics of Fear*. Oxford: Alta Mira Press.
Altheide, D.L., Gray, B., Janisch, R., Korbin, L., Maratea, R., Neill, D., Reaves, J. and Van Deman, F. (2001) 'News Constructions of Fear and Victim: An Exploration through Triangulated Qualitative Document Analysis', *Qualitative Inquiry*, 7(3): 304–322.
Beck, U. (1999) *World Risk Society*. Oxford: Wiley.
Berger, P.L. and Luckmann, T. (1966) *The Social Construction of Reality: A Treatise in the Sociology of Knowledge*. New York: Doubleday.
Best, J. (2008) *Social Problems*. New York: W.W. Norton and Company, Inc.
Chalecki, E.L. (2002) 'A New Vigilance: Identifying and Reducing the Risks of Environmental Terrorism', *Global Environmental Politics*, 2(1): 46–64.
Chibnall, S. (1977) *Law and Order News: An Analysis of Crime Reporting in the British Press*. London: Tavistock.
Eyres, J. and Altheide, D.L. (1999) 'News Themes and Ethnic Identity: *Los Angeles Times* News Reports of Vietnamese, Black, and Hispanic Gangs', *Social Problems*, 11: 85–103.

Fox News (2008) 'FBI: Eco-Terrorism Remains No. 1 Domestic Terror Threat'. Available at: http://www.foxnews.com/story/0,2933,343768,00.html. Accessed 21 September 2010.

Furedi, F. (2002) *Culture of Fear: Revised Edition*. London: Continuum.

Greenpeace (2014) 'The Bombing of the Rainbow Warrior'. Available at: http://www.greenpeace.org/international/en/about/history/the-bombing-of-the-rainbow-war/. Accessed 5 May 2014.

Greer, C. (2005) 'Crime and Media', in C. Hale, K. Hayward, A. Wahidin and E. Wincup (eds), *Criminology*. Oxford: Oxford University Press, 157–182.

Hall, S. (1978) *Policing the Crisis*. London: Macmillan.

Jewkes, Y. (2004) *Media and Crime*. London: Sage.

Joose, P. (2012) 'Elves, Eenvironmentalism, and "Eco-Terror": Leaderless Resistance and Media Coverage of the Earth Liberation Front', *Crime, Media, Culture*, 8(1): 75–93.

Lamb, J.R. (1985) 'Cities Squawk at Plan to Save Dwindling Bird', *The San Diego Union-Tribune*. 31 July.

Lippmann, W. [1922] (2008) *Public Opinion*. London: Collier-Macmillan.

Loadenthal, M. (2013) 'Deconstructing "Eco-Terrorism": Rhetoric, Framing and Statecraft as Seen through the Insight Approach', *Critical Studies on Terrorism, Special Issue. Terrorism and Peace and Conflict Studies: Investigating the Crossroad*, 6(1): 92–117.

McCombs, M.E. (2006) *Setting the Agenda: The Mass Media and Public Opinion*. Cambridge: Polity Press.

McCombs, M.E. and Shaw, D.L. (1972) 'The Agenda-Setting Function of Mass Media', *Public Opinion Quarterly*, 36(2): 176–187.

McNair, B. (1998) *The Sociology of Journalism*. London: Arnold Publishers.

Orange County Weekly (2005) 'Don't Gloat Yet'. 30 December.

Ramos, A. (2013) 'Smuggling of GMO Seeds Is Biopiracy', *Amandala: Belize's Leading Newspaper*. Available at: http://amandala.com.bz/news/smuggling-gmo-seeds-bio-piracy-bagmo/. Accessed 28 April 2014.

Rosenthal, A. (1991) WAR IN THE GULF: The President; Bush Calls Gulf Oil Spill A 'Sick' Act by Hussein'. Available at: http://www.nytimes.com/1991/01/26/world/war-in-the-gulf-the-president-bush-calls-gulf-oil-spill-a-sick-act-by-hussein.html. Accessed 4 August 2014.

Schmid, A.P. (2008) *Terrorism: Revised Academic Definition*. Online: Knol: A Unit of Knowledge: http://knol.google.com/k/alex-schmid/terrorism/dd3psyh8k3c3/2# (26 July 2008) [Accessed 3 January 2009].

Schudson, M. (2003). *The Sociology of News*. New York: Norton.

Sumner, D.T. and Weidman, L. (2013) 'Eco-terrorism or Eco-tage: An Argument for the Proper Frame', *Interdisciplinary Studies of Literature and the Environment*. Doi: 10.1093/isle/ist086.

The Globe and Mail (Canada) (1989) 'Letter Warns of Spikes in Trees', *The Globe and Mail*, 15 September.

4
The Visual Acuity of Climate Change

Avi Brisman

Introduction

In '"Multicolored" Green Criminology and Climate Change's Achromatopsia' (Brisman, forthcoming), I contemplated whether we might regard climate change as *achromatopsic* – whether we might consider it colorblind in that it 'affects us all, regardless of where we live, regardless of skin colour, income, ethnicity, religion and gender' (White 2010: 10). After exploring whether the impacts of climate change will be distributed unevenly/unequally, I suggested that we seem to be facing a situation in which the *achromatopsia* of climate change – the indiscriminate way in which greenhouse gases know no bounds (see, e.g., Leech 2012; Walters 2013; see generally, Fountain and Gillis, 2013) and climate change affects the entire planet – will, because of existing inequalities and differential abilities to adapt, produce *greater inequalities* between developed and developing, rich and poor, white and non-white groups and countries.

In the present chapter, I again consider climate change in visual or ophthalmological terms.[1] Here I examine our visual acuity of climate change – our acuteness or clearness of vision of climate change. I begin with some general comments about our sensory experience of environmental harms and crimes in general, and climate change, in particular, before considering how we are 'seeing' climate change and how our sight is being/has become impaired. Following Kramer (2013: 155), who contends that the lag between emissions and their effects on climate makes it 'uniquely difficult to mobilize political will to address the problem,' I argue that our failure to see the signs that our climate is changing is playing a part in political inaction on climate change, as well as our reluctance to curb our individual and collective consumptive practices contributing to it. Although the purpose of this chapter is to describe and diagnose, rather than prescribe, I conclude with some suggestions for improving our visual acuity of climate change.

Sensory experiences: environmental harm and climate change

According to Mares (2010: 286), '[c]rimes are generally seen as specific instances of harm inflicted by some specifically identifiable people on other identifiable people. Even many ecological crimes often have identifiable actors such as the recent oil spill in the Gulf of Mexico.' But many harms to the environment, its ecosystems, its biodiversity and to human and non-human animal health lack an 'identifiable actor' – lack either a discrete individual or group (e.g., corporate) perpetrator. Writing about the environmental pollution of the late 1970s and early 1980s, Michalowski (1985: 341) observed:

> [d]espite its greater demonstrable costs in both dollars and damaged human health, environmental pollution does not evoke the same nearly unanimous public demand for protection as does common crime. Part of the reason for this is that the effects of pollution are seldom immediately obvious. There are occasional environmental disasters such as the smog inversion in New York City in 1973, which took 400 lives. For the most part, however, the effects of pollution are subtle and cumulative. Individuals may become sick, feel nauseated, or develop cancer, but this is generally perceived as a failure of their own body [sic], not the consequences of living in a polluted environment. Additionally, because the pollution of air and water leading to illness and other costs is most often the cumulative result of the actions of a multiplicity of industries, some at great distances from the affected city or region, it is difficult to identify a guilty party. The lack of an easily identifiable cause–effect relationship between polluting and its consequences for human lives often produces a sense of resignation among those who live with unsafe water and air [internal footnote omitted].

Thus, Michalowski implies, in order for public consciousness and concern to become animated, we require three things: a distinguishable actor or guilty party, a specific victim or set of victims, and a recognisable injury to that victim or group thereof. For consciousness and concern to translate into action and response, White (2013: 121) suggests, the 'solution' must be 'apparent, immediate and targeted'. Using the decline and potential extinction of a species as an example, White (2013: 121–122) contends that if '[s]pecific culprits are seen to bear the responsibility for the demise of certain species...law enforcement action is constructed accordingly'. Otherwise, the environmental problem at hand is put in the '"too hard" basket' (White 2013: 122), resulting in stasis.

What, then, of climate change?

There are many signs that our climate is changing. A few of them are:

- rising average global temperatures (with many of the warmest years on record coming within the last decade [2000–2010]);
- changing patterns of precipitation;
- rising sea and ocean levels (largely due to diminished ice sheets);
- increases in extreme weather events, including heat cyclones, droughts, floods (especially of coastal areas, deltas, low-lying islands and river basins), heat waves, hurricanes and wildfires;
- changes in species habitats, leading to an almost unprecedented loss of biodiversity;
- among other effects (for overviews, see, e.g., Lee 2009; McNall 2011; Washington and Cook 2011; Agnew 2012a, b; Franz 2012; Sollund 2012; Hall 2013; Pretty 2013; Brisman 2013; forthcoming).

But while we may be experiencing the impacts of anthropogenic climate change, and while 'climate change' may be a part of our public discourse (see, e.g., Brisman and South 2013a, 2013b; Brisman 2012, 2013; McClanahan and Brisman 2013), we may not be *seeing* the evidence of our climate changing and consciously processing what has been coming into our field of vision. In other words, while we may intellectually grasp the *idea of climate change* and have some experience of climate change – or some experience that we *attribute to* climate change (see, e.g., Ross 1991: 6) – we do not *see* climate change or *feel* it the way we might other discrete environmental 'events' (e.g., a blizzard, an earthquake, a flood, a tornado, a tsunami). As such, climate change is more akin to the environmental pollution described by Michalowski above than to the more tangible events with visible damage, such as the Exxon Valdez oil spill in March 1987, the Deepwater Horizon oil spill in April 2010, or the Ajka alumina sludge spill in western Hungary in October 2010 (see generally Rachlinski 2000: 306; Dybing 2012).

Indeed, a number of commentators have weighed in on whether and the extent to which climate change can be or has been *seen* and/or *felt*.

According to Hulme (2009: 196), 'no-one can see climate changing or feel it happening'. Similarly, Anderegg (2010: 28) contends that 'human-caused climate change is intangible. On a day-to-day basis, we experience weather, not climate'. Likewise, Moser and Dilling (2004: 34) state that '[t]he day-to-day changes one might notice are small, if noticeable at all,' while Dean (2006: D4) describes climate change as an environmental problem that develops 'imperceptibly', making it 'hard for people to see rising sea levels as a threat'. McCright and Dunlap (2003: 367) conceptualise climate change as 'a crescive – i.e., cumulative, incremental, long-term – problem with no definitive beginning and no specific, conventional location' [citations omitted] – a description akin to Agnew's (2012b: 15) reference to climate change as 'a problem of a special sort – it is a "slow crisis". Its worst consequences will not appear for many years (e.g., a substantial rise in sea level), but people and groups are inclined to respond to immediate rather than delayed threats [internal citation omitted]'.[2]

For some commentators, it is more appropriate to employ the language of *invisibility*. For example, Tákacs-Sánta (2007: 30) finds that because 'for the vast majority of us visual perception is the most important device in sensing the surrounding world, the greatest difficulty arises when the problematic environmental factors or their effects are invisible' (citing Winter and Koger 2004). Krugman (2010a: A25) maintains that 'as visible pollution has diminished, so has public concern over environmental issues.... This decline in concern would be fine if visible pollution were all that mattered – but it isn't, of course. In particular, greenhouse gases pose a greater threat than smog or burning rivers ever did.' Whereas Tákacs-Sánta (2007: 30) leaves open the possibility that 'sometimes imperceptibility... might enhance concern' (citing Johnson 1993), Krugman (2010a: A25) asserts that 'it's hard to get the public focused on a form of pollution that's invisible, and whose effects unfold over decades rather than days' – a position that resonates with Giddens's (2011: 2) statement that 'since the dangers posed by global warming aren't tangible, immediate or visible in the course of day-to-day life, many will sit on their hands and do nothing of concrete nature about them'.

I would contend that while we may not see the climate *change* – we may not see a glacier actually recede or the level of the sea rise or the bleaching of a colony of corals – we are able to see evidence that the climate *has changed* and we will continue to do so (see, e.g., Dhar 2013; Pappas 2012; Dickel 2013; Malik 2014; Neuhauser 2014; Turrentine 2014). Unfortunately, *whether* we do so depends on our visual acuity and I would suggest that ours has been somewhat impaired and that this impairment has affected our perception of the need to act, our recognition of the need to act *now*, our willingness to act, and our sense of responsibility to act.

Two types of impairment could describe our visual acuity of climate change: (1) *climate change micropsia*; and (2) *climate change myopia*. I briefly describe each of these in turn.

Climate change micropsia

Micropsia is a condition that affects human visual perception, whereby objects are perceived to be smaller than they actually are (see Ceriani et al. 1998; see generally Michaeli-Cohen et al. 1996).[3] Those who suffer from *micropsia* may see objects as more distant than they really are or objects may appear smaller as they approach the subject – a condition known as *convergence-accommodative micropsia* (see Hollins 1976). *Climate change micropsia* refers to the condition in which the effects of climate change are seen as smaller than they really are (e.g., glaciers are not melting that much and certainly not to the point where it could contribute to rising sea levels or adversely affect the 60 million people dependent on ice and snow melt for water supply) or the impacts of climate change seem more distant than they really are (e.g., between 18 and 35 per cent of plant and animal species could become extinct by *2500*, not *2050*, as Thomas and colleagues (2004) project; two-thirds of the world's polar bear population may be lost within *500* years, not *50*, as Washington and Cook (2011: 60) claim). For those suffering from *convergence-accommodative climate change micropsia*, the impacts of climate change appear smaller as they (have continued to) come closer to the subject.[4]

Individuals afflicted with *climate change micropsia* exhibit many of the same symptoms as 'impact skeptics' – Washington and Cook's (2011: 11) term for 'those who accept human causation of the warming trend but claim that the impacts will be beneficial or benign'. As Rahmstorf (2005: 79), from whom Washington and Cook borrow the term 'impact skeptic', explains, such skeptics 'underscore the possible positive consequences of climatic warming, like a potential extension of agriculture into higher latitudes'. Rahmstorf (2005: 79) acknowledges that 'a warm climate is not necessarily worse than a colder one'. He continues:

> we must bear in mind that rapid changes will have predominantly adverse effects because society and ecosystems are highly adapted to the recent climate. Higher runoff amounts after heavy precipitation, for example, are not a problem per se. But if river beds and human

infrastructure are not adapted for this, the result is water standing in Prague and Dresden (as in 2002). Nor is a higher sea-level bad in itself – it is just unfortunate that our cities tend to be located along the present coastlines. Not least, global warming will make our living conditions more unpredictable – we are travelling into uncharted waters without being able to foresee all the consequences.

In the absence of climate protection measures, we will probably see a warming by several degrees in this century. The most recent comparable period of major global warming occurred when the last ice age ended ~15,000 years ago: at that time, the climate warmed by approx. 5°C in global mean. This warming had serious implications for man and ecosystems. But the process unfolded over a period of 5,000 years – humankind is now threatening to bring about a similarly large climate change within the space of a century. This extraordinarily rapid change would most likely exceed the adaptive capacity of man and nature.

To understand the difference between *climate change micropsia* and the 'impact skepticism' identified by Washington and Cook (2011) and Rahmstorf (2005), consider the type of impact that climate change may have on agriculture. According to Washington and Cook (2011: 59), increased global temperatures as a result of human activity may well lead to some or all of the following impacts: decreased water supplies for human consumption; increased wildfire frequency (associated with higher temperatures and earlier spring snowmelt); changes to ecosystems (including expanded deserts and encroachment of shrubs into grasslands, rendering unsuitable rangeland currently used for domestic livestock grazing); and decline in rice yields (as a result of warmer night-time minimum temperatures). For the individual afflicted with *climate change micropsia*, global temperatures have not risen that much and will do so only minimally, if at all. Climate change may have already or may in the future decrease the supply of fresh water, but only a little bit; deserts may expand, but only slightly; shrubs may encroach into grasslands, but only minimally – and hardly enough to render rangeland unsuitable for grazing; rice yields may decline, but only a little bit. For the 'impact skeptic', the impacts of climate change are not (or will not be) smaller than they are (or are predicted to be). Rather, the effects will be *positive*, rather than *negative*. Thus, for the 'impact skeptic', anthropogenic climate change, such as human-caused global warming, will *improve* agriculture in some high-latitude regions, *increase the growing season* in Greenland, and *increase the productivity* of sour orange trees (see Washington and Cook 2011: 59 for a discussion).[5]

While 'impact skepticism' is more misguided and Machiavellian than *climate change micropsia*, neither sees climate change as a really serious problem (or, in the case of the 'impact skeptic', a problem at all). More importantly, inaction accompanies both. As Agnew (2012b: 16) explains: 'there will not be a meaningful response to climate change until the negative consequences of such change become more apparent. At that point, climate change will become an immediate problem for much of the world; its seriousness difficult to deny. Many will feel an obligation to act, given that climate change will become an *obvious* threat to humanity – as well as to economic prosperity and development.'

Climate change myopia

Myopia (known as 'nearsightedness' in American English and 'shortsightedness' in British English) is a condition that causes distant objects to appear out of focus. Whereas, for most myopes, close objects appear in focus, for those suffering from 'high myopia', objects must be extremely close to the eyes in order for them to see clearly without eyeglasses (see generally Grosvenor 1987; Morgan and Rose 2005).

Climate change myopia bears a strong resemblance to what Brooks (2009: A27) has called 'perverse cosmic myopia' – the 'inability to focus attention on the most perilous matter at hand'. *Climate change myopia* refers to the inability to focus attention on climate change and is a condition with two different symptoms, either of which may present in the afflicted individual: in the first, the effects of climate change – especially those anticipated impacts – appear hazy or fuzzy; in the second, the effects of climate change – especially those occurring in regions far away from where one lives – appear blurry or out of focus.[6] Whereas for someone suffering from *climate change micropsia*, the impacts of climate change may seem more distant than they really are (e.g., about 150 million city dwellers – primarily in Bangladesh, China, India, Florida, Myanmar, Thailand and Vietnam – could be in danger due to climate change by the year *2700*, not *2070*, as Weeks (2009: 103) reports), for someone exhibiting the first kind of symptom of *climate change myopia*, the uncertainty of climate models might seem even more pronounced and the variation in predicted global surface temperature change or sea-level rise Arctic sea-ice melt might appear greater (or the range of predicted global surface temperature change or sea-level rise or Arctic sea-ice melt might look ill-defined). For someone presenting the second type of symptom of *climate change myopia*, evidence of climate change (or lack thereof) is based solely on one's experience within a small geographic radius. Thus, for example, while January 2010 was seen as unusually cold in much of the United States, from a global perspective, it was the second-hottest January since surface temperatures were first measured more than 130 years ago (Gore 2010). For someone living in the United States and suffering from *climate change myopia*, the atypical frost on his/her windshield would appear as clear evidence of global *cooling*, irrespective of the warmer than average weather experienced far away in Africa, Asia and Canada at that time. Finally, someone suffering from *high climate change myopia* – recall that with *high myopia*, near vision is affected in addition to blurry distance vision – would have difficulty seeing clearly both the impacts of climate change around him/her and those in other parts of his/her country or in other nation-states. Thus, someone living in northern Arizona might not be able to discern that decreased winter snowfall in the mountains is enabling elk to forage at higher elevations throughout the winter, causing a decline in seasonal plants and leading to elk consumption of maple and aspen, which, in turn, is contributing to a decline in songbirds that rely on these trees for their habitat (Pappas 2012); the same individual would also not recognise the changing migration patterns of polar bears in the Canadian or Russian Arctic (see, e.g., Angier 2004; Barringer 2007; Revkin 2007a, 2007b; Gessen 2012; Ungar 2013a, 2013b; White 2013).

Unfortunately, Western mainstream media has failed to inform and educate the public about the causes, evidence and anticipated impacts of climate change – and it has insisted on providing a forum for the extreme minority views of climate change contrarians and deniers in the name of 'balanced' reporting (see Washington and Cook 2011: 93–94; Brisman 2012; Brisman and South 2013b; McClanahan and Brisman 2013). This obfuscation has impeded the 'advancement of public acknowledgement of, concern about and action with respect to climate change' (McClanahan and Brisman 2013: 3) and has presented a formidable challenge to those seeking to retard the progression of *climate change myopia*. To make matters worse, Rachlinski (2000: 312) attributes climate change to human shortsightedness about the impact of fossil fuels. This raises the question of whether *climate change myopia* (which I identified above as a condition wherein the *effects* of climate change – both those anticipated effects and those presently occurring in faraway geographic regions – appear blurry or out of focus) might be a similar or related (or perhaps even the same) clinical entity as the shortsightedness Rachlinski identified with respect to the *causes* of climate change. Moreover, it appears that the management of *climate change myopia* may be frustrated by what Shiva (2008: 31) has referred to as 'myopic scientists' who, she claims, believe that the problems associated with climate change can be addressed through 'technological fixes' which, we can infer, will not address the root causes of either climate change or *climate change myopia*.[7]

On the bright side, it seems that *climate change myopia* is not a genetic or hereditary disorder for there are no known instances of *congenital climate change myopia* (also known as *infantile climate change myopia*). This leaves open the possibility that accurate information about climate change and education related to climate science could forestall *youth onset climate change myopia* (which occurs in the early childhood or adolescent years) and *school climate change myopia* (which appears during childhood, particularly in the school-age years, and is attributed to the work one does – or does *not* do – in school (see, generally, Goss et al. 1997; Morgan and Rose 2005)). Indeed, a proper regimen during childhood and adolescence could affect the likelihood of *adult onset climate change myopia* (both *early onset climate change myopia*, which occurs between the ages of 20 and 40, and *late adult onset climate change myopia*, which occurs after age 40 [see, generally, Goss et al. 1997]), although more research is needed in this area. For now – and for the millions already afflicted with *climate change myopia* – corrective lenses are in order. Without them – without a dose of *hyperopia* (Thompson 2009), to mix prescriptive metaphors – those suffering from *climate change myopia* will continue to emphasise near-term benefits over long-term interests, such as the health and vitality of human, non-human animal and plant species, which are threatened by anthropogenic climate change.

Visual acuity, behavioural and political inaction

Whether we can *see* climate change or cannot – whether climate change is *invisible* or whether we suffer from *micropsia*, *myopia* or some other ophthalmological ailment – may be the subject of academic debate over the appropriate metaphor. What is clear, however, is that our failure to see the signs that our climate is changing, as well as our inability to perceive the connections between our individual and collective consumptive practices and the physical evidence of our rapidly changing climate, is contributing to our behavioural and political inaction (see Kramer 2013: 155).

Fifteen years ago, McKibben (1999) contemplated our inaction with respect to climate change, including taking 'the baby step represented by the 1997 Kyoto accords, which would [have] return[ed] us to 1990 levels by 2010'. He posited:

> The reason ... is that we don't yet feel viscerally the wrongness of what we're doing. ...
>
> I used to wonder why my parents' generation had been so blind to the wrongness of segregation; they were people of good conscience, so why had inertia ruled for so long? Now I think I understand better. It took the emotional shock of seeing police dogs rip the flesh of protesters for white people to really understand the day-to-day corrosiveness of Jim Crow.
>
> We need that same gut understanding of our environmental situation if we are to take the giant steps we must take soon. ... We don't live on the planet we were born on. We live on a new, poorer, simpler planet, and we continue to impoverish it with every ounce of oil and pound of coal that we burn.

McKibben concluded:

> In retrospect it will be clear. A hundred years from now, people may well remember the 1990's not as the decade of the Internet's spread or the Dow's ascension but as the years when global temperatures began spiking upward – as the years when rain and wind and ice and sea water began irrefutably to reflect the power and heedlessness of our species. But how bad it will get depends on how deeply and how quickly we can feel.'

For McKibben, then, our inaction stems from our lack of visceral feeling and, in particular, our lack of *shock*. Since McKibben's writing, we have had two occasions in the United States when we could have – or should have – been shocked: Hurricane Katrina in 2005, the costliest natural disaster, as well as one of the five deadliest hurricanes, in the history of the United States, which left us with lasting images of survivors, stranded by floodwaters, dotting the tops of houses across New Orleans, and Hurricane Sandy in 2012, the second-costliest hurricane in US history, which provided us with poignant pictures of a flooded New York City subway system, taxis floating in Hoboken, New Jersey, and boats resting on streets along the Atlantic coastline. These storms and the images that accompanied them may have temporarily awakened us from our 'sleepwalk to extinction' to borrow from Shiva (2008: 144) and mix metaphors.[8] But now, once again, we seem unenthused, uninspired, unmoved.[9]

According to White (2010: 3), '[p]art of the reason why responses to climate change have been so little and so late has to do with the nature of "slow crisis"', a phrase/term I noted above. 'Floods in Brazil, Australia and Sri Lanka in early 2011', White (2010: 3) continues, 'have generally been interpreted publicly as once-in-a-hundred-year phenomena. Cyclones and hurricanes are "normal" to certain regions of the world, even though the frequency and intensity might be changing. There is no one single earth-shattering event that demarcates the "crisis" of climate change. Transformation is progressive and longitudinal. It is not abrupt, completed or singularly global in impact.' I will leave the Malthusian suggestion that Mother Nature may need to up the voltage on her shocks for another day – that we need a 'single earth-shattering event that demarcates the "crisis" of climate change'.[10] For now, I will simply assert that we need a much, much stronger pair of glasses, for the ones that we have on right now may only be helpful in viewing things *retrospectively*, as McKibben suggests.

Geographic and social discontinuities

In 'Environmental Discontinuities: The Production and Regulation of an Eco-experience', Halsey (1999) examines the socio-ecological effects of formal and informal regulatory strategies governing the movement of tourists (with)in and around the Great Australian Bight Marine Park in a remote region of South Australia. Prior to the designation of the area as a 'Marine Park', Halsey (1999: 229) explains, 'there was no gate, no fences and no signs saying who owned or leased what. Instead there was a dirt track which preserved the feeling of continuity of the land, sky and sea that often builds over the course of travelling in a car, or on a bike or on foot for long periods. There was, in other words, no sense of entering a place of *dis*continuity – of moving *in*to a place'. According to Halsey (1999: 229), '[a] gate is the concrete manifestation of a discontinuity. It is a means for establishing relations of power through the erection of insides and outsides – significances and insignificances. Things "outside" are usually thought of as foreign or waste (*other*) whereas things "inside" are usually thought of as endemic or useful (self). The implication... is that things "inside" the membrane are more "valuable" than everything "exterior" to it'. As a result, Halsey (1999: 229) rues, 'people's primary environmental concern' has come to be for the conservation of that which 'lies "within" the membrane', while ignoring that which 'occurs "outside" this privileged space'. For Halsey (1999: 248), the worry is that such dynamics – such divisions and segmentations – can foster a sentiment that '"the natural environment" [is] something "removed" or *dis*located from everyday practice' – that humans are separate from, rather than part of, our planet's ecosystems.

Halsey's piece is a Deleuzian critique of space and movement (or lack thereof), but it is also about (selective) seeing or not seeing. Essentially, Halsey's point is that we are creating geographic and social discontinuities and that this runs the risk of making us less able to recognise how complex systems in the world and across the planet relate to one another and how changes in one variable or in one part can affect another part and possibly the entire system. In other words, our propensity for creating divisions, segmentations and zones has prevented our conceptualising '*the Earth* as a closed system...that can be tipped out of balance' (McNall 2011: 3), and that we are toying with that balance through our individual and collective actions, behaviours, customs, patterns, practices and routines. McNall (2011: 48) observes: 'Each of our lives – through the numerous choices we make daily – affects the climate and has a role in creating the future. Yet these connections are often invisible. If we cannot see the consequences of our actions, how can we change?'

Conclusion

In this chapter, as in previous work (see, e.g., Brisman 2005), I have argued our failure to prevent or respond, through mitigation or adaptation, to (an) environmental harm is a *visual* or *opthalmological* problem. It is not so much that the connections between our (daily) decisions and the consequences of actions are *invisible*, as McNall (2011) contends, but that we suffer from the ophthalmological ailments of *climate change micropsia* (i.e., the effects of climate change are seen as smaller than they really are; the impacts of climate change seem more distant than they really are) and *climate change myopia* (i.e., the effects of climate change – especially those anticipated impacts – appear hazy or fuzzy; the effects of climate change – especially those occurring in regions far away from where one lives – appear blurry or out of focus).

White (2013: 146) has remarked that '[t]he survival of the human species is contingent upon how we, collectively, address climate change and ecological degradation'. To this I would add that whether and how we, collectively, address climate change and ecological degradation, more generally, is linked to our visual acuity and the extent to which we will continue to exhibit/possess ophthalmological maladies. While this chapter has focused on diagnosing and describing a problem, rather than prescribing a regimen to retard or prevent the onset of or cure such visual impairments, it has noted the importance of accurate information about climate change and education related to climate science, especially for forestalling *youth onset climate change myopia* and *school climate change myopia*. In addition, I would suggest: (1) a heightened sensitivity to creating and disseminating images that 'create a feeling of the importance of climate change as an issue while empowering the viewer to do something about it' (Braasch 2013: 37) – a responsibility that must be borne not just by those involved in climate-change research and education, but to anyone concerned about environmental harm and the future of the planet; and (2) a healthy dose of 'outdoor time' for all (http://www.nwf.org/be-out-there/why-be-out-there.aspx; see also Louv 2006; Brisman and Rau 2009), spending time outside is something that we can all strive to do, for, as Washington and Cook (2011: 91) explain, 'it is hard for many people to feel a sense of urgency, as ecological degradation is just not *real* to them. ... [O]ur society in the West is now more isolated from the natural world than were preceding generations. People don't spend as much time out in nature and spend less time in "witness" of nature [citation omitted].' Otherwise, we may find ourselves afflicted with 'boiling frog' syndrome (see Krugman 2006) – unable or unwilling to react to significant changes that occur gradually, unresistingly allowing ourselves to be boiled to death.

Notes

1. The terms, 'climate change', 'global warming' and 'weather' are often used interchangeably, but they are not synonymous. As White (2012: 2) explains,

    [g]*lobal warming* describes the rising of the earth's temperature over a relatively short time span. *Climate change* describes the interrelated effects of this rise in temperature: from changing sea levels and changing ocean currents, through to the impacts of temperature change on local environments that affect the endemic flora and fauna in varying ways (for instance, the death of coral due to temperature rises in sea water or the changed migration patterns of birds). *Weather* is the name we give to the direct local experience of things such as sunshine, wind, rain, snow and the general disposition of the elements. It is about the short-term and personal, not the long-term patterns associated with climate in general. As the planet warms up, the climate will change in ways that disrupt previous weather patterns, and will in some places even

bring colder weather, although overall temperatures are on the rise [citation omitted].

In light of these differences and to maintain consistency with my previous work, which employs the term 'climate change', rather than 'global warming' (see, e.g., Brisman 2005; 2013; forthcoming), this chapter will use the term 'climate change' to refer to the consequences of build-up of carbon dioxide and other greenhouse gases that make up the Earth's atmosphere and trap heat. Occasionally, I refer to 'anthropogenic climate change' to emphasise the human impact on the environment and the world's atmosphere.

2. For a somewhat competing perspective to those presented by Hulme (2009), Anderegg (2010), Moser and Dilling (2004), Dean (2006), McCright and Dunlap (2003) and Agnew (2012b), see, for example, Lowe and colleagues (2006: 435, 451), who note the 'uncertainty and complexity surrounding climate change', but find that 'there is an internalization of climate change, that people have identified evidence of the phenomenon' and that people possess a sensitivity to and an awareness of a changing climate. Similarly, Rachlinksi (2000: 312) contends that '[t]he climate itself is difficult for laypersons to track, but the alleged symptoms of global climate change are easy to imagine. With or without a dramatic change in climate, bad weather constantly finds its way into the news. Droughts, tornadoes, hurricanes, floods, and heat waves consistently receive coverage on the nightly news, whether or not they are the products of global climate change. This attention makes it easier to recall instances of weather-related tragedies, making the prospect of a disastrous change in the climate seem likely.' Doyle (2007: 129) states: 'Images of melting glaciers dominate the pictorial language of climate change, powerful symbols of a fragile earth at risk from the impacts of climate change. ... [P]hotographs of glaciers represent temporally the already seen effects of climate change.' Later, however, Doyle (2007: 136) clarifies her position, explaining that 'the first impacts [of climate change] are "being felt" rather than explicitly seen'; she concludes by suggesting that 'rather than proving that climate change is real through visible means, it might be more useful for environmental [non-governmental organizations], and environmental scientists, to persuade the public that not all environmental problems can be seen' (2007: 147). Most recently, Howe and Leiserowitz (2013: 1488) note that 'global warming has manifested gradually over many decades and at spatial scales well beyond the direct perceptual capabilities of any individual human being (e.g., the global or continental scale)'. Using national survey data collected in the United States in 2011, they find that '[w]hile people are capable of recognizing and adapting to short- and long-term climate variability and change, these processes depend, at least in part, on the changes in local climate conditions being perceived by the affected individuals, either through personal experience or description', and conclude that the subjective experience of local climate change is dependent not only on external climate conditions, but also on individual beliefs, with perceptions seemingly biased by prior beliefs about global warming (2013: 1499).

3. Alice-in-Wonderland syndrome (AIWS, named after the novel written by Lewis Carroll), also known as Todd's syndrome (named after the physician John Todd, who first documented it), is a disorienting neurological condition

affecting human visual perception. Those suffering from AIWS may experience either micropsia or macropsia, in which objects in the affected section of the visual field appear larger than normal, causing the subject to feel smaller than he/she actually is (Cinbis and Aysun 1992; Todd 1955).
4. *Climate change micropsia* should not be confused with 'centennial blindness' – what Coupland (2010: 219) has identified as '[t]he inability of most people to understand future time frames longer than about a hundred years'. Whereas those suffering from *climate change micropsia* can see things that are far away (but just think that they are farther away than they actually are) and those afflicted with *climate change myopia* find faraway things blurry, hazy or ill-defined, those plagued by 'centennial blindness' cannot see those far away things at all – and their blindness is not limited to the impacts of climate change. The really unfortunate are those with 'decimal blindness', which Coupland (2010: 219) describes as 'the inability to think beyond a ten-year time span'. Rarer still is 'crastinal blindess', a high-speed version of 'decimal blindness' in which the subject cannot see or think past tomorrow (Coupland 2010: 219).
5. For a comparison of the negative impacts (or potential negative impacts) of anthropogenic climate change, as identified by climate scientists, and the positive impacts (or potential positive impacts) of climate-change deniers with respect to agriculture, glacier melt, economics, Arctic melt, health, environment, ocean acidification and sea-level rise, see Washington and Cook (2011: 59–62).
6. *Climate change myopia* might be considered a kind of 'environmental myopia' – an 'unsophisticated lack of appreciation and knowledge of the extent and gravity of' an environmental problem, often caused by misperceptions about the sustainability of a resource (Herbig 2010: 114). Under such a conceptualisation, *climate change myopia* would refer to the lack of appreciation and knowledge of the extent and gravity of climate change; misperceptions about the availability of finite resources, such as fossil fuels, and the sustainability of certain energy sources, might also be causes of or indicative of this type of *climate change myopia*.
7. In a similar vein to Shiva (2008), Kramer (2013: 159) contends that '[t]he pathological promotion and pursuit of endless economic growth on a planet with finite resources, such as fossil fuels, is unsustainable in the long run. It also produces "tunnel vision" which restricts people from considering any solution to the global warming problem other than a technological one that would facilitate continued high levels of consumption, only at a "cleaner" level [citing Hamilton 2010].'
8. Commentators disagree as to whether climate change will result in the extinction of humans. For example, White (2013: 146) shares Shiva's pessimism: 'The survival of the human species is contingent upon how we, collectively, address climate change and ecological degradation.' For a slightly more sanguine perspective on the future of humanity, see Washington and Cook (2011: 82), who write: 'Few climate scientists argue that global warming will send humans extinct, but that it could lead to major water and food shortages and vastly impoverish the world we share with other species.'

9. Arguably we do not even seem to *see* the things we do *right* with respect to mitigation and adaptation to climate change. For example, in the aftermath of Hurricane Katrina, Arcadis, the international consulting, design, engineering and management services company, helped design a $1.1 billion, two-mile-long barrier that protected New Orleans from a 13.6-foot storm surge in the summer of 2012, when Hurricane Isaac hit the Gulf Coast of the United States. According to Folger (2013: 55), '[t]he Lower Ninth Ward, which suffered so greatly during Hurricane Katrina, was unscathed'. As Piet Dircke, an Arcadis executive, lamented to me one night over dinner in Rotterdam., 'Isaac was a tremendous victory for New Orleans. All the barriers were closed; all the levees held; all the pumps worked. You didn't hear about it? No, because nothing happened.'
10. One UN climate official has come close to making such a suggestion. Mr. Halldor Thorgeirsson, Director for Strategy, United Nations Framework Convention on Climate Change, has, according to Satter (2013) implied that 'a global solution to the issue [i]sn't likely until the effects of climate change c[o]me barreling down on peoples' heads or flooding into their homes'.

References

Agnew, R. (2012a) 'Dire Forecast: A Theoretical Model of the Impact of Climate Change on Crime', *Theoretical Criminology*, 16(1): 21–42.
—— (2012b) 'It's the End of the World as We Know It: The Advance of Climate Change from a Criminological Perspective', in R. White (ed.), *Climate Change from a Criminological Perspective*. New York: Springer, 13–25.
Anderegg, W.R.L. (2010) 'Diagnosis Earth: The Climate Change Debate', *Thought & Action: The NEA Higher Education Journal*, 26: 23–36.
Angier, N. (2004) 'Built for the Arctic: A Species' Splendid Adaptations', *The New York Times*, January 27: D1, D4.
Barringer, F. (2007) 'Protocol Is Cited in Limiting Scientists' Talks on Climate', *The New York Times*, March 9: A15.
Braasch, G. (2013) 'Climate Change: Is Seeing Believing?', *Bulletin of the Atomic Scientists*, 69(6): 33–41.
Brisman, A. (2005) 'The Aesthetics of Wind Energy Systems', *New York University Environmental Law Journal*, 13(1): 1–133.
—— (2012) 'The Cultural Silence of Climate Change Contrarianism', in R. White (ed.), *Climate Change from a Criminological Perspective*. New York: Springer, 41–70.
—— (2013) 'Not a Bedtime Story: Climate Change, Neoliberalism, and the Future of the Arctic', *Michigan State International Law Review*, 22(1): 241–289.
—— (forthcoming) '"Multicolored" Green Criminology and Climate Change's Achromatopsia', *Contemporary Justice Review*.
Brisman, A. and Rau, A. (2009) 'From Fear of Crime to Fear of Nature: The Problem with Permitting Loaded, Concealed Firearms in National Parks', *Golden Gate University Environmental Law Journal*, 2(2): 255–272.
Brisman, A. and South, N. (2013a) *Folk Devils, Denial, Climate Change and Environmental Crime: Applying the Work of Stan Cohen to Green Criminology*. Paper presented at the 41st Annual Conference of the European Group for the Study of Deviance and Social Control. Oslo, Norway (30 August 2013).

—— (2013b) 'A Green-Cultural Criminology: An Exploratory Outline', *Crime Media Culture*, 9(2): 115–135.
Brooks, D. (2009) 'Perverse Cosmic Myopia', *The New York Times*, March 20: A27.
Ceriani, F., Gentileschi, V., Muggia, S. and Spinnler, H. (1998) 'Seeing Objects Smaller Than They Are: Micropsia Following Right Temporo-Parietal Infarction', *Third Neurological Department of the University of Milan*, 34(1): 131–138.
Cinbis, M. and Aysun, S. (1992) 'Alice in Wonderland Syndrome as an Initial Manifestation of Epstein-Barr Virus Infection', *British Journal of Ophthalmology*, 76(5) [May]: 316.
Coupland, D. (2010) *Player One: What Is to Become of Us*. Toronto: Anansi.
Dean, C. (2006) 'Next Victim of Warming: The Beaches', *The New York Times*, June 20: D1, D4.
Dhar, M. (2013) 'Why Autumn Leaves May Be Dulled by Climate Change', *LiveScience*, September 20. Available at: http://news.yahoo.com/why-autumn-leaves-may-dulled-climate-change-163649087.html. Accessed 1 October 2013.
Dickel, S. (2013) 'Beyond Cynicism: Climate Engineering Technologies and Vegan Diets as Alternative Solutions for Climate Change', in A. Maas, B. Bodó, C. Burnley, I. Comardicea and R. Roffey (eds), *Global Environmental Change: New Drivers for Resistance, Crime and Terrorism?*, Baden-Baden, Germany: Nomos Verlagsgesellschaft, 243–259.
Doyle, J. (2007) 'Picturing the Clima(c)tic: Greenpeace and the Representational Politics of Climate Change Communication', *Science as Culture*, 16(2): 129–150.
Dybing, S.S. (2012) 'Environmental Harm: Social Causes and Shifting Legislative Dynamics', in R. Ellefsen, R. Sollund and G. Larsen (eds), *Eco-global Crimes: Contemporary Problems and Future Challenges*. Surrey, UK: Ashgate, 273–294.
Folger, T. (2013) 'Rising Seas', *National Geographic*, September: 30–59.
Fountain, H. and Gillis, J. (2013) 'Typhoon in Philippines Casts Long Shadow Over U.N. Talks on Climate Treaty', *The New York Times*, November 12: A3.
Franz, A. (2012) 'Climate Change in the Courts: A US and Global Perspective', in R. White (ed.), *Climate Change from a Criminological Perspective*. New York: Springer 89–107.
Gessen, K. (2012) 'Polar Express', *The New Yorker*, December 24 and 31: 98–116.
Giddens, A. (2011) *The Politics of Climate Change*, 2nd edn. Cambridge: Polity Press.
Gore, A. (2010) 'We Can't Wish Away Climate Change', *The New York Times*, February 28: WK11.
Goss, D.A., Grosvenor, T.P., Keller, J.T., Marsh-Tootle, W., Norton, T.T. and Zadnik, K. (American Optometric Association Consensus Panel on Care of the Patient with Myopia) (1997) *Optometric Clinical Practice Guide: Care for the Patient with Myopia*. St. Louis: American Optometric Association. Available at: http://www.aoa.org/documents/optometrists/CPG-15.pdf. Accessed 20 December 2013.
Grosvenor, T. (1987) 'A Review and a Suggested Classification System for Myopia on the Basis of Age-Related Prevalence and Age of Onset', *American Journal of Optometry and Physiological Optics*, 64(7) [July]: 545–554.
Hall, M. (2013) *Victims of Environmental Harm: Rights, Recognition and Redress under National and International Law*. London and New York: Routledge.
Halsey, M. (1999) 'Environmental Discontinuities: The Production and Regulation of an Eco-experience', *Criminal Justice Policy Review*, 10(2): 213–255.

Hamilton, C. (2010) *Requiem for a Species: Why We Resist the Truth about Climate Change*. London: Earthscan.
Herbig, J. (2010) 'The Illegal Reptile Trade as a Form of Conservation Crime: A South African Criminological Investigation', in R. White (ed.), *Global Environmental Harm: Criminological Perspectives*, Cullompton: Willan, 110–131.
Hollins, M. (1976) 'Does Accommodative Micropsia Exist?', *American Journal of Psychology*, 89(3) [September]: 443–454.
Howe, P.D. and Leiserowitz, A. (2013) 'Who Remembers a Hot Summer or a Cold Winter? The Asymmetric Effect of Beliefs about Global Warming on Perceptions of Local Climate Conditions in the U.S.', *Global Environmental Change*, 23(6): 1488–1500.
Hulme, M. (2009) *Why We Disagree About Climate Change: Understanding Controversy, Inaction and Opportunity*. Cambridge: Cambridge University Press.
Johnson, B.B. (1993) 'Advancing Understanding of Knowledge's Role in Lay Risk Perception', *Risk — Issues in Health and Safety*, 4, 189–211.
Kramer, R.C. (2013) 'Carbon in the Atmosphere and Power in America: Climate Change as State-Corporate Crime', *Journal of Crime and Justice*, 36(2): 153–170.
Krugman, P. (2006) 'A Test of Our Character', *The New York Times*, May 26: A19.
—— (2010a) 'Drilling, Disaster, Denial', *The New York Times*, May 3: A25.
Lee, J.R. (2009) *Climate Change and Armed Conflict: Hot and Cold Wars*. London and New York: Routledge.
Leech, G. (2012) *Capitalism: A Structural Genocide*. London and New York: Zed Books.
Louv, R. (2006) *Last Child in the Woods: Saving Our Children from Nature-Deficit Disorder*. Chapel Hill, NC: Algonquin.
Lowe, T., Brown, K., Dessai, S., de França Doria, M., Haynes, K. and Vincent, K. (2006) 'Does Tomorrow Ever Come? Disaster Narrative and Public Perceptions of Climate Change', *Public Understanding of Science*, 15: 435–457.
Malik, T. (2014) 'Effects of Climate Change Visible from Space, NASA Chief Says', *Yahoo! News*, May 6. Available at: http://news.yahoo.com/effects-climate-change-visible-space-nasa-chief-says-221720003.html. Accessed 11 August 2014.
Mares, D. (2010) 'Criminalizing Ecological Harm: Crimes Against Carrying Capacity and the Criminalization of Eco-Sinners', *Critical Criminology*, 18(4): 279–293.
McClanahan, B. and Brisman, A. (2013) 'A Peace on Climate Change', *The Critical Criminologist*, 22(1): 2–7.
McCright, A.M. and Dunlap, R.E. (2003) 'Defeating Kyoto: The Conservative Movement's Impact on U.S. Climate Change Policy', *Social Problems*, 50(3): 348–373.
McKibben, B. (1999) 'Indifferent to a Planet in Pain', *The New York Times*, Sept. 4.
McNall, S. (2011) *Rapid Climate Change: Causes, Consequences, and Solutions*. New York and London: Routledge.
Michaeli-Cohen, A., Almog, Y., Loewenstein, A., Stolovitch, C., Gutman, I. and Lazar, M. (1996) 'Presumed Ocular Myasthenia and Micropsia: A Case Report', *Journal of Neuro-Opthalmology*, 16(1): 18–20.
Michalowski, R.J. (1985) *Order, Law, and Crime: An Introduction to Criminology*. New York: McGraw-Hill.

Morgan, I. and Rose, K. (2005) 'How Genetic Is School Myopia?', *Progress in Retinal and Eye Research*, 24(1) [January]: 1–38.

Moser, S. and Dilling, L. (2004) 'Making Climate Hot: Communicating the Urgency and Challenge of Global Climate Change', *Environment*, 46(10): 32–46.

Neuhauser, A. (2014) 'Poll: Americans Still Unconcerned About Global Warming', *U.S. News & World Report*, April 4. Available at: http://www.usnews.com/news/blogs/data-mine/2014/04/04/poll-americans-still-unconcerned-about-global-warming. Accessed 11 August 2014.

Pappas, S. (2012) '8 Ways Global Warming Is Already Changing the World', *LiveScience*, September 12. Accessed at: http://www.livescience.com/23026-global-warming-changing-world.html. [Accessed 20 December 2013].

Pretty, J. (2013) 'The Consumption of a Finite Planet: Well-Being, Convergence, Divergence and the Nascent Green Economy', *Environmental and Resource Economics*, 55(4): 475–499.

Rachlinski, J. (2000) 'The Psychology of Climate Change', *University of Illinois Law Review*: 299–319.

Rahmstorf, S. (2005) 'The Climate Skeptics', in Munich Reinsurance Company [Munich Re] (ed.), *Weather Catastrophes and Climate Change*. Munich: PG Verlag, 76–83.

Revkin, A. (2007a) 'Arctic Melt Unnerves the Experts', *The New York Times*, October 2: D1, D4.

—— (2007b) 'Grim Outlook for Polar Bears', *The New York Times*, October 2: D4.

Ross, A. (1991) 'Is Global Culture Warming Up?', *Social Text*, 28: 3–30.

Satter, R. (2013). 'UN Official: World Failing Over Climate Change', *Associated Press/Yahoo! News*, September 17. Available at: http://news.yahoo.com/un-official-world-failing-over-climate-change-180628550.html. Accessed 11 August 2014.

Shiva, V. (2008) *Soil Not Oil: Environmental Justice in a Time of Climate Crisis*. Cambridge, MA: South End Press.

Sollund, R. (2012) 'Oil Production, Climate Change and Species Decline: The Case of Norway', in R. White (ed.), *Climate Change from a Criminological Perspective*. New York: Springer, 135–147.

Tákacs-Sánta, A. (2007) 'Barriers to Environmental Concern', *Human Ecology Review*, 14(1): 26–38.

Thomas, C.A., Cameron, A., Green, R.E., Bakkenes, M., Beaumont, L.J., Collingham, Y.C., Erasmus, B.F.N., Ferreira de Siqueira, M., Grainger, A., Hannah, L., Hughes, L., Huntley, B., Jaarsveld, A.S., Midgley, G.F., Miles, L., Ortega-Huerta, M.A., Townsend Peterson, A., Phillips, O.L. and Williams, S.E. (2004) 'Extinction Risk from Climate Change', *Nature*, 427(6970) [January 4]: 145–148.

Thompson, C. (2009) 'Don't Work All the Time – You'll Live to Regret It', *Wired*, 17(08) [July 15]. Available at: http://www.wired.com/culture/lifestyle/magazine/17–08/by_work. [Accessed 1 October 2013]

Todd, J. (1955) 'The Syndrome of Alice in Wonderland', *Canadian Medical Association Journal*, 73(9) [November]: 701–704.

Turrentine, J. (2014) 'The Facts Are Not Enough', *Oneearth*, April 7. Available at: http://www.onearth.org/articles/2014/04/katharine-hayhoe-on-the-ipcc-climate-report-showtime-years-of-living-dangerously. Accessed 11 August 2014.

Ungar, Z. (2013a) 'The Fuzzy Face of Climate Change', *Pacific Standard*, (January/February): 40–51.

—— (2013b) *Never Look a Polar Bear in the Eye: A Family Field Trip to the Arctic's Edge in Search of Adventure, Truth, and Mini-Marshmallows*. Boston: Da Capo Press.
Walters, R. (2013) 'Air Crimes and Atmospheric Justice', in N. South and A. Brisman (eds), *Routledge International Handbook of Green Criminology*. London and New York: Routledge, 134–149.
Washington, H. and Cook, J. (2011) *Climate Change Denial: Heads in the Sand*. London and Washington, DC: Earthscan.
Weeks, J. (2009) 'Rapid Urbanization: Can Cities Cope With Rampant Growth?', *CQ Global Researcher*, 3(4) [April]: 91–118.
White, R. (2010) 'Globalisation and Environmental Harm', in R. White (ed.), *Global Environmental Harm: Criminological Perspectives*, Cullompton: Willan, 3–19.
—— (2012) 'The Criminology of Climate Change', in R. White (ed.), *Climate Change from a Criminological Perspective*. New York: Springer, 1–11.
—— (2013) *Environmental Harm: An Eco-Justice Perspective*. Bristol: Policy Press.
Winter, D.D.N. and Koger, S.M. (2004) *The Psychology of Environmental Problems*. 2nd edn. Mahwah, NJ: Lawrence Erlbaum Associates.

5
'Honour' Crimes
Alexandra Hall

Introduction

In the United Kingdom a number of high-profile cases related to forced marriage and 'honour' killing have sparked media attention to so-called 'honour' crimes and 'honour-based' violence (HBV). In response, recent scholarly research has focused on the impact of honour-based practices on the lives of Black and Minority Ethnic (BME) women, particularly incidents that culminate in violence and aggression (Akpinar 2003; Welchman and Hossain 2005; Meetoo and Mirza 2007; Gill 2009; Idriss and Abbas 2011). However, this form of violence and abuse remains largely under-reported and underestimated. It is only partially understood and therefore susceptible to prejudicial cultural stereotypes and media sensationalism (Dustin and Phillips 2008). This chapter unpacks these emerging debates around 'honour' crime and victimisation while acknowledging the cultural and political sensitivity associated with these issues. After an initial overview of what constitutes a 'crime of honour' and how we might move beyond the contested nature of the term to understand its specificities, the discussion analyses the nature and extent of 'honour' crimes in the United Kingdom. This is followed by a discussion of the concept of *izzat*, which occupies the centre of the distinct honour/shame complex that plays an important reproductive role in specific South Asian cultural groups, with a particular focus on British-Pakistani diasporic communities. The aim is to explore the aetiology of HBV in a specific cultural context before moving on to discuss how forms of HBV among South Asian groups can be categorised as invisible crimes. In doing so debates inspired by feminist criminology are drawn upon, including relations between the body and the family, all of which are located in the broader criminological field of violence against women (VAW). The approach suggests that gendered and familial relations and their associated cultural codes can constitute a barrier to the reporting and recording of incidents, potentially jeopardising the human rights of individuals, predominantly young women. These relations and codes can also constitute barriers to conducting social-scientific research. Finally, at the level of policy and practice, the chapter explores how incidents and structural patterns of honour-related crime are made visible to governmental agencies and accessible to social-scientific inquiry.

'Honour' crime: a working definition of a contested concept

Crimes such as forced marriage, kidnap, rape, murder, false imprisonment, female genital mutilation and interpersonal violence – as well as less physical harms involving financial, emotional and psychological abuse – are sometimes committed in families as part of the maintenance of 'honour'. This is seen by some as a vital vehicle for the cultural reproduction of a particular social structure and way of life (Welchman and Hossain 2005; Dustin 2006). However, so-called 'honour' crimes and HBV are inherently contested concepts whose symbolic and abstract underpinning leaves them open to much debate (Gill 2009: 476). To conceptualise and categorise the concealment of such crimes and understand why these powerful underlying social structures and cultural forces exist, how they reproduce themselves and how they can be interrupted and transformed, it is important to begin with a working definition of the key concept under scrutiny. Gill (2009: 476) argues that incidents of HBV:

> constitute any form of violence perpetrated against females within a framework of patriarchal family structures, communities, and/or societies, where the main justification for the perpetration of violence is the protection of a social construction of honour as value system, norm, or tradition.

Typically, forms of HBV occur in families as a violent response to a female family member's transgression of a strict set of 'traditional' gendered norms relating to sexual purity, which is perceived to bring shame on the family (Siddiqui 2005: 263). Although evidence suggests that victims of 'honour' crimes are usually women and perpetrators male, it must also be noted that there have also been incidents in which female family members have committed or been complicit in acts of violence, the most recent example being the case of Shafilea Ahmed, in which both of her parents were charged with her murder and sentenced to life imprisonment (see discussion below). Moreover, albeit less frequently, there have been cases with male victims, for example, in the United Kingdom the cases of Awais Akram and Ahmed Bashir, where both men were targeted by the male family members of their girlfriends in 'revenge attacks'. In 2009, Akram was left severely disfigured after being stabbed and having sulphuric acid poured over his face and body. Back in 1996, Bashir was attacked in his garden and died after having been stabbed and slashed 43 times; his perpetrators, one the brother of his girlfriend, were handed life sentences in 2005 (see Coleman 2011). That said, male-on-male violence is usually the outcome of 'feuds over land or property' (Siddiqui 2005: 264; see also Hall 2014). However, this chapter will focus on the most common motivation for 'honour' crimes: the control of female sexuality. Usually in these instances a female who may have sought a divorce, refused a marriage proposal or engaged in extramarital affairs is perceived as transgressing the cultural boundaries of her permitted sexual behaviour and is therefore seen to be shaming the reputation of her family. Having had her behaviour and sexuality monitored by family members – who act to regulate and restore their family honour in the eyes of others – she becomes the victim of violent crime.

In recent years, public discourse in the UK has paid more attention to forced marriage and 'honour' killing (Dustin and Phillips 2008: 407). Most often these social harms and violent crimes are associated with Middle Eastern and South Asian communities and are reported as entrenched in their cultural practices. However, this homogenous view of ethnocultural groups is misleading. When discussing HBV it is important to avoid essentialising the abuse or violence and thus subscribing to religious, cultural or racial stereotypes and discriminatory discourses which serve to stigmatise BME groups, undermine the complex issues victims face and further reduce the visibility of these specific social harms. Much of the literature on HBV warns readers about the stereotyping of cultural groups, acknowledging that generalised accounts of violent crimes by members of BME, particularly Muslim groups, can feed Islamophobia and reactionary views on immigration control (Sen 2005; Warrier 2008; Abbas 2011). Some proponents therefore locate HBV within the broader transcultural framework of violence against women (VAW) (Meetoo and Mirza 2007; Gill 2009). For example, Meetoo and Mirza call for the adoption of a human rights approach to tackle 'honour' killing. They blame the 'gender trap' of the prevailing multicultural discourse, which attempts to validate cultural and ethnic differences while failing to recognise or tackle gendered oppressions within some communities. This, along with Islamophobia and fear of the 'other' – more common in Western liberal democracies since 9/11 – can limit responses to the control of female sexuality, HBV and homicide. Academic work has also criticised Eurocentric views of HBV as problem-focused accounts that label any 'other' culture as backward and barbaric. They tend to argue that the sensationalising accounts of 'honour' killings and forced marriages are a way to intensify the ruling ideology and hegemony of the West (see Akpinar 2003; Meetoo and Mirza 2007; Abbas 2011).

Furthermore, there is a justified amount of sensitivity surrounding the term 'honour' when it is used in association with crime and violence. In this context, it is often placed in quotation marks, as it is in this chapter, to highlight the untenable discourses that perceive the crimes to be honourable and encourage perpetrators to defend their actions on moral grounds (Dustin and Phillips 2008: 412). However, problematising the term always brings up difficulties. As Gill (2006: 1) warns,

> We must guard against two dangers: on the one hand the danger of universalising what are merely western feminist ideas of morality, and on the other of tolerating human rights violations for the sake of multicultural accommodation.

Although social scientists and policy-makers should be careful not to sensationalise 'honour' crimes or stereotype BME communities, there is a need to recognise the specificities and trends associated with the crimes (Dustin and Phillips 2008: 413). Where possible – although still located within the broader category of VAW – the specific dynamics of each offence categorised as HBV should be established in order to protect victims, build cases against perpetrators and offer appropriate criminal justice and public-policy responses.

However, it is also important to attempt to understand the universal nature of honour. Historically, honour and shame have been deeply rooted in the cultural and social norms of various groups and societies around the world (see Pitt-Rivers et al. 1961; Campbell 1964; Peristiany 1965). Honour is therefore not peculiar to particular cultures; however, formal variations can be distinguished in different cultural contexts. What needs to be examined and tackled are violent acts committed *in the name* of various sociocultural conceptualisations of honour. Aase's (2002) work highlights the problems associated with understanding the concept of honour. He argues that we need comparisons and we must be specific about 'defining its semantic content'. This is important because, on the one hand, honour is subjective, yet simultaneously acted upon in similar ways in various cultural contexts. On the other hand, we might encounter different conceptualisations of honour within a given culture, such as in Pakistan where a distinction is often made between *izzat* (honour and respect) and *ghairat* (valour), which is discussed below. These must be understood as comparative yet 'similar phenomena' (Aase 2002: 6). Overall, Aase's empirical evidence points to associating honour with the courage and capacity to defend, but in the absence of practical norms: 'apart from violations of women's sexual chastity there rarely exist any prescribed norms according to which honourable vengeance must be taken' (Aase 2002: 10). It is therefore more important to ask if behaving honourably – generally conceptualised as 'the legitimate use of power in order to protect one's interests' (Aase 2002: 10) – appears to take place in specific political-economic and sociocultural contexts and to analyse and contextualise the nature and dynamics of the prescribed norms on which acts of HBV are manifested.

Even though we are focusing on 'honour' crimes in the context of South Asian, specifically Pakistani, diasporic groups in the United Kingdom, this is not to suggest that violence against women and killing in the name of 'honour' happens solely in Asian communities; similar phenomena can be found in white European communities, such as Greece, Italy or the United Kingdom (see Campbell 1964; Spierenburg 2008). In the United Kingdom, for example, similar instances of domestic violence occurring among white British groups are commonly referred to as 'crimes of passion', yet they are also entrenched in ideas of shame, pride, honour and respect. The broader relevance to be drawn from this specific cultural context is a need to revisit 'face', vengeance and honour as concepts that have not been lost in the process of modernity to be replaced by feelings of dignity, as many modernisation theorists would have us believe (see, for example, Berger 1974). These normative concepts in their various guises still have a formative effect on societal expectations which can govern the behaviour of individuals and sometimes culminate in violence or victimisation, while simultaneously leading to misconceptions and inappropriate responses to criminality and victimisation. Therefore, it is important to evaluate complexities, contexts and motivations, while remaining cautious of both universalism and cultural relativism. In this way we can avoid disassociating the abuse from the wider issue of domestic violence and regarding it simply as a manifestation of a specific culture (Thiara and Gill 2010: 45). The chapter will now offer an overview of the shape and extent of HBV in the United Kingdom, before moving on to explore the cultural specificities of the honour/shame complex among Pakistanis, in order to better understand the complex and context-specific aetiology of 'honour' crimes.

The size and shape of 'honour' crimes in the United Kingdom

There is not space here to fully explore the range of 'honour' crimes happening across the globe. An interesting collection of internationalised comparative work can be found in Welchman and Hossain (2005). It is important, however, to identify the size, shape and extent of HBV in the United Kingdom in comparative terms. What do we know about 'honour' crime and how big a problem is it?

Globally, the United Nations estimates 5,000 women on average dying each year in 'honour' killings, but that number significantly decreases in the United Kingdom, with estimates as low as 10 to 12 'honour' killings per annum (see Brandon and Hafez 2008). Other notable figures available include those released by UK police in 2011 highlighting a 47 per cent increase in reported incidents of HBV over a two-year period, with 2,823 incidents in 2011, 500 of which happened in London (BBC Online 2011). However, as Janssen (2006) argues, cases of HBV cannot be thoroughly quantified and no reliable statistics exist. It is widely argued that there is a huge dark figure of this type of crime and victimisation, with a large proportion of HBV, including 'honour' killings, not reported. Reasons for this will be explored in depth below, but in terms of murder the dark figure includes the disappearance of women who have been taken 'back home' to their ancestral country where they are abused and killed. Another crucial issue is the cases of suicide that have been reported as responses to HBV, which increases underestimation because suicide is not categorised as 'honour' killing (see Siddiqui 2005). Therefore these incidents remain outside of UK law-enforcement provision and statistics. As discussed above, cases can range from financial and emotional abuse to murder, and, as will become clear, our lack of knowledge and response is due to a range of complex factors preventing disclosure and clear understanding of victimisation.

In terms of what we know about 'honour' crimes, there have been a number of high-profile cases of 'honour' killing in the United Kingdom which act as exemplars of these crimes in UK public discourse. One such case is that of British-Pakistani Shafilea Ahmed. Shafilea was 17 years old in 2003 when she was reported missing from her home in Cheshire, England. Her mutilated body was found six months later in the River Kent, Cumbria, in the Northwest of England. After initial police information suggested that she had turned down an arranged marriage in Pakistan, drinking bleach in a suicide attempt during her visit there, they began to suspect that her parents had played a part in her disappearance. Eventually her younger sister disclosed that after years of abuse her parents had suffocated her sister and dumped her body. On 3 August 2012, they were found guilty of their daughter's murder and sentenced to life imprisonment. Another high-profile case was that of 16-year-old Heshu Yones who died at the hands of her Iraqi Kurd father in 2002. It was revealed that Heshu's father had stabbed her 17 times and slit her throat before attempting his own suicide. It was reported that problems began after her father found out Heshu was in a relationship with an 18-year-old Lebanese Christian. In both of these cases, the actions of daughters were deemed to be bringing shame on their families. Most media reports in cases such as these offer a simplified account of cultural tension between the traditions of an older generation and the desires of their children for a more liberal 'Westernised' lifestyle (see Gill 2006). There will be a fuller discussion of this in the context of British-Pakistanis below, but for now these cases illustrate the complexities and tensions inherent in accounts of HBV.

Although the majority of 'honour' killings reported in the United Kingdom have involved women from South Asian and Middle Eastern backgrounds, the notion of behaving honourably is universal. Crimes committed in the name of honour occur across a broad range of social and cultural groups. That said, Siddiqui (2005: 265) argues that 'notions of "shame" and "honour" are strong and influential in tight-knit minority communities propped up by orthodox and conservative cultural and religious values'. Therefore, bearing in mind these complexities, the chapter will now focus further on the honour/shame complex among a specific yet differentiated sociocultural group in order to both add detail and contextualise the various similarities and differences in the ways in which individuals, families and communities conceptualise honour and shame and how this can sometimes lead to acts of abuse and violence.

Izzat, honour and shame: the aetiology of 'honour-based' violence among South Asian groups

Usually, the two concepts 'honour' and 'shame' are seen as opposite means of social evaluation, 'the reflection of the social personality in the mirror of social ideals' of a given society (Peristiany 1965: 9). Honour represents a specific set of social standards against which an individual's behaviour is evaluated. This evaluation is connected to recognition and feeds into an individual's and/or group's social standing and status. Shame, on the other hand, is behaviour that can disgrace and erode the individual's or the family's honour. Various honour and shame complexes are reproduced and sometimes change over time in specific social, political, cultural and economic contexts. However, it is widely argued that, among modern-day South Asian groups, evaluations of behaviour remain largely honour-based (see, for example, Werbner 1990; Lefebvre 1999; Shaw 2000; Aase 2002; Ballard 2008). But what are the specific characteristics of honour and shame expressed in the social judgements and actions among South Asian groups?

The concept of *izzat* is fundamental to South Asian honour/shame complexes (Werbner 1990; Lefebvre 1999; Shaw 2000; Aase 2002; Ballard 2008). *Izzat* is a fluid form of symbolic capital that can be gained, lost and converted in various ways (Hall 2014). Put simply, it refers to the individual's and the family's reputation, level of respect and prominence in the community. It is an extremely broad and complex concept with an inherently dynamic and fluid nature. It can refer to caste and class status or to public reputation, and it is deeply embedded in the politics of identity, family, marriage and community. It is recognised throughout Pakistan, the wider South Asian subcontinent and the South Asian diaspora worldwide.

Soni's work highlights the fluidity of *izzat* and its powerful influence on most aspects of social and cultural life among South Asian groups. It not only confers status and feeds into a community's hierarchical nature, it also can offer moral guidelines and be a base for social identity (Soni 2006: 7). In other words, it feeds into norms and values and can fundamentally shape an individual's or group's behaviour. *Izzat* is constantly sought, either because individuals have a vested interest in increasing their status, or out of fear that they might bring shame (*sharam*) on themselves and their family, which in effect reduces the family's *izzat*. However, despite sharing the value of *izzat*, South Asian groups are by no means homogenous, stable and culturally cohesive. Therefore, what one Pakistani individual, for example, views as dishonourable – an affront to social norms, values and attitudes – may differ from another. Nothing is fixed and the broad labels 'South Asian', 'Pakistani' or 'Muslim' are essentialising distortions of the heterogeneous nature of societies and social groups. The implications are that analyses of HBV should take an intersectional approach (Thiara and Gill 2010: 47) that encompasses gendered, 'raced' and classed realities (Brah 1996). Intersectionality is an anti-essentialist framework that attempts to capture 'power in its multiple modalities' constituted by the complex dynamics of social relations, subjectivity, identity and experience (Brah 1996: 211). It aims to analyse the multiple and simultaneous links between and across axes of power based on, for example, 'race', class and gender taking place in specific economic, political and cultural contexts. Understanding the relationships between and across forms of power can aid our analysis of HBV because it allows for a more nuanced analysis of the varied and fluid conceptualisations of *izzat* and the complex structural, social and subjective dynamics of their formation which, on occasion, result in acts of violence.

If *izzat* is seen as a fluid form of symbolic capital which can govern rules, actions and dispositions among diverse South Asian groups whose lived experiences and social relations are embedded in various and intersecting modalities of power, then it is clear that there will be various conceptualisations of *izzat*. On the one hand, certain groups and individuals relate their degree of *izzat* in terms of status, wealth, education, caste and class background. On the other, it can be viewed in terms of 'internally defined gendered criteria' (Gill 2009: 477) in which specific cultural notions of gender ideals are signified by the female body, and where the actions of females are relied upon to symbolically and materially preserve a group's cultural values (Dwyer 2000; see discussion below). In the latter case, rules for women can include projecting a specific image of femininity – one which is chaste and self-effacing – by, for example, covering, wearing loose clothing and having no male relationships outside of their immediate family. For men, it is their willingness to protect these gender ideals by responding if a female family member deviates from them. However, this 'protection' also includes the maintenance of status and power relations. For these men higher *izzat* is achieved as a result of 'defending familial honour in feuding relations and protecting the chastity of its women, endow[ing] a person, as he grows older...with political influence, power and authority' (Werbner 2007: 166). The capacity and willingness to actively defend their respect and social standing is *ghairat* for many social groups from the Northwest of Pakistan. According to Aase, among these groups *ghairat* and *izzat* are two different 'forms' of honour. Whereas *ghairat* is 'dichotomous' – you either have it or not – *izzat* is 'continuous' or held in degrees and fluctuating (Aase 2002: 92). However, although *ghairat* is associated with the tribes of Northern Pakistan as an important feature of their particular honour/shame complex, it is not universally recognised by all Pakistanis.

Patriarchal gendered norms that feature in particular Pakistani social relations are widely argued to impact on the social attitudes and customs of the diaspora in Britain. Bolognani, analysing nonconformity among females in a Pakistani diaspora in Britain, points to the 'double moral burden' some women encounter. On the one hand, 'an individual one based on their conduct as thought appropriate to their gender' and, on the other, 'a family one, based on their successful maintenance of the family honour (*izzat*)' (Bolognani 2008: 152). These individual and familial levels of the honour/shame complex will be explored in relation to HBV below. However, at this stage it is important to highlight that these gendered norms and values intrinsic to some Pakistani cultures have been reproduced in the United Kingdom and still remain embedded in notions of honour and shame, transgressions from which sometimes result in HBV. Moreover, these norms and values have diverse dynamics determined by intersecting social and cultural identities based on, for instance, class, caste, political affiliation and regional ethnicity, as well as varying transnational political-economic and socio-cultural contexts.

Marriage rules also play a significant role in the kinship/family structure in transnational Pakistani social relations. Broken *rishtas* (marriage proposals) – the refusal of a marriage proposal between kin – can cause huge rifts among members (Shaw and Charsley 2006). The consequences of refusing to maintain certain cultural codes among trusted relatives are extremely varied. Some Pakistani women who refuse a *rishta* may be disowned by their wider *biradari* (extended family) (Shaw 2000: 185) or, in extreme cases, such as Shafilea Ahmed, may be forced into a marriage, suffer abuse or be murdered because they are perceived as shaming their family honour. Furthermore, marriage proposals for daughters can depend on the reputation of their mothers, which serves to increase the pressure for all women to conform to specific 'honourable' behaviours throughout the generations, fearful that their reputation could lead to their offspring failing to find an appropriate match. Siddiqui (2005: 264) reports of one mother who committed suicide in order to protect her daughters' reputations following the news from her husband that he was going to divorce her and falsely spread rumours of her adultery in the community. There is an ongoing debate surrounding Pakistani marriage rules, particularly transnational marriages between first cousins. Some arguments reduce the arranged marriage to a basic socio-economic function, as merely satisfying the material and migratory desires of the kinship group, but the cultural issues of emotional ties and protection also play an important role (Shaw and Charsley 2006: 407). Likewise, the generalised view of all arranged marriages as forced, where women have no choice in their spouse, can be challenged. It is important to distinguish between arranged and forced marriages and avoid representing 'love' marriages in the West as 'natural' and arranged marriages as 'backward' or merely economic in nature (for more on the forced marriage debate see Gill and Anitha 2011).

Moreover, it is important not to slip into simple binary categorisations and not to represent all Pakistani women as passive victims and men as inherently violent. This, again, highlights the need for an intersectional approach that is sensitive to the various and interrelated oppressions some women and men face. This can help us to construct a more nuanced analysis of the contextual specificities of acts of HBV, thus avoiding cultural and racial stereotyping. After all, as demonstrated, such communities are not homogenous, and HBV is not universally practised. Various means can be employed to acquire symbolic capital (*izzat*), which depends on intersecting and diverse social categories, contexts and histories, and which vary in terms of their acceptability and function. This explains why some Pakistanis may remain committed to conservative gender ideals and will act violently to restore broken rituals, while others may be more committed to liberal/modernist values. Theorising the aetiology, nature and dynamics of these crimes in their fluid, complex and diverse contexts is a daunting task, yet necessary if we are to increase their visibility.

The (in)visibility of 'honour' crime: personal and familial contributions to hidden crimes and harms

As suggested, honour and shame are normative categories in flux, therefore what is required is a better understanding of their complex dynamics. This is just one of the tasks criminological inquiry must address if increasing the visibility of HBV is to be taken seriously. To date, despite heightened public interest, mainly generated through sensationalised media reports, crimes committed in the name of 'honour' are not well understood. This lack of knowledge is just one issue impacting the resources and criminal justice responses required to render them visible in order to better support and protect victims.

As the section above has shown, the control of female sexuality is prevalent in patriarchal social systems based on honour and shame. Female chastity and fidelity are cornerstones of such value systems, and a family's reputation can depend on its female members' behaviour, particularly with regard to what the community might view as shameful sexual relations. A good deal of feminist literature has challenged these honour codes and gender ideals as products of patriarchy, where shame is used to discriminate against women, control their sexuality and maintain unjust power relations between the genders (see, for example, Akpinar 2003; Meetoo and Mirza 2007; Wilson 2006). This is evident in Wilson's (2006) research which explores the experiences of South Asian women and draws attention to the control of women's bodies and sexuality by their families. For these feminist thinkers, 'concepts like *izzat* are ... used as excuses for intimidation and extortion' (Wilson 2006: 15). Similarly, Akpinar (2003: 470) argues that the implicit association between hierarchically specified gender roles and honour and shame are a way of 'controlling female sexuality [whereby] men and women are constituted as complementary contrasts to each other'. Therefore, the female embodiment of these gendered social norms and subsequent control of their bodies and sexuality maintains HBV's invisibility because female victims, facing a variety of social barriers, are unable to disclose their abuse (Thiara and Gill 2010: 45) or, further hampering both understanding and the development of appropriate responses, some victims may not comprehend their victimisation at all.

Latif's research also emphasises this central problem. Drawing on the case studies of five Mirpuri-Pakistani women in violent relationships, she explores the nature and dynamics of domestic violence among a Pakistani diaspora in England. She notes that 'traditional' sociocultural norms impact on the victims of domestic violence and their capacity to reveal their abuse (Latif 2011: 29). Focusing on the intricacies of customs in relation to Mirpuri-Pakistani women who are victims of domestic violence, her work analyses the honour and shame complex and emphasises the fluid nature of *izzat*. In the case of this particular community, Latif found that female honour was in need of protection and usually associated with the values of 'virginity, chastity and fidelity', which are represented by 'traditional' female cultural practices such as 'long hair, being softly spoken and lowering and covering one's head in the presence of elders' (Latif 2011: 35). Her findings highlight the role of 'spiritual abuse', 'marital practices' and 'perceived moral conformity' in the victim–perpetrator relationship and suggest that the response to such violence requires a better understanding of the complexity of the challenges South Asian women face. This work reveals two of the ways 'honour' crimes remain invisible: first, that the honour code prevents the disclosure of the crimes, especially where they have been embedded in spiritual and psychological abuse, and, second, that the state institutions from which victims seek help lack a comprehensive understanding of their victimisation.

For women in the diaspora these complexities can become complicated even further. Some younger females may struggle with their hybrid cultural experiences, where the ideals on which their sexuality is prescribed by members of their diasporic community, commonly signified by sexual purity, is in juxtaposition to a cultural political economy based on liberalism and hyper-individualism in which womanhood is publicly sexualised (Mohammad 2005). Harriss and Shaw (2009: 106) offer an interesting analysis of the political economy of the Pakistani household, critically examining the distribution of power within families of Pakistani migrants to Britain. Focusing on what they call 'intermediary institutions', they argue that gender and generation shape 'normative expectations about family roles and flows of obligation and responsibility between kin'. Younger generation South Asian women can find themselves negotiating their diasporic identities in terms of the expectations of their family while also feeling the pressure from the political, economic and sociocultural environment that surrounds them. Where some members of the older generation remain committed to, or reassert their commitment to, a range of 'traditional' values and practices, the younger generation can find themselves living separate lives in public and in private – hybridised diasporic identities (see Dwyer 2000). This public/private conflict, where the close-knit nature of community and family structures conceals problems in private, can also control the actions of daughters in public.

However, a family's reputation – and therefore honour or *izzat* – still depends on female family members, predominantly daughters, acting in a culturally accepted way. Therefore the close-knit nature of family/kinship relations among 'honour-based' cultural groups leads to the privatisation of violence, which plays a prevalent role in the continued invisibility of HBV. Here HBV can be analysed as a form of domestic violence, commonly occurring in the private realm. This privatisation of HBV, whereby the family is the site of prescribed gender relations (see Ray 2011), results in shame, often enforcing certain rules and boundaries on women, and violence and abuse remain hidden from view:

> On one hand it is used by the perpetrators as an excuse or a mitigating factor when they commit acts of violence against women.… From the perspective of the women themselves the concept works differently. What is particular about the concept of 'honour' and the fear of 'shame' is that it isolates women further and this results in preventing them seeking outside help when affected by domestic violence. (Meetoo and Mirza 2007: 188)

Victims can be subjected to abuse and threats which prevent them from seeking help outside the family structure because they fear they will put themselves at risk or dishonour their family name further. Often the perpetrators are close family members who, although they may feel limited in terms of their ability to act on cultural codes in public, are violent in private where these practices are sanctioned. Family members may seek to 'cover up' HBV and it is therefore rarely reported to the police. Sometimes, as mentioned above, victims are unaware of their own victimisation (Gill 2009: 478). This too emphasises the difficulties with public/private manifestations of power relating to gender among groups where HBV is prevalent, compounding the victim's inability to comprehend and acknowledge – let alone voice – their victimisation (see Beckett and Macey 2001).

This can include a lack of resources – some women cannot speak English, do not have any financial freedom, are forcefully kept in the home or disappear after being abducted and are never reported missing (Gill 2009: 480). In some instances the state's immigration policies with regard to marriage and partnerships contributes to the proliferation of these problems for victims. The five-year rule and 'no recourse' to public funds create specific barriers for abused women. The UK immigration rules now state that an initial grant to remain in the United Kingdom for a non-EEA spouse lasts 30 months, during which time they are able to take employment but cannot access public funds such as welfare benefits. After the initial 30-month period another application must be made which allows further leave to stay in the United Kingdom for five years. Individual settlement is only available after this five-year period. This can prolong the time women stay in violent relationships because those with insecure immigration status, without access to public money, fear losing their children, being deported or left destitute. Therefore, some victims do not have the power or ability to seek help even if they want to.

Furthermore, all of this has impacted upon responses to harm and victimisation in terms of public-policy and criminal justice. According to Gill, 'because honour crime takes place within families, many states have traditionally used its private context as a pretext for non-intervention' (Gill 2006: 1). This lack of intervention, she argues, has been intensified as a result of 'multicultural accommodation', which has further contributed to HBV's invisibility. This prolongs and intensifies the lack of visibility because it is underestimated and under-reported, seen by many as a new phenomenon, too complex or culturally sensitive, and subsequently skirted over out of fear of being 'politically incorrect'.

Overall, for Gill (2006) – who calls for a human rights approach – this lack of stricter legal responses is in part to be blamed on the depoliticisation of the term 'honour crime'. This highlights the contentious nature of the subject and the problems associated with developing effective measures in the criminal justice system to tackle HBV and increase its visibility.

To sum up so far, in cases of HBV, honour and shame are normative mechanisms of social and cultural reproduction that focus on the female body, and the overwhelming majority of cases occur within the family structure and in the home. Victims are forced to deal with social barriers that make it difficult to report their victimisation, and for this primary reason they remain invisible to the criminal justice system and social-scientific inquiry. That said, outside of the need for the criminal justice system and social-scientific research to address the complexities of the causalities and victimisations characteristic of 'honour' crimes, there has been a relative amount of increased awareness of HBV in public discourse in recent times. The following section will now summarise what has been addressed to date in terms of practice and policy in the United Kingdom to increase the visibility of HBV, and suggest what still needs to be done.

Working to increase visibility

Academics and activists have been attempting to increase our awareness of VAW for decades. In the United Kingdom since the 1970s efforts have been made by Black feminists such as Southall Black Sisters to respond to the particular needs of BME women (Dustin and Phillips 2008: 408). Their work in particular has helped publicise VAW in these contexts and helped spur on governmental and institutional responses (see Siddiqui 2005). A number of activists and community-level projects continue to campaign and lobby for BME women's rights at the local, national and international level, working hard to raise awareness and empower women. Women's shelters and community and women's groups across the United Kingdom provide safe spaces for victims of HBV. One such organisation is Karma Nirvana, set up in Derby by a woman who had experienced HBV. It provides a bi-lingual helpline for victims, campaigns around the country in schools and to local governments and tries to maintain a social media presence. These and many other community and activist organisations have paved the way for progressive change and preceded any official responses from public and social policy (Dustin and Phillips 2008).

However, following extensive UK media coverage of the murder of Heshu Yones (see discussion above), the need for constitutional and legal safeguards for victims of HBV began to make some inroads into policies addressing violence in BME communities, which included forced marriage and 'honour' killing. As Dustin and Phillips (2008: 412) note, '[t]he media categorisation of this as an "honour" crime helped make this visible as a new area of public policy'. To date, public-policy and criminal justice responses are driven by the EU's attempt to share good practice among member states, with conferences and initiatives set up in various countries aimed at creating a 'knowledge base about HBV'. In the United Kingdom in 2000, a project focusing on combating 'honour' crimes with data collection, documentation and practice-sharing ran for five years, jointly coordinated by the Centre of Islamic and Middle Eastern Law at the University of London and the International Centre for the Legal Protection of Human Rights (INTERRIGHTS). A 'significant moment for action', according to Dustin and Phillips, occurred in 2003 when a domestic violence report from the Metropolitan Police Service 'identified "honour" crime as an important area for future work, set up a Strategic Homicide Prevention Working Group on Honour Killings, and began to develop its strategy, including training for front-line staff' (2008: 412). In addition, a Crown Prosecution Service pilot scheme began in 2007 which offered specialist HBV training to 25 prosecutors in consultation with activists and academics working in the field. A Home Affairs Select Committee inquiry and report into domestic violence, forced marriage and 'honour-based' violence appeared in the same year. Some changes to legislation have also been implemented. The term 'honour killing' entered the British legal system in 2003 and changes to legislation were introduced which saw harsher sentencing and discarded the 'cultural defence' which had been accepted throughout the 1990s in cases brought to court, often with a reduction of the charge to manslaughter (Gill 2009: 481). Furthermore, the Forced Marriage (Civil Protection) Act was passed in 2007 which enables the victims of forced marriages to apply for court orders for their protection. This included setting up the forced marriage unit which provides practical support and information to those who have been affected. As of June 2012, forced marriage was officially deemed an illegal offence in the United Kingdom. However, there is some concern that this recent criminalisation could render forced marriage even less visible because women who don't want to criminalise their families are less likely to report it.

However, despite these developments, police still 'lack basic knowledge and understanding' of HBV, public discourse and media representations remain largely sensationalist and the state offers inadequate responses to cases in court (Gill 2009: 482). Urgent improvements are needed in order to offer adequate domestic violence provision and legislation, much of which goes beyond the punitive response. Specialist services, appropriate legal representation and institutional frameworks are only the tip of the iceberg. The deeper structural problems reproducing gendered oppressions and unequal socio-economic realities – which are beyond the scope of this chapter – constitute a very difficult and intractable context for the everyday experiences of the individuals affected by HBV. More resources and funding are needed for safe spaces, community organisations and third sector NGOs who work directly with individuals affected by HBV. We also need to formulate future strategies, which should not only aim at punishment but prevention, for appropriate criminal justice and public-policy responses drawn up in consultation and engagement with these organisations. As Dustin and Phillips (2008: 420) argue, 'the greater involvement of women's NGOs in formulating strategies and initiatives helps secure better ways to tackle abuses of women without inadvertently promoting abuses of culture'. Working with those on the ground in these communities is vital. Information about the communities in question and their diverse sociocultural practices should not only assist the evaluation of current policy impact but also highlight potential changes that could benefit the community.

At a time of limited public resources it is more important than ever for policy-makers and institutional representatives to make informed decisions during the development of future policy related to HBV. It is also essential to begin to address the possibilities for both institutional intervention in relation to 'honour' crime and to consider the possibility and scope of changing attitudes at the local level by mobilising advocates of cohesion in the community, such as progressive religious groups and community activist groups. Currently the possibility of this actually happening is doubtful. Instead, the voluntary and community sector and activist organisations that support victims face huge economic uncertainty and pressures caused by the austerity measures imposed on the nation by the current Coalition government. As a result, services are closing down and advocates are losing platforms from which to raise issues about HBV. Because of this, the project to increase visibility will proceed at a much slower rate and more victims will slip through the gaps in the welfare state.

Conclusion

As this chapter has shown, 'honour' crimes and HBV are inherently contested concepts which, for a variety of reasons, lack visibility. The research discussed above highlights the central role of the female body and the tension between the individual and familial dimensions in which 'honour' crimes are manifested, and consistently shows that the privatisation of violence, lack of response and knowledge of the complexities, as well as lack of disclosure, combine to decrease its visibility. Therefore, from the levels of the individual and family to the state, there are many reasons why social harms committed in the name of 'honour' remain under-reported, underestimated and misrecognised or denied.

These issues have complex dynamics, but they also have a range of specificities. The tension between misrepresenting a religious and cultural 'group' and misrecognising the abuse and oppression that impact on some individuals is a politically and culturally sensitive subject to approach. Academic work must achieve a more accurate picture of the motivations and victimisations, address the diverse experiences and needs of communities and social groups affected and tackle these social harms in their various contexts with cultural and political sensitivity. Awareness of cultural differences within ethnic groups that are wrongly presumed to be homogenous and of inherent cultural stereotypes is therefore required. Yet political correctness should not gloss over the issue of HBV in these communities and prevent action on human rights violations or penetrative research on the issue. Public-policy and criminal justice responses are also needed to challenge 'honour' crime, which, in consultation with community and women's groups, seek to increase its visibility in terms of knowledge and action and offer relevant support to victims. It is in consultation with these existing and emerging organisations, which have varied but informed ideas and suggestions for improvement to the policy agenda to tackle HBV, that the issue can be made more visible.

Overall, social-scientific knowledge of the extent and nature of honour-based practices and HBV in British communities is deficient and the issue warrants further exploration. To move beyond both essentialist and relativist discourses, more nuanced interdisciplinary work with empirical breadth and theoretical depth is required which addresses the specificities of various honour/shame complexes in order to fully analyse HBV's motivations and complex victimisations. This, along with the huge amount of work that has been done on the ground for decades, can help inform future criminal justice responses and make these crime types more visible.

References

Aase, T. (ed.) (2002) *Tournaments of Power: Honour and Revenge in the Contemporary World*. Aldershot: Ashgate.

Abbas, T. (2011) 'Honour-Related Violence towards South Asian Muslim Women in the UK: A Crisis of Masculinity and Cultural Relativism in the Context of Islamaphobia and the "War on Terror', in M.M. Idriss and T. Abbas (eds), *Honour, Violence, Women and Islam*. Abingdon: Routledge, 16–28.

Akpinar, A. (2003) 'The Honour/Shame Complex Revisited: Violence against Women in the Migration Context', *Women's Studies International Forum*, 26(5): 425–442.

Ballard, R. (2008) 'Inside and Outside: Contrasting Perspectives on the Dynamics of Kinship and Marriage in Contemporary South Asian Transnational Networks', in R. Grillo (ed.), *The Family in Question: Immigrants and Minorities in Multicultural Europe*. Amsterdam: Amsterdam University Press, 36–70.

BBC Online (2011) '"Honour" Attack Numbers Revealed by UK Police Forces', BBC News UK [online]. Available at: http://www.bbc.co.uk/news/uk-16014368. Accessed 7 January 2014.

Beckett, C. and Macey, M. (2001) 'Race, Gender and Sexuality: the Oppression of Multiculturalism', *Women's Studies International Forum*, 24 (3): 309–319.

Berger, P.L. (1974) *Pyramids of Sacrifice: Political Ethics and Social Change*. New York: Anchor Books.

Bolognani, M. (2008) '"These Girls Want to Get Married as Well": Normality, Double Deviance and Reintegration amongst British Pakistani Women', in V.S. Kalra (ed.), *Pakistani Diasporas: Culture, Conflict and Change*. Oxford: Oxford University Press, 150–166.

Brah, A. (1996) *Cartographies of Diaspora, Contesting Identities*. London: Routledge.

Brandon, J. and Hafez, S. (2008) *Crimes of the Community: Honour-Based Violence in the UK*. London: Centre for Social Cohesion.

Campbell, J.K. (1964) *Honour, Family and Patronage: A Study of Institutions and Moral Values in a Greek Mountain Community*. Oxford: Oxford University Press.

Coleman, J. (2011) '"Honour" Crimes: Six Cases', *The Guardian* [online]. Available at: http://www.theguardian.com/uk/2011/dec/03/honour-crimes-cases. Accessed 3 December 2013.

Dustin, M. (2006) *Gender Equality, Cultural Diversity: European Comparisons and Lessons*. London: London School of Economics.

Dustin, M. and Phillips, A. (2008) 'Whose Agenda Is It? Abuses of Women and Abuses of "Culture" in Britain', *Ethnicities*, 8(3): 405–424.

Dwyer, C. (2000) 'Negotiating Diasporic Identities: Young British South Asian Muslim Women', *Women's Studies International Forum*, 23(4): 475–486.

Gill, A. (2006) 'Patriarchal Violence in the Name of Honour', *International Journal of Criminal Justice Sciences*, 1(1): 1–12.

—— (2009) '"Honour" Killings and the Quest for Justice in Black and Minority Ethnic Communities in the UK', *Criminal Justice Policy Review*, 20(4): 475–494.

Gill, A. and Anitha, S. (eds) (2011) *Forced Marriage: Introducing a Social Justice and Human Rights Perspective*. London: Zed Books.

Hall, A. (forthcoming 2014) *Reconceptualising Izzat: Honour, Respect & Social Status among a Pakistani Diaspora in Britain*. Ph.D. thesis. Newcastle upon Tyne: University of Northumbria.

Harris, K. and Shaw, A. (2009) 'Kinship Obligations, Gender and the Life Course: Re-writing Migration from Pakistan to Britain', in V.S. Kalra (ed.), *Pakistani Diasporas: Culture, Conflict and Change*. Oxford: Oxford University Press.

Idriss, M.M. and Abbas, T. (eds) (2011) *Honour, Violence, Women and Islam*. Abingdon: Routledge.

Janssen, J. (2006) *Your Honour or Your Life? An Exploration of Honour Cases for Police Officers and Other Professionals*. The Hague: Stapel & De Koning.

Latif, Z. (2011) 'The Silencing of Women from the Pakistani Muslim Mirpuri Community in Violent Relationships', in M.M. Idriss and T. Abass (eds), *Honour, Violence, Women and Islam*. Abingdon: Routledge 29–41.

Lefevbre, A. (1999) *Kinship, Honour and Money in Rural Pakistan: Subsistence Economy and the Effects of Internal Migration*. Richmond: Curzon.

Meetoo, V. and Mirza, H.S. (2007) '"There is Nothing 'Honourable' about Honour Killings": Gender, Violence and the Limits of Multiculturalism', *Women's Studies International Forum*, 30(3): 187–200.

Mohammad, R. (2005) 'Negotiating Spaces of the Home, the Education System and the Labour Market: The Case of Young, Working-class, British Pakistani Women', in G.W. Falah and C. Nagel (eds), *Geographies of Muslim Women: Gender, Religion, and Space*. New York: Guilford Press, 178–202.

Peristiany, J.G. (ed.) (1965) *Honour and Shame: The Values of Mediterranean Society*. London: Weidenfeld and Nicolson.

Pitt-Rivers, J. (1961) *The People of the Sierra*. Chicago: University of Chicago Press.

Ray, L. (2011) *Violence & Society*. London: Sage.

Sen, P. (2005) '"Crimes of Honour", Value and Meaning', in L. Welchman and S. Hossain (eds), *Honour: Crimes, Paradigms and Violence Against Women*. London: Zed Books, 42–63.

Shaw, A. (2000) *Kinship and Continuity: Pakistani Families in Britain*. London: Routledge.

Shaw, A. and Charsley, K. (2006) 'Rishtas: Adding Emotion to Strategy in Understanding British Pakistani Transnational Marriages', *Global Networks*, 6(4): 405–421.

Siddiqui, H. (2005) 'There Is No "Honour" in Domestic Violence, Only Shame! Women's Struggles against "Honour" Crimes in the UK', in L. Welchman and S. Hossain (eds), *Honour: Crimes, Paradigms and Violence against Women*. London: Zed Books.

Soni, S. (2006) 'Encountering "Izzat" in Asian Communities – A Reflection on Youth Work Practice', *Youth & Policy*, 90: 5–17.

Spierenburg, P. (2008) *A History of Murder. Personal Violence in Europe from the Middle Ages to the Present*. Cambridge: Polity Press.

Thiara, R.K. and Gill, A.K. (eds) (2010) *Violence Against Women in South Asian Communities: Issues for Policy and Practice*. London: Jessica Kingsley.

Warrier, S. (2008) '"It's in Their Culture": Fairness and Cultural Considerations in Domestic Violence', *Family Court Review*, 46(3): 537–542.

Welchman, L. and Hossain, S. (eds) (2005) *Honour: Crimes, Paradigms and Violence Against Women*. London: Zed Books.

Werbner, P. (1990) *The Migration Process: Capital, Gifts and Offerings among British Pakistanis*. Oxford: Berg.

—— (2007) '"Veiled Interventions in Pure Space: Shame and Embodied Struggles among Muslims in Britain and France", special issue on "Authority and Islam"', *Theory, Culture and Society*, 24 (2): 161–186.

Wilson, A. (2006) *Dreams, Questions, Struggles: South Asian Women in Britain*. London: Pluto.

6
Elder Abuse

Matthew Hall

Introduction

In this chapter I will examine the concept of elder abuse, arguing that this extends beyond the more limited notion of the 'criminal victimisation' of the elderly. Drawing on examples of research studies and legislation from the United Kingdom, Canada and the United States, the principal argument of the chapter is that the traditionally positivistic methods adopted by criminologists to count and otherwise understand crime (mainly in the form of victimisation surveys and police data) underestimate greatly the prevalence of elder victimisation, particularly when such victimisation is understood to encompass broader 'social harms' not necessarily recognised as official 'crimes' by the criminal law and in any case not often coming to the attention of the criminal justice system.

In adopting a broader approach to the questions of social harms befalling older people, this chapter reflects the arguments of the critical schools of criminology and victimology which hold that criminologists and victimologists have for most of their history focused the majority of their attention on those notions of crime and criminal justice espoused by *states* (McBarnet 1983). Thus, the argument goes, mainstream criminology and victimology still fail to take account of 'real, complex, contradictory and often politically inconvenient victims' (Kearon and Godey 2007: 31). It is submitted that this is precisely what renders the true scale of elder abuse relatively 'invisible' (to the criminal justice system and to society as whole) along with many of the other forms of victimisation discussed in this volume. As an alternative, critical criminology is more concerned with notions of 'social harms', regardless of state-sanctioned criminal definitions, and in achieving social justice (Barak 1990).

In pursuing the above agenda, this chapter does not set out to draw normative judgements as to the *desirability* of criminalising harms perpetrated against the elderly more extensively, but rather adopts the critical perspective as a means of illustrating how the present approach systematically ignores (and thus renders invisible) large components of such abuse as well as the associated question of who is perpetrating the abuse, why and in what settings. As an alternative to the traditional positivist view, it is argued that elder victimisation could be approached from a critical perspective informed by a social constructivist epistemology. Such an approach acknowledges that social phenomena – including 'crime', 'abuse' and 'old age' itself – are being constantly revised. In advocating this perspective, the chapter will show how revealing the true extent and nature of elder abuse relies on critical commentators also understanding the significance of social perceptions of older people, age and ageing. It is argued that such a perspective better reflects the fast-paced changes witnessed in our understanding of the true level of harm suffered by elderly people falling under the broader descriptor of 'elder abuse'.

The remainder of this chapter begins by examining critically various standing conceptualisations of 'elder abuse' and in so doing exposing it as a multifaceted issue heavily contingent on societal understandings. The chapter will then move on to discuss and critique traditional dismissal by some criminologists of elder victimisation as a 'non problem', based on positivistic surveying methods. It will then demonstrate three areas in which more detailed study of elder abuse *has* occurred and argue that, while this literature has provided invaluable insight into the wider social harms experienced by the elderly, much of it still tends to conceive of elder abuse as constrained to immediate situational factors, as opposed to heavily influenced by socially constructed variables. The chapter will then demonstrate the applicability of a broader perspective on elder abuse informed by critical criminology and a social constructivist epistemology. It will demonstrate how, in so doing, the net of elder abuse can be cast far wider and that the interactions between this form of social harm and others is complex and multifaceted, raising important issues in terms of citizenship and human rights. In its closing remarks the chapter advocates an interdisciplinary approach be taken to the future study of elder abuse informed by the critical school.

Conceptualising 'elder abuse'

'Elder abuse' as a concept has been variously defined, not always consistently. Thus, Castle et al. (2013: 21) have recently remarked on the 'lack of definitional clarity related to elder abuse, mistreatment, neglect, and exploitation'. In the United Kingdom, the government has adopted the following understanding of abuse in its official policy document concerning the protection afforded to 'vulnerable adults', entitled 'No More Secrets':

> a violation of an individual's human and civil rights by any other person or persons. (Home Office and Department of Health 2000)

Notably this definition does not confine abuse to the requirements of specified crimes, although it does imply there has been a breach of recognised 'rights' (on which, see below). Compare this to the definition of elder abuse presented in the Toronto Declaration on the Global Prevention of Elder Abuse (World Health Organization 2002: 3):

> Elder Abuse is a single or repeated act, or lack of appropriate action, occurring within any relationship where there is an expectation of trust which causes harm or distress to an older person. It can be of various forms: physical, psychological/emotional, sexual, financial or simply reflect intentional or unintentional neglect.

This understanding includes both actions and omissions and generally embodies principles more common to the civil law than the criminal law, including 'duty of care', 'expectation of trust' and 'negligence'. Thus, under this definition, we can predict that much elder abuse would be unlikely to figure in official crime statistics. For its part, the 'No More Secrets' document mentioned above elaborates on the definition of abuse as covering physical, sexual, psychological and financial/material abuse as well as neglect, and acts or omission which withhold the necessities of life, such as medication, adequate nutrition and heating. Of course a critical appraisal of 'elder victimisation' covers not only what we think of as 'harm', 'abuse' or 'crime', but also how we define 'the elderly' or 'older people' in this context. For simplicity, this chapter (along with much of the literature [Shenfield 2013]) will adopt the age of 65 and over as indicating an elderly person, although it is important to realise that this is to some extent arbitrary (Castle et al. 2013). Indeed, Powell et al. (2007) expose the complexities of the interactions between Beck's (1992) notion of the 'risk society' and old age as a *social* construction. On the latter point, Penhale (2013: 179) notes:

> Of importance also within the field of elder abuse are the societal views and attitudes, which are commonly held concerning older

people. The discrimination and lowered social status experienced by older people; the routinized devaluation which elders experience from living in an ageist society can exacerbate vulnerability which may already exist due to deterioration in physical and mental health. The risk of abuse may thus be increased for individuals.

A similar point is raised by Dow and Joosten (2012: 853) in their critique of more simplistic ideas of 'elder abuse':

> The focus is mainly on carer stress or family dysfunction and thereby fails to address the systemic context in which elder abuse is allowed to occur. This focus also encourages an acceptance of the victim–perpetrator dichotomy, and does not take into account the complexity of relationships between two adults, or the societal pressures and assumptions that affect individuals.

Furthermore, Penhale (2013) concludes that the term 'elder abuse' hides the gendered nature of much of the activities under discussion, that is, the fact that it is older *women* who are far more often the victims of such abuse compared to older men. As such, the author argues:

> [T]he term elder abuse, by virtue of its gender-neutral status, may disempower older women who are the majority of elders who experience abuse in later life. Links with the feminist movement to end violence against women may serve to empower older women and to promote their rights to full citizenship. (170)

If we are to adopt a socially situated and comprehensive approach to elder abuse, it therefore seems appropriate to extend 'beyond criminology' (Hillyard and Toombs 2003) to incorporate health and social services and, as we will see below, 'justice' concerns. This will become an important theme as this chapter progresses.

Challenging traditional thinking on elder victimisation

As indicated above, in some ways the invisibility of elder abuse can be attributed to the generally positivistic perspective (and thus methodologies) of much mainstream criminology. Although criminological study of elderly victimisation has continued to develop since at least the 1970s (see Shichor and Kobrin 1978), until recently a reliance by many criminologists on crime statistics (mainly derived from victim surveys) has fostered the overriding impression that for many kinds of offending it is the younger age bracket who both tend to commit crimes and become the victims of crime (Chaplin et al. 2011). As well as being generally 'not affected' by crime, survey methods have tended to suggest that elderly people also fear crime to a greater extent than other sectors of the population (Clarke and Lewis 1982). As summarised by Pain (1995: 584):

> [O]ne of the paradoxes arising in criminological discussions of 'risk' and 'fear' remains that while elderly people seem to suffer as much or more from the fear of crime as young people, they appear to be the least likely of all groups to be victimized.

In recent years this prevailing wisdom has been challenged in two key ways. First, closer inspection of the official crime figures has revealed that such a simplistic understanding of the relationship between older people and crime underplays considerable complexities. For example, Lindesay (1996), Klaus (2005) and Bulman (2010) subscribe to the basic proposition that, while older people may indeed be less prone to the forms of criminal victimisation captured via victimisation surveys, this in fact only represents the tip of the iceberg when one considers less visible victimisations occurring in private, including elder abuse and the effects of occupational and/or 'white-collar' crime (Powell and Wahidin 2004). Similarly, in relation to older people's fear of crime there is now much evidence to suggest that *gender* rather than *age* is the more determinative demographic (Pain 1995), depending precisely on how one conceives the notoriously complex subject of 'fear of crime' (see Farrall et al. 1997).

A second challenge to traditional thinking on the subject of older victims can be levied at those components of the literature which draw conclusions almost exclusively from officially recognised crime that is picked up by crime surveys (Powell et al. 2007). This ignores the much wider concepts of victimisation now being utilised both by academic commentators and by governments in official policies on victimisation which have increasingly steered the question away from rigid legalistic definitions of 'victimhood' towards wider discussions of 'harm' (Hall 2010). In the next section we will see how a limited understanding and literature has developed concerning elder victimisation outside the criminal statistics, although at the same time this literature has tended to be confined to certain situations and has fully conceptualised neither elder abuse itself (its victims or its perpetrators) nor its implications in a wider societal context.

What we know and what we think we know: situations of elder abuse

While this chapter (and this volume as a whole) is concerned with the absence of detailed knowledge concerning victimisation, as noted above this does not mean that criminologists have entirely ignored the subject of older people as victims of abuse or that knowledge about the scale of such abuse is completely lacking. To give an example, the preliminaries of the US 2009 Elder Abuse Act (discussed in more detail later in this chapter) cite a figure of 'between 500,000 and 5,000,000 elders (people over 60) in the United States' as being abused, neglected or exploited each year. Nevertheless, the breadth of this estimate is itself indicative of the lack of clear or certain figures on this issue. More recent US research from Acierno et al. (2010) cites a figure of 10 per cent of individuals over the age of 60 reporting that they have experienced some type of mistreatment in the year prior to being surveyed.

The above data notwithstanding, when elder abuse has received more detailed examination by researchers, most attention has focused on three distinct situations in which such abuse occurs: in care homes; in domestic settings; and in the financial abuse (often fraud) perpetrated by individuals, and sometimes corporations, against the elderly. We will now examine each of these in turn with particular reference to why such abuse often falls outside official crime statistics.

Abuse of the elderly in care homes

Abuse in care homes is an aspect of elder abuse that has arguably received the most attention, at least in the public sphere, including several high-profile media exposés of care homes under investigation for alleged incidence of abusing residents (BBC 2012). Significantly, however, because crime surveys tend to be carried out on households, potential victims of such abuse almost never appear in official crime statistics. This absence of elderly people resident in care homes from the crime figures is significant not just because of the raw numbers of people excluded from the survey but, more importantly, because it effectively also excludes a whole classification of abuse and victimisation occurring within institutional settings. In relation to residential care homes, there have been very few definitive studies of such victimisation in the United Kingdom. Research by Speight and Purdon (2007) (part of a wider National Centre for Social Research Study of Abuse and Neglect of the elderly) attempted to map out the feasibility of such a project. The authors concluded that such a study was feasible but that more work was needed to clarify the scope and definitions of concepts like 'elder abuse' before it could yield meaningful results.

Wolhunter et al. (2009) provide a concise summary of relevant research that has been carried out in residential homes in Germany (Goergen 2004) and the United States (Lachs et al. 2007; Payne and Gainey 2006). The former study (Wolhunter et al. 2009) concluded that verbal victimisation and neglect at the hands of nursing staff were more regularly reported than physical violence. Lach et al.'s research, however, indicates that when residents do suffer violence, it is often at the hands of other residents competing for scarce resources. More detailed examination of older people both as victims *and perpetrators* of elder abuse is still a major omission from the literature.

In contrast to both the above findings, Payne and Gainey's (2006) study revealed far greater incidents of violent victimisation perpetrated by nursing care staff, which the authors attribute not to instructional factors, but rather to individual characteristics of offenders and – in accordance with routine-activities theory (Cohen and Felson 1979) – the fact that victims had been systematically placed in vulnerable positions. On this point Pain (1995) similarly concludes that routine-activities theory has an important role in explaining some elderly victimisation. In addition, Payne and Gainey (2006) argue that general-strain theory (Agnew 1992) can also be applied in relation to the role of caregiver burden when such caregivers become victimisers of the elderly both in nursing homes and in the victims' own home (on which, see below). Importantly such findings have prompted some commentators to point out that while the victimisation of elderly and other vulnerable adults is poorly understood and certainly under-researched, so too are the long-term effects of caring for someone in declining health, both in a professional and a personal/family capacity. As such, Grunfeld et al. (2004: 1796) conclude:

> Caregivers' depression and perceived burden increase as patients' functional status declines. Strategies are needed to help reduce the psychosocial, occupational and economic burden associated with caregiving.

While Grunfeld's empirical work focused on family caregivers of relatives with advanced breast cancer, the principle that the abuser as well as the abused needs to be the topic of more criminological study is well advocated.

More recently, Castle et al. (2013) have provided an updated review of the (US-based) literature and findings on care-home mistreatment of elderly people (here defined as those of age 65 and above). Their review indicates a number of factors can contribute to caregiver stress, including: decreased satisfaction, long hours, low pay, physical demands, staff shortages (increased workload), and minimal education and training. Nevertheless, as noted above, still vastly under-researched is 'resident to resident' abuse which can take the form of: invasion of privacy or personal integrity; roommate problems; hostile interpersonal interactions; unprovoked actions; and inappropriate sexual behaviour (Pillemer et al. 2011). Work by Thomson et al. (2011) noted that not only did the elderly in care homes themselves often not report abuse, but medical personnel and staff were often unable to detect abuse because of the lack of education and/or training. Overall, Castle et al. (2013: 25) conclude that, in the case of care homes: 'Despite the growth in empirical studies, the literature, in general, was limited in providing a nuanced understanding of abuse.'

Abuse of the elderly in domestic settings

Running in parallel to the growth and development in understanding of elder abuse in care homes, recent years have also seen increasing recognition of abuse of the elderly in their own homes, usually by family members, as potentially constituting domestic violence. This may make sense as, according to some estimates, two-thirds of acts of elder abuse are committed at home by someone in a position of trust (Help the Aged 2008). It was noted above that several commentators have used the concept of 'caregiver burden' to explain the prevalence of elder abuse both in nursing homes and in the domestic setting. Cooper et al. (2010) have expanded on the determinants of family carers' abuse of elderly relatives more specifically, arguing that these include: anxiety and depression; spending more hours caring; experiencing more abusive behaviour from care recipients; and higher burden. That said, Finkelhor and Pillemer (1985) have emphasised that elderly abuse may be a reaction against the position of dependency in which an abuser finds him/herself rather than the responsibilities of caregiving.

In the United Kingdom, the official (albeit non-statutory) definition of domestic violence does not restrict the concept to younger people but instead defines it as 'any incident or pattern of incidents of controlling, coercive or threatening behaviour, violence or abuse between those aged 16 or over who are or have been intimate partners or family members regardless of gender or sexuality' (Home Office 2012). Consequently, some have debated the relative merits and demerits of the conceptual overlaps between the two concepts. Certainly the utility of combining investigations of elder abuse with domestic violence research is a matter of some debate. One early contribution to these debates was made by Finkelhor and Pillemer (1985) who compared elder abuse with domestic violence generally and that perpetrated against children specifically. The authors concluded that the structural relationships between abused and abuser makes elder abuse more akin to spousal abuse than to the abuse of children. Approaching elder abuse in this manner, they argue, brings a number of advantages in that 'it does not infantilize the elderly, emphasises initiatives they can take on their own behalf, and allows for the dependency of the abuser on the abused' (Finkelhor and Pillemer 1985: 12). Penhale (2013: 179) is critical of simply amalgamating the two areas of discussion because 'elder abuse is similar to and yet different from other types of family violence'. The author argues:

> The spectrum of elder abuse, if viewed as a continuum, encompasses both abuse between partners in later life and child abuse and many variations in between. It also encompasses abuse that occurs within institutions, either due to the regime within the institution, or abuse that occurs directed at an individual in that setting (from a relative, paid carer, or indeed another resident). This form of abuse is indeed different from violence occurring within the domestic setting and is an indication of the extra care that needs to be taken when considering the abuse of older women. (179)

Notwithstanding such reservations, one further link between the issues of elder abuse and domestic violence is the realisation that the latter may in fact constitute a long-term continuation of the former. This was a key conclusion presented by Hightower et al. (2001) following a major empirical study of abuse and violence in the lives of older women in British Columbia and Yukon. That said, Kilbane and Spira, in the US context, have pointed out that the distinction between domestic violence and elder abuse does matter for practical reasons because US states tend to have different processes and systems in place for dealing with 'domestic violence' compared with 'adult protection services'. Thus the classification of harm into one category or the other in fact has very important implications for the types and levels of services victims have access to.

Occupational and corporate abuse of the elderly

Abuses carried out by carers in residential homes are often classified as occupational or white-collar crime, given that such abuse takes place in the context of the perpetrator's professional duties. That said, Payne et al. (2012) have argued that in the nursing home context it is important to emphasise the differences between elder abuse and elder neglect. Neglect cases, they argue, are more likely to be white-collar crimes rather than occupational crimes. They also note that neglect cases are more likely than abuse cases to be committed in groups, involve multiple victims and result in more serious consequences for victims. Another perspective is provided by Policastro et al. (2013), whose empirical work indicated that although white-collar crimes targeting older victims are more likely to occur in a workplace (such as a care-home), nearly a quarter of these crimes occur in the victim's home.

Of course the concepts of 'white-collar', 'corporate' and 'occupation' crimes have themselves been the subject of long-term debate and the differences between them are not always clear cut (Sutherland 1949; Nelken 2007). Here the critical focus is on social harm and 'abuse' rather than crime and therefore this chapter is more concerned with how older people may find themselves subject to legal or semi-legal exploitations by professionals and corporate actors. Indeed, one important observation to make here is that studies in the United States and Sweden (Larsson and Alalehto 2013) all confirm that while they are not necessarily the most frequent victims of white-collar crime, the demographic component of society most likely to think such crimes are 'seriously wrong' are elderly women from a minority ethnic group who do not use the Internet regularly.

Generally, however, the susceptibility of older people to abuses by professionals and corporations has received very little attention in the literature. One key exception is the work of Powell and Wahidin (2004) on the embezzlement of funds from older people's pensions by legal banking corporations. Evans and Porche (2005) have also examined the defrauding of older people by occupational and speech therapists both within and outside nursing home environments. These findings suggest that older people were targeted for such fraud principally based on the belief that they would be less likely to report crime to the authorities and that the authorities for their part would be less likely to believe their reports event when they did. Evidence of the impact of such crime on elderly victims in particular is provided by Spalek's (1999) empirical work with victims of a major pension fraud perpetrated in the United Kingdom by newspaper owner Robert Maxwell, in which pension funds were essentially stolen from investors. Spalek's analysis of first-hand interviews with some of those affected revealed that the impact of this 'white-collar crime' on victims was comparable to that experienced by victims of sexual, violent and property crime, including similar psychological, emotional, physical, financial and behavioural impacts.

As with some of the other characteristics routinely attributed to 'older people' discussed above, it is equally important when reviewing this kind of data to ascertain whether age itself is in fact the defining variable. In the cases of older people's alleged susceptibility to fraud, for example, Smith (1999: 4) argues:

> Generally, however, the extent to which older persons are defrauded is directly proportional to the vulnerabilities which arise out of the circumstances in which they live. Old age, of itself, does not predispose someone to being deceived and defrauded any more than does gender or nationality. Indeed, the experiences of a lifetime may make older persons more able to detect a fraudulent proposal when it is made and to avoid its consequences, than others who are younger and less knowledgeable concerning life's pitfalls.

The above view notwithstanding, Smith (1999: 21) does point out that while 'being old' does not of itself necessarily leave one more open to fraud, 'some older people do possess some characteristics which make them more vulnerable than younger people'. These include: being less mentally alert; being more trusting of people; being more tolerant; having time to devote to a new venture; possessing savings one wishes to invest; and being in straitened circumstances where one might be willing to take risks in order to advance one's financial position which one might otherwise avoid. Furthermore, Levi (1999: 7) offers extended argument to the effect that, in terms of impact, fraud can have significant extra effects on the elderly compared to younger victims:

> Not only does fraud lead to broken dreams, it also closes off opportunities which, once passed, are irrecoverable. For older people, vulnerable anyway to loss of confidence in themselves, frauds can destroy happiness permanently, just as readily as any other crime such as mugging or a more serious burglary. Indeed, more so, because victims know that they have supplied funds or goods voluntarily and because the loss of their financial cushion makes meaningless all their lifelong savings and sacrifices.

Lee and Geistfield (1999) have offered further discussion of elderly people's susceptibility to telemarketing fraud. Their conclusion is that some older people again may be more vulnerable to this if they are seeking social interaction with fraudulent telemarketers and thus are oblivious to their scams. In addition, Croall (2007) has argued that older people may find themselves the targets of more aggressive sales practices in relation to security devices. Again the critical focus here – and looking at abuse rather than crime – is important because such practices may not in fact (legalistically) constitute criminal activity, and may indeed be seen by corporate actors as 'good business'. Croall (2009: 132) also highlights a number of other commercial or occupational activities adversely affecting the elderly 'such as the sale of "assistive products" for older people, and the activities of cowboy builders referred to above may have a disproportionate impact on the elderly with many press reports playing on vulnerable elderly victims'. Again, a critical approach is imperative here if we are to question which activities are and are not subject to criminal prosecution (assuming they were reported, recorded and charged by the police) and the wider societal factors that have made this the case.

Exposing hidden abuse: new approaches to elder victimisation

While the above literature may give an impression that our knowledge of elder abuse is in fact fairly healthy, it is important to emphasise that much of this work (including the application of strain theory and routine-activities theory to the elderly) has in most cases failed to deliver truly sophisticated understandings of elder abuse which engage with the wider context of historical and structural factors that (from a critical perspective) keep certain crimes and victims hidden and not taken seriously. For example, while we have estimates of the scale of elder abuse taking place in certain well-researched contexts, this work provides very little information on, for example, the *offenders* who target older people. Furthermore, the situations described above in which elder abuse has been examined are somewhat arbitrary. So while we know something of how elder abuse is perpetrated in care homes, the abuse and victimisation of elderly people in hospital settings (for example) remains largely hidden.

The advantage of adopting a critical criminological perspective in this context is that critical criminology tends to cast light specifically on forms of social harm that systematically fail to be included both by researchers' and by policy-makers' sampling. The focus is therefore on the presence or absence of *harm* rather than how that harm falls within proscribed legal categories or existing methodological instruments. In keeping with social constructivism, a critical perspective would also question prevailing understandings of 'victimisation', 'old age', 'abuse' and so on, often in terms of power inequalities present in society. Indeed, on this point in a relatively early contribution to the critical elder abuse literature, Leroux and Petrunik (1990: 651) observed in Canada that much legislation being touted as addressing 'elder abuse' failed to genuinely address the needs of those abused largely as a result of difficulties experienced in developing a strong lobbying basis for social action to develop relevant legislation:

> the absence of a strong elder lobby group and the absence of developed ideologies (e.g., feminism in the case of wife abuse and child sexual abuse) have resulted in elder abuse receiving much less attention than other problems grouped under the family violence rubric. Indeed, most of the legislation that presently exists in Canada deals not with the abuse of the elderly as a class but with the provision of services to dependent, incompetent adults whether they are elderly or not.

Of course for academic criminologists this more 'politicised' approach to the study of elder victimisation may justifiably raise alarm bells in terms of the objectivity of the research exercise. Insofar as the more critical perspective (arguably) promotes politicisation, and perhaps activism, it is perhaps worth noting at this point that the study of victimisation as a whole (criminal or otherwise) has often been an area in which activist and academic branches have overlapped. For example, speaking of Gloria Egbuji, the Nigerian lawyer and campaigner for victims' rights, Jan van Dijk (1998: 2), himself a major figure in the proliferation of victimology across Europe, notes: 'Like many of us, our Nigerian colleague resists to be qualified as either researcher or activist. Most of us are happy to wear both hats.' Methodologically this might imply that as with other victimological questions, this is an area in which positivistic values of 'objectivity' are less useful. It is a perspective that has previously been argued to apply to feminist study, Mies (1993) going so far as to argue that 'value free research' is not only impossible but also manifestly undesirable in that area. Her argument is that feminist work should be written for women by researchers who are indeed 'consciously partial'. A move away from positivism in this area is also foreshadowed by the very real deficiencies noted above in the statistical picture being painted of elder abuse by standard crime-counting tools.

Indeed, following the arguments made in the previous paragraph, the 'notion of elder justice' has itself grown into something of a political movement since before the use of the term in the 1965 US Older Americans Act, and certainly since the World Health Organisation's spearheading of the Toronto Declaration on the Global Prevention of Elder Abuse in 2002. The Declaration (World Health Organization 2002: 2) is presented as a call for action aimed at the prevention of elder abuse and in particular highlights that in many parts of the world 'legal frameworks are missing. Cases of elder abuse, when identified are often not addressed for lack of proper legal instruments to respond and deal with them.' Such perspectives have further fostered arguments that such abuse (or 'ageism' more broadly) needs to be treated in the same way as the abuse of other victimised/marginalised groups in society, that is, in the same way as homophobia, transphobia, xenophobia, sexism and so on. Certainly, in criminological terms there has been debate in the literature over whether elder abuse should be categorised as a form of hate crime. Garland (2011: 30) has reflected on both the advantages and disadvantages of such a classification. On the positive side the author notes that hate crime and elder abuse do share some key characteristics:

> [J]ust as forms of recognized hate crime, such as homophobic or transphobic (for instance), occur within a social context characterized by open or latent hostility towards those groups, arguably elder abuse also occurs in a social context in which older people are not valued. Instead, they are stigmatized by, and marginalized from, mainstream society in a fashion similar to that of the acknowledged hate crime victim groups.

In addition, Sherry (2010) has argued that much of the literature and policy-making context has failed to explore the clear overlap between elder abuse and disability hate crime. That said, Garland is also keen to point out that notions of hate crime inevitably tend to compartmentalise victims into set social groupings with assumed, homogenous characteristics. Given the great variation in wealth and social status among the elderly, he argues, this would be a mistake.

From a critical criminological perspective, then, it is argued that future studies of elder victimisation need to encompass wider conceptions of crime and of the 'elderly' as a victimised 'group', understanding that the categorisation of this group as simply 'those who are over 65' or 'those resident in care homes' is in fact a gross simplification of the multifaceted nature of such victimisation, encompassing structural inequalities in society among various groups of marginalised 'others', some of whom happen to have reached old age.

A further step in the application of a critical criminology to elder victimisation/abuse may be – in keeping with critical criminology's overarching goal of achieving social justice (Taylor et al. 2011) – to consider 'elder abuse' as a breach of human rights rather than a discrete offence or set of offences designated by criminal law (Schwendinger and Schwendinger 2011; Biggs and Haapala 2013). More recent developments in the United States in particular have seemed to reflect this perspective, thus the 2009 Elder Abuse Act (s.2011(6)) defines elder abuse in the following terms:

> (A) from a societal perspective, efforts to (i) prevent, detect, treat, intervene in, and prosecute elder abuse, neglect, and exploitation; and (ii) protect elders with diminished capacity while maximizing their autonomy; and (B) from an individual perspective, the recognition of an elder's rights, including the right to be free of abuse, neglect, and exploitation.

The understanding of elder abuse as a human rights issue was also recently backed by the UN in its statement to mark the first annual 'World Elder Abuse Awareness Day' on 15 June 2013 (UN 2013). Indeed, such views have also galvanised worldwide political support and activism in favour of a UN declaration on the rights of older people, principally in the form of the Age Demands Action campaign (HelpAge International 2013). Others have placed the elder abuse issue within the context of citizenship debates, arguing that such abuse represents a (continuing) denial of the social inclusion and participation of older people in civil society (at the local, national and international levels) (see Phelan 2008; Carney 2010). This discussion in fact returns us to the earlier observations of how society views older people and 'ageing' itself. Arguably much in the same way feminists have argued that domestic violence and the crime of rape cannot be understood without appreciating the systemic denial of equal rights to women, so some commentators have suggested that elder abuse must be examined by reference to ageism. As argued by Phelan (2008: 325):

> there is scant literature on elder abuse viewed through the lens of ageism and its sway on human rights and citizenship. These three

perspectives on the topic allow for a meaningful and equitable benchmark from which elder abuse may be considered. Ageism influences the way human rights and citizenship are articulated for older people and is conceptualised as stereotypical views of older people leading to prejudiced attitudes, actions and societal marginalisation. Such attitudes function to both disadvantage and devalue older people providing a covert basis for societal tolerance of elder abuse.

Having reached a position of understanding elder abuse as far more than a 'crime' issue, it follows that criminology alone (even the broadest conceptions of critical criminology) cannot hope to fully encapsulate all of its constituent qualities. Thus what is needed is for criminologists to work with other disciplines, and indeed other sectors. Again, US policy on elder abuse is increasingly accepting this reality. A succession of Elder Justice Acts (2002, 2003 and 2009) have enhanced relevant provisions to achieve these aims in a host of different contexts, including criminal justice, medical services, social services, economic reforms, legal issues, housing and law enforcement (see Blancato 2004). Ultimately, then, what is needed in this area is not only a critical criminology, but a broader critical gerontology (see Wild et al. 2013).

Conclusion

We have seen that the traditional criminological tools of positivistic inquiry have by their nature omitted elder abuse and indeed elderly victims of crime more specifically. In keeping with the critique of critical criminology, the area represents a form of social harms that frequently fall outside official categories of offending behaviour. As a group the victims of such abuse are often invisible largely because they do not appear in crime statistics which at worst may have given the false impression that elder abuse as a whole is not a significant social issue.

This is not to say criminological knowledge of elder abuse is wholly lacking. Thus we have seen extensive evidence demonstrating that elder abuse is widespread in care homes and in domestic settings. Aggressive occupational and corporate practices may also specifically target the elderly and affect them in different ways than younger people. However, the picture these sources have drawn of elder abuse and elder victimisation is also confused and, crucially, often ignores the reality that elder abuse is in fact situated within a much broader social constructivist debate around the construction of age, ageism, harm and justice. The critical perspective adopted in this chapter, it is argued, better reflects these complexities. At the same time critical criminology acknowledges that 'the elderly' are not a homogenous victimised group with identical needs, wishes and expectations, but instead represent a diverse 'group' potentially suffering human rights abuses, regardless of the official criminal classification (or otherwise) of those abuses.

In closing, one final point of importance is that detailed research is lacking in, which the victims of elder abuse *themselves* are consulted. Thus even the best theoretical discussion will arguably be guilty of further marginalising this 'group' if the voices of that group do not make a more regular appearance in this research. In other areas of victimisation, authors have pointed out that the position and views of victims of crime are often assumed by policy-makers and academics (see Rock 1990). Victims of elder abuse are in danger of being marginalised as a result of assumptions about what 'old people' want and how they react to abuse, and this starts with the still often-cited assumption that fear of crime among the elderly is 'irrational'. In promoting discussion and policy development around elder abuse, we must therefore be very wary of making the same mistake of proceeding without taking into account the direct views of those affected.

The galvanising of political and activist support has helped raise the profile of elder abuse, as has the application of the human rights critique. Fundamentally more research is needed from a social constructivist perspective, acknowledging that what lies behind 'elder abuse' is often much more ingrained societal attitudes to age and the elderly, if we are to better understand these issues and offer meaningful assistance. Such research must ensure the views of elder abuse victims themselves are derived and incorporated into analysis and into any future policy recommendations.

References

Acierno, R., Hernandez, M., Amstadter, A., Resnick, H., Steve, K., Muzzy, W. and Kilpatrick, D. (2010) 'Prevalence and Correlates of Emotional, Physical, Sexual, and Financial Abuse and Potential Neglect in the United States: The National Elder Mistreatment Study', *American Journal of Public Health*, 100(2): 292–297.

Agnew, R. (1992) 'Foundation for a General Strain Theory of Crime and Delinquency', *Criminology*, 30(1): 47–87.

Barak, G. (1990) 'Crime, Criminology and Human Rights: Towards an Understanding of State Criminality', *Critical Criminology*, 2(1): 11–28.

BBC (2012) Lime Trees Care Home in Sheffield to Close [online]. Available at: http://www.bbc.co.uk/news/uk-england-south-yorkshire-19061808. Accessed 27 August 2013.

Beck, U. (1992) *Risk Society: Towards a New Modernity*. New Delhi: Sage.

Biggs, S. and Haapala, I. (2013) 'Elder Mistreatment, Ageism, and Human Rights', *International Psychogeriatrics*, 25(8): 1–8.
Blancato, R. (2004) 'The Elder Justice Act: A Landmark Policy Initiative', *Journal of Elder Abuse & Neglect*, 14(2–3): 181–183.
Bulman, P. (2010) 'Elder Abuse Emerges from the Shadows of Public Consciousness', *National Institute of Justice Journal*, 265: 4–9.
Carney, G. (2010) 'Citizenship and Structured Dependency: The Implications of Policy Design for Senior Political Power', *Ageing and Society*, 30(2): 229–251.
Castle, C., Ferguson-Rome, C. and Teresi, J. (2013) Elder Abuse in Residential Long-Term Care: An Update to the 2003 National Research Council Report, *Journal of Applied Gerontology*, 20(10): 1–37.
Chaplin, R., Flatley, J. and Smith, K. (2011) *Crime in England and Wales 2010/22*, HOSB 10/11. London: Home Office.
Clarke, A. and Lewis, M. (1982) 'Fear of Crime among the Elderly: An Explanatory Study', *British Journal of Criminology*, 22(1): 49–78.
Cohen, L. and Felson, M. (1979) 'Social Change and Crime Rate Trends: A Routine Activity Approach', *American Sociological Review*, 44(4): 588–608.
Cooper, C., Selwood, A., Blanchard, M., Walker, Z., Blizard, R. and Livingston, G. (2010) '"The Determinants of Family Carers" Abusive Behaviour to People with Dementia: Results of the CARD Study', *Journal of Affective Disorders*, 121(1–2): 136–142.
Croall, H. (2007) 'Victims of White-Collar and Corporate Crime', in P. Davies, P. Francis and C. Greer (eds), *Victims, Crime and Society*. London: Sage, 79–108.
—— (2009) 'White Collar Crime, Consumers and Victimization', *Crime, Law and Social Change*, 51(1): 127–146.
Dow, B. and Joosten, M. (2012) 'Understanding Elder Abuse: A Social Rights Perspective', *International Psychogeriatrics*, 24(6): 853–855.
Evans, R. and Porche, D. (2005) 'The Nature and Frequency of Medicare/Medicaid Fraud and Neutralization Techniques among Speech, Occupational, and Physical Therapists', *Deviant Behaviour*, 26(3): 253–270.
Farrall, S., Bannister, J., Ditton, J. and Gilchrist, E. (1997) 'Questioning the Measurement of the "Fear of Crime": Findings from a Major Methodological Study', *British Journal of Criminology*, 37(4): 658–679.
Finkelhor, D. and Pillemer, K. (1985) *Elder Abuse: Its Relationship to Other Forms of Domestic Violence*. Washington, DC: US Department of Justice.
Garland, J. (2011) 'Difficulties in Defining Hate Crime Victimization', *International Review of Victimology*, 18(1): 25–37.
Goergen, T. (2004) 'A Multi-method Study on Elder Abuse and Neglect in Nursing Homes', *The Journal of Adult Protection*, 6(3): 15–25.
Greer, C. (2007) 'News Media, Victims and Crime', in P. Davies, P. Francis and C. Greer (eds), *Victims, Crime and Society*. London: Sage, 20–49.
Grunfeld, E., Coyle, D., Whelan, T., Clinch, J., Reyno, L., Earle, C. and Willan, A. (2004) 'Family Caregiver Burden: Results of a Longitudinal Study of Breast Cancer Patients and Their Principal Caregivers', *Canadian Medical Association Journal*, 170(12): 1795–1801.
Hall, M. (2010) *Victims and Policy Making: A Comparative Approach*. Cullompton: Willan Publishing.
HelpAge International (2013) *Age Demands Action for Rights* [online]. Available at: http://www.helpage.org/get-involved/campaigns/ada-for-rights/. Accessed 22 August 2013.

Help the Aged (2008) *The Financial Abuse of Older People: A Review of the Literature.* London: Help the Aged.
Hightower, J., Smith, M. and Hightower, H. (2001) *Silent and Invisible: A Report on Abuse and Violence in the Lives of Older Women in British Columbia and Yukon.* Vancouver: Yukon Society of Transition Houses.
Hillyard, P. and Toombs, D. (2003) 'Introduction', in P. Hillyard, D. Toomb and C. Pantazis (eds), *Beyond Criminology: Taking Harm Seriously.* London: Pluto Press, 1–9.
Home Office (2012) *A New Definition of Domestic Violence.* Press Release of 18 September 2012 [online]. Available at: http://www.homeoffice.gov.uk/media-centre/news/domestic-violence-definition. Accessed 3 August 2013.
Home Office and Department of Health (2000) *No Secrets: Guidance on Developing and Implementing Multi-Agency Policies and Procedures to Protect Vulnerable Adults from Abuse.* London: Department of Health.
Kearon, T. and Godey, B. (2007) 'Setting the Scene: A Question of History', in S. Walklate (ed.), *Handbook of Victims and Victimology.* Cullompton: Willan Publishing, 17–36.
Kilbane, T. and Spira, M. (2010) 'Domestic Violence or Elder Abuse? Why It Matters for Older Women', *Families in Society*, 91(2): 165–170.
Klaus, P. (2005) *Crimes Against Persons Age 65 or Older, 1993–2002.* Washington, DC: US Department of Justice, Bureau of Justice Statistics.
Lachs, M., Bachman, R., Williams, C. and O'Leary J. (2007) 'Resident-to-Resident Elder Mistreatment and Police Contact in Nursing Homes: Findings from a Population-Based Cohort', *Journal of American Geriatrics Society*, 55: 840–845.
Larsson, D. and Alalehto, T. (2013) 'The Reaction towards White Collar Crime: When White Collar Crime Matters', *The Open Criminology Journal*, 6: 1–9
Lee, J. and Geistfield, G.L. (1999) 'Elderly Consumers' Receptiveness to Telemarketing Scams', *Journal of Public Policy & Marketing*, 18(2): 208–217.
Leroux, T. and Petrunik, M. (1990) 'The Construction of Elder Abuse as a Social Problem: A Canadian Perspective', *International Journal of Health Services*, 20(4): 651–663.
Levi, M. (1999) 'The Impact of Fraud', *Criminal Justice Matters*, 36 (Summer): 5–8.
Lindesay, J. (1996) 'Elderly People and Crime', *Reviews in Clinical Gerontology*, 6(2): 199–204.
McBarnet, D. (1983) 'Victim in the Witness Box: Confronting Victimology's Stereotype', *Crime, Law and Social Change*, 7: 293–303.
Mies, M. (1993) 'Towards a Methodology for Feminist Research', in M. Hammersley (ed.), *Social Research: Philosophy, Politics and Practice.* London: Sage, 64–80.
Nelken, D. (2007) 'White Collar and Corporate Crime', in M. Mahuire, R. Morgan and R. Reiner (eds), *The Oxford Handbook of Criminology.* 4th edn. Oxford: Oxford University Press, 733–770.
Pain, R. (1995) 'Elderly Women and Fear of Violent Crime: The Least Likely Victims? A Reconsideration of the Extent and Nature of Risk', *British Journal of Criminology*, 35(4): 584–598.
Payne, B., Blowers, A. and Jarvis, D. (2012) 'The Neglect of Elder Neglect as a White-Collar Crime: Distinguishing Patient Neglect from Physical Abuse and the Criminal Justice System's Response', *Justice Quarterly*, 29(3): 448–468.

Payne, B. and Gainey, R. (2006) 'The Criminal Justice Response to Elder Abuse in Nursing Homes: A Routine Activities Perspective', *Western Criminology Review*, 7(3): 67–81.

Penhale, B. (2013) 'Older Women, Domestic Violence, and Elder Abuse: A Review of Commonalities, Differences, and Shared Approaches', *Journal of Elder Abuse & Neglect*, 15(3–4): 163–183.

Phelan, A. (2008) 'Elder Abuse, Ageism, Human Rights and Citizenship: Implications for Nursing Discourse', *Nursing Inquiry*, 15(4): 320–329.

Pillemer K., Chen E., Van Haitsma, K., Teresi, J., Ramirez, M., Silver, S. and Lachs, M. (2011) 'Resident-to-Resident Aggression in Nursing Homes: Results from a Qualitative Event Reconstruction Study', *The Gerontologist*, 52: 24–33.

Policastro, C., Gainey, R. and Payne, B. (2013) 'Conceptualizing Crimes against Older Persons: Elder Abuse, Domestic Violence, White Collar Offending, or Just Regular 'Old' Crime', *Journal of Crime and Justice*, Online pre-access only at time of writing. Available at: http://www.tandfonline.com/doi/full/10.1080/0735648X.2013.76753. Accessed 27 August 2013.

Powell, J. and Wahidin, A. (2004) 'Aging and Corporate Crime', *Journal of Societal and Social Policy*, 3(1): 47–59.

Powell, J. and Wahidin, A. and Zinn, J. (2007) 'Understanding Risk and Old Age in Western Society', *International Journal of Sociology and Social Policy*, 27(1): 65–76.

Rock, P. (1990) *Helping Victims of Crime: The Home Office and the Rise of Victim Support in England and Wales*. Oxford: Oxford University Press.

Schwendinger, H. and Schwendinger, J. (2011) 'Defenders of Order or Guardians of Human Rights?' in I. Taylor, P. Walkton and J. Young (eds), *Critical Criminology (Routledge Revivals)*. Oxon: Routledge: 113–146.

Shenfield, B. (2013) *Social Policies for Old Age: A Review of Social Provision for Old Age in Great Britain*. Oxon: Routledge.

Sherry, M. (2010) *Disability Hate Crimes: Does Anyone Really Hate Disabled People?* Farnham: Ashgate.

Shichor, D. and Kobrin, S. (1978) 'Criminal Behavior Among the Elderly', *The Gerontologist*, 18(2): 213–218.

Smith, R. (1999) 'Fraud & Financial Abuse of Older Persons', *Trends & Issues in Crime and Criminal Justice*, No. 132. Canberra: Australian Institute of Criminology.

Spalek, B. (1999) 'Exploring the Impact of Financial Crime: A Study Looking into the Effects of the Maxwell Scandal upon the Maxwell Pensioners', *International Review of Victimology*, 6(3): 213–230.

Speight, S. and Purdon, S. (2007) *UK Study of Abuse and Neglect of Older People: A Feasibility Study in Care Homes*. London: National Centre for Social Research.

Sutherland, E. (1949) *White Collar Crime*. New York: Dryden.

Taylor, I., Walton, P. and Young, J. (2011) 'Critical Criminology in Britain: Review and Prospects', in I. Taylor, P. Walkton and J. Young (eds), *Critical Criminology (Routledge Revivals)*. Oxon: Routledge, 6–62.

Thomson M., Lietzau, L., Doty, M., Cieslik, L., Williams, R. and Meurer, L. (2011) 'An Analysis of Elder Abuse Rates in Milwaukee County', *Wisconsin Medical Journal*, 110: 271–276

United Nations (UN) (2013) *World Elder Abuse Awareness Day* [online]. Available at: http://www.un.org/en/events/elderabuse/background.shtml. Accessed 22 August 2013.

Van Dijk, J. (1998) 'A New Society of Victimology? A Letter from the President', *The Victimologist*, 1, 2–3.

Wild, K., Wiles, J. and Allen, R. (2013) 'Resilience: Thoughts on the Value of the Concept for Critical Gerontology, *Ageing and Society*, 33(1): 137–158.

Wolhunter, L., Olley, N. and Denham, D. (2009) *Victimology: Victimisation and Victims' Rights*. London: Routledge.

World Health Organization (2002) *Toronto Declaration on the Global Prevention of Elder Abuse*. Geneva: WHO.

7
Selling Sex Invisibly: Solicitation as an Invisible Crime

Mary Laing

Introduction

Sex work is conceptualised in a multiplicity of nuanced ways in the academic literature, including (among others) as a bounded, yet 'authentic' intimate practice, as labour, as an economic survival strategy and as a type of therapy (see inter alia Bernstein 2007; Sanders 2005; Ditmore et al. 2010; Smith 2013). In addition, victimisation, criminalisation, as well as conceptual and material understandings of violence are key themes. There has been little exploration specifically, however, of sex work as an 'invisible crime'[1] yet there is potential for the criminalisation and victimisation of sex workers (and many would argue the two are inextricably linked) to be explored through the invisible crime typology of *the body*. Within this analysis, I am not seeking to position sex workers as criminals, but instead will draw on parts of the legal system in England and Wales that criminalise aspects of the commercial sexual exchange. It is indisputable that sex work discourse is as much underpinned by criminological and legalistic frameworks as it is infused with moralistic, ideological and ethical debates.

The incisive previous volume of this collection looked at crime types including crimes committed by employees against organisations (and vice versa), fraudulent behaviour and cybercrime (Davies et al. 1999). The opening chapter states that: 'some criminal acts are not transparent, even to the most vigilant observer. That is, they are not readily visible.' Taking the practice of sex work as a new illustration of an invisible crime, this chapter moves beyond the first volume of *Invisible Crimes* empirically, but draws conceptually on the themes running through this earlier work to explore the criminalised practice of street solicitation by male sex workers in Manchester (UK). Drawing on 28 interviews with key stakeholders and over 600 hours of participant observation while delivering services to male sex workers as a volunteer outreach worker in street and bar spaces, I argue that the ways in which men seek clients on the streets can be understood through the lens of 'relative invisibility'. In short, they are visible to some (e.g., clients, outreach workers) but are largely invisible to others. I will argue that this relative invisibility is achieved through the performance of solicitation, which I conceptualise as a type of *sexual choreography* – a useful lens which enables the micro-politics of solicitation to be un-picked and, specifically explores how sex workers use embodied tactics of walking, looking and dressing to solicit for business (see also Williams 2013).

But first to contextualise men as sellers of sex; male sex work permeates all areas of the sex industry. Men sell sex in a multitude of sociocultural contexts and spaces, including on the streets, online, independently, through agencies and in pornography; there is at least one male brothel in the United Kingdom, and many other indoor club and sauna spaces where sex is exchanged and sold. These spaces are more-or-less visible depending on how you read the cityscape, who you ask, or what you type into your Internet search engine. However, what is very visible is the gendered and feminised nature of sex work in policy, practice and research discourse which more often than not positions women as sex workers and men as clients or exploiters (although see Smith and Laing 2014 and Laing et al. forthcoming). Indeed, the contours of invisibility (no knowledge, no statistics, no theory, no research, no control, no politics, no panic!) are, for the most part, applicable. Acknowledging those few colleagues who have written and published on male sex work (Gaffney 2007; Morrison and Whitehead 2007; Wilcox and Christmann 2008; Atkins and Laing 2012; Smith 2012; Minichiello and Scott 2014), it is notable that there is less research on male sex workers working in any space in the United Kingdom and international context when compared to their female counterparts. In addition, the national policy context in England and Wales up until the publication of the Coalition Government's new national strategy document (Home Office 2012) was deeply feminised, and positioned men as clients, pimps, traffickers and abusers rather than as sex workers or as being potentially vulnerable to sexual exploitation (Home Office 2004, 2006; Whowell and Gaffney 2009; Kingston 2010; Whowell 2010). Although the current strategy document does recognise gender diversity in the sex industry, the dominant narrative is still that of the female worker and male client (Home Office 2012). This gender-narrow reading of the sex industry in England and Wales is reflected in the limited service provision for male and trans*

sex workers nationally; and as this chapter will illustrate, this relative invisibility is reflected in localised practices of male street sex work.

In England and Wales, sex work is managed through a regulationist approach. Within this framework, the exchange of sex between consenting adults for remuneration is legal – but there are a number of laws in place which limit where, when and between whom this transaction can take place. Originating in France in the 1800s, it could be argued that the primary focus of the approach is to *contain*; as Hubbard (2012: 44) outlines: 'Designed to concentrate vice, the idea was that this system of regulation would purge the streets of prostitutes, but perhaps more importantly, would allow prostitutes to be surveyed, compartmentalized and hierarchized.' Regulationism seeks to filter out what are (and are not) socially acceptable performances and embodiments of public sexualities and crucially what sorts of paid (or unpaid) sex can and should be visible in cityscapes. Those manifestations which are deemed dangerous or deviant are often driven out or removed.

Throughout history street sex workers have consistently been moved or displaced from public city spaces. Often constructed as a challenge to dominant hetero- and homo-normative values, as well as neoliberal practices of gentrification and consumption, the street sex worker is often perceived to present a deviant and unwelcome figure in family and community spaces. Men, women and trans* individuals who sell sex are 'othered', positioned as abject and threatening, as 'bad bodies ... distanced through processes designed to purify or sanitize' (Hubbard 2012: 97; see also Sibley 1995). This 'casting out' not only dehumanises sex workers, but their removal from the landscape has had violent and fatal consequences. Nowhere is this more visible than in the case of the missing women in the Downtown Eastside area in Vancouver, where between 1995 and 2001 (although the exact dates/years are difficult to confirm) more than 65 women were murdered or went missing. When reports were made to the Vancouver Police Department (VPD), they responded with a positivistic approach, suggesting that it was normal for women (particularly sex workers, often with an addiction, often from first nations communities) living in and around the neighbourhood to simply disappear. The women were constructed as non-ideal victims, as somehow complicit in their disappearance and having precipitated their 'missing' status; the positivistic approach used by the VPD rendered them, in essence, invisible (see also Ross 2010).

That sex workers are often positioned as invisible or 'undeserving' is therefore linked not only to their often tacit criminalisation, but is also their socio-moral construction. They are often, in both a material and empirical sense as Davies et al. (this volume) argue, driven 'into the dark'. Like other invisible crimes situated in the typology of *the body*, '[m]orality and ethics ... are [the] underpinnings of why some harms and crimes remain invisible though they cause suffering and injury. They enable victims to be "othered" and [are] therefore outside of the gaze of the criminal justice system' (Davies et al. this volume).

Although the victimisation of sex workers is an important debate to be had in the context of invisible criminality and victimisation, and there have been a number of interesting developments in this field of late – for example the National Ugly Mugs Scheme[2] – this chapter moves beyond this reading of invisible victimisation and instead, perhaps more fittingly, discusses a type of invisible criminality associated with sex work. To this end, solicitation will be explored through a case study of male sex workers seeking clients on the streets and in public sex environments (PSEs) in Manchester, UK. It will be argued that solicitation of clients through embodied sexual choreographies enables those men selling sex to maintain a 'relative invisibility' in the city. This chapter will explicitly consider the solicitation performed by male sex workers the 'degrees of invisibility associated with particular act[s] and event[s], and their relations to mechanisms of enforcement, regulation and control' (Davies et al. 1999: 5).

Solicitation: an invisible crime?

The spaces discussed in the research presented here[3] are two areas situated in Manchester, UK: the Village and the Industry Street area. Each of these is considered in turn before conceptual work on solicitation and public sex is briefly considered.

The Village

The Village is an LGBTQ[4] night-time leisure/pleasure space located in the city of Manchester. It constitutes multiple streets, some connected by alleyways, and was identified as an area of street sex work by Manchester City Council (Manchester City Council 2009). The area comprises mostly bars and clubs, the primary function of which are to cater to clubbers and other night-time revellers; however, many also open through the day and serve food, coffee and drinks. There are also a number of shops, a sauna, hairdresser, doctor's surgery, takeaways, taxi firms as well as other small businesses, car parks and a large bus station. A number of charity organisations also work from the Village. Spaces like this are now commonplace in larger urban centres in the United

Kingdom and beyond (Bell and Jayne 2004). Notably, such spaces have been critiqued as offering only 'safe' expressions of LGBTQ sexualities, with more liminal practices, including public sex cultures as well as other fetishised performances of sex and sexualities, commonly being erased or invisibilised. As (Binnie 2001: 104) has argued, where 'cappuccino culture thrives the more overtly sexual, threatening and queer have been pushed out'. It is therefore notable that street sex-working has persisted despite the increased marketisation of the Village as a cosmopolitan space of consumption.

Industry Street area

The second case study space is a PSE and cruising space (a space where men meet other men for sex) which, although situated close to the street spaces described above, comprises a series of overground and underground tunnels which run alongside a canal. It offers a walking route into the city centre from outlying residential areas and, over the past decade, adjacent wastelands, and parts of the space itself, have undergone significant regeneration: shops, apartments, car parks and murals have been installed. The space has also been subject to multiple situational crime-prevention mechanisms, including lighting, walls being painted white, CCTV being fitted, police signage warning that those engaging in 'obscene or lewd behaviour' are committing criminal offences, and regular street cleansing to remove sex litter and explicit graffiti – both of which ritually return after short periods of time. The space is used by men seeking both paid and unpaid sexual encounters. The name 'Industry Street area' is a pseudonym.

Walking for sex in the city: conceptualising solicitation

The discreet solicitation of paid and unpaid sex in the city is not a new practice. The city itself has long been renowned as a space of sexual encounter; according to the sexologists of the 1900s, the city was a space where one could experience 'dangerous' pleasures (Brickell 2006). The architecture, crowds, flow and anonymity of the urban has often been cited as central to the seeking out of anonymous sexual partners. Walking, cruising and soliciting 'exploit[s] the ambivalences and uncertainties in the city' (Turner 2003: 7), and it has been documented that men seeking anonymous public sex with other men have often drawn on the ambiance, noise, light and hustle and bustle as cover to seek out illicit sexual encounters (Turner 2003). In the nineteenth century, there were 'urban ramblers' who were self-identifying heterosexual men walking in the city in pursuit of pleasure (Rendell 2000). It was not uncommon for rambler magazines to publish lists, locations and descriptions of sex workers . Rendell (2000: 198) defined the concept of rambling, noting that:

> In the pursuit of pleasure, in constant motion, rambling represents the city as multiple and changing sites of desire. In traversing the city, looking in its open and interior spaces for adventure and entertainment, the rambler re-maps the city, both conceptually and physically, as spaces of social interactions, rather than as a series of static objects. Rambling represents urban space as fluid and complex, varying according to time and specific urban location.

Through the footsteps of the rambler, the city is re-mapped through sexual seeking and interaction; sex workers' adverts in magazines attest to the ability of the rambler to rewrite the city in the context of its erotic topography. The spaces used become known and defined by their use, and remade through practice (Atkins and Laing 2012); as Ingold (2000: 26) has argued, 'perceptual skills...emerge, for each and every being, through a process of development in a historically specific environment'.

Research on public sex notes the importance of walking in the city as a method for seeking out sexual encounter and emphasises that movement is also central to being concealed. Being hidden may be facilitated by the physical space in which the sex takes place (for example, in toilet cubicles, or hidden outdoor spaces [Brown 2008]). Alternatively, being hidden or discreet in the landscape may be made possible by processes of blending in, for example the ephemeral backward glance in a busy street that goes unnoticed by the majority (Turner 2003). The glance embodies the erotic, with walking, gazing and being looked at linked to the potential for touch, intimacy and sex itself (Humphreys 1970; Turner 2003; Brown 2008). The position of the person seeking sexual encounter is maintained through performances of ambiguity and movement (Turner 2003; Atkins 2007). Atkins noted in his research that moving around spaces of public space in circuits made you noticeable to those walking the circuit too (others seeking out public sex), but ambiguous to others; you could be walking to home, to work or waiting to meet someone. Williams (2013: 31) also found this in her research, noting that sex workers 'reappropriate public spaces through tactics of visibility that allow them to remain visible and easily accessible for customers, while at the same time [they] employ tactics of purpose whereby these spaces justify their purpose in specific places'.

Walking for sex then is a useful strategy for those seeking sex in the city, as by moving through the city in this quite mundane fashion, those seeking, and providing sex are able to remain ambiguous and 'normal' in the landscape. As Wunderlich (2008: 126–127) suggests, walking (for whatever purpose) is 'an unquestioned form of movement through the city, often unnoticed and not regarded in itself as being a particular singular or insightful experience'. In the case study areas, men working the streets engage in spatial performances or 'choreographies' (embodied tactics used to solicit) which enable them to sell sex while simultaneously concealing their sex-working identities. The notion of choreography is not new and Iveson (2007) draws on the work of Dowsett (1996: 143–146) to describe the sexual skilling of men engaged in anonymous same-sex encounters:

> The sexual skilling that occurs in such encounters starts with the sex acts themselves. It is about the physical possibilities of the body; what hands, mouths, penises, and anuses can achieve. A second level of skilling occurs in learning the choreography of sexual encounters. By choreography is meant the subtle and nuanced movement of bodies in sexual encounters; the stalking of partners, the shifting of attention from the general possibility of sex to the specific opportunity of sex, the inviting glance, the suggestive movements of bodies, and so on. Beyond those sensate discoveries it involves a familiarity with the context, the local sexual economy; a recognition of sites for sex as being not limited to their defined purposes and subject to certain rules of conduct.

The analysis presented seeks to develop this conceptual framing further to encompass commercial sex and to explore the 'micro-politics of solicitation' (see also Whowell 2010). The crux of the argument is that performing the invisible crime of solicitation through choreographies of walking, looking and dressing allows men selling sex on the streets to be obviously visible to some, while remaining ambiguous and 'in place' to others.

Walking (stopping) and looking for business

The men I met while on outreach described how they sought clients within and when walking between the Village and the Industry Street Area. It was observed and communicated in interviews with both the men and outreach workers that walking and stopping in the areas indicated that they may be seeking paying clients.

> I suppose when you're on Industry Street, Industry Street is quite a popular cruise area as well, round that side of the canal as well so really I think when you're going to be up there, you're either cruising, you're looking to buy sex or you're selling sex. (interview with outreach worker)

Further, it was indicated that particular streets and smaller areas were known for different activities:

> Smith Street[5] is for getting drunk, and then if you go along Richardson Street that's for picking up rent boys, and then sometimes outside the [space] that as well, they drive down back alleys and wait there and then flash you when you walk past. (interview with sex-work project service use)

Notable in the above quote is the subtle method the client uses to catch the attention of the worker, with the flash of headlights easily lost in the hustle and bustle of the space and meaningless to those not offering sexual services (Whowell 2010).

Walking routes around the Village and between the Industry Street Area in order to remain 'in place' and 'normal' while stopping at various points or 'patches' enabled the men to identify themselves as being available for clients. Atkins (2007) noted in his ethnography of PSEs that stillness of bodies in spaces of public sex can indicate commitment to a sexual encounter. The space in which the men are walking contributes methodologically to how they sell sex and their presence on the beat acts as a signifier as to their reason for being there. An outreach worker commented on the men's use of the beat space:

> Although they still have their identified standing corner, the lads will cruise the whole area of the Village really, walking round, and opportunistically striking up conversations with people, or they might just start having a drink with somebody, and after they've had three or four drinks you know [they ask about business]. (interview with outreach worker)

Here there is recognition that those selling sex are redefining the primary purpose of the streets and built landscape to solicit for business. Reflecting Dowsett's earlier definition of 'choreography', they are manipulating local (sexual) consumption and economies, and reshaping these to meet their own needs. Hubbard (1999: 172) refers to this as a type of strategic resistance; with sex workers re-working and diverting spaces 'to create an alternative meaning of space – a space that has its own alternative morality'. This also includes the tactic of targeting potential customers in bars and having a drink before bringing up the subject of business (see also Williams 2013 on targeting customers). Through this the men are able to remain discreet and 'in place'. Cresswell (1996) has critically explored notions of being in – or out of place and the social construction of discursive boundaries to exclude some but not others. As the data presented suggests the men seek to negotiate these boundaries through discreet choreographies of solicitation:

> You can feel relaxed in a bar. ... If you're nice to a person you're guaranteed to get a drink, so if you get a drink off the person then you can always compromise on if they want the sex, and if they want sex, you can always charge whatever you want. You can say 'look I'm like this, I'm trying to make money, how are you fixed?' (interview with sex-work project participant)

The process of solicitation in this case is social, reflecting the intended use of the Village space, contributing to the discretion with which the exchange takes place. Sex worker and client having a drink together in a pub 'normalises' their visibility in the Village. However, after months on outreach, outreach workers could often spot couples who they thought might be engaged in sexual exchange; age was often a giveaway, as was demeanour and dress.

Walking and being on the move also enabled the men to retain a low profile, escape police attention and retain a non-sex-working normative persona. The following excerpt from an interview reflects this:

> *Participant:* We sometimes sort of like stay in one area for a little bit to see if anyone's driving round and if they're not, we'll go into certain pubs and if they're not in there then we'll just go round, mooching [walking] around, seeing what's what. ...
> *Mary:* Right so you'll mooch round to see where business is rather than having like a favourite space and always staying there?
> *Participant:* That's right aye, because it helps us to get away from the police as well, because if we see the police presence then we go and move away to a different areas as well where it doesn't look too much on top.
> *Mary:* So moving around keeps the police off your back?
> *Participant:* Yeah exactly.

The movement of men around the Village, particularly when the police enter, is indicative of the geographical mobility of the men. Their ability to spot the police entering the Village was a skill nearly all the men I encountered had. While on outreach, I was able to observe the men, their peers and others considered 'undesirable' by the police and authorities in the Village (this also included the homeless community and the street sellers who sold flashing tiaras, fluffy bunny ears and the like, and others not engaging in 'approved' forms of commerce and consumption) walk to the periphery of the Village if a police officer was sighted entering the space. An excerpt from my research diary reflects this:

> When the police entered the Village I didn't notice but one of the guys noticed them enter the Village from the tip of Smith Street. The area's working lads and others immediately dispersed – not a fast run away or anything, they just calmly turned and walked away.

The movement of certain social groups out of the Village when police presence is visible not only raises questions about the regulation and policing of the space, but poses perhaps more fundamental questions about who has the 'right to the city', who can (and cannot) occupy and use public spaces. Don Mitchell (2003: 9) has written extensively on this in relation to homeless populations, and argues that the removal of those groups or identities that are seen by regulators as problematic leads to 'a specific and highly constricted, sort of public sphere ... a highly sanitized city and a fully deracinated politics – a politics that elevates the importance of aesthetics over the needs of people to simply survive'. This politics reflects the earlier described framework of being 'in' or 'out' of place (Cresswell 1996); and it is this discordant positioning of sex workers which pushes them to be, as far as possible, 'invisible' in street spaces.

Indeed, the Village and Industry Street Area constitutes a significant source of income for all of the men (n = 40+) I encountered over the fieldwork period. Many stated its key function to them was as an area in which they could 'make money', not just through selling sex but through other clandestine activities such as selling 'fake drugs' or copied DVDs. Who can walk and wait on the streets and for what reason is therefore a topic of interest and debate to these men. The police's desire for the men to be moved out of the Village, or alternatively stopping and questioning the men for 'hanging round' or simply 'being there', was described as 'embarrassing' in interview. One police officer commented on the disruptive presence of the men in the area:

> Male sex workers are hanging about street corners near the pubs and the gay community are concerned that they are making the place look a mess. They make it look unruly, un-wanted, more seedy. They're disrespecting them [the gay community] because this is where they drink. This is the area they have created for themselves. So when people come through the Village and they see the young lad hanging round in a tracksuit they're not too keen on it. It looks threatening. (interview with police officer)

So not only do they have to exit the space because of concerns they will get 'pulled' by the police, but also because they are positioned as contra to the desired clientele of the Village. One man described how he reacts when the police enter the Village:

> We don't actually need to be caught and have our reputation as a prostitute on our mind so we want to try and go under cover like rats basically. That's how it is, it's like that's how we feel like at the moment, we've got to be scuttering like rats, once we see the police we scutter like hell. (interview with sex-work project participant)

The movements of the men described as 'rats scuttering' is emotive and symbolic; a report from the local specialist sex-work project stated that the men often use symbolism as part of the art work projects they completed with them, and that it is 'the beginning, for the boys, of reflection on a "secret" and maybe shameful set of knowledges: making something visible and safer through symbol' (Blue Room 2009: 9). In the same report, the 'rats' and 'dirt' descriptor is used again as a quote from one of the men when describing the sex work he is engaged in:

> Make [male sex work] more visible. It's about time we had a voice. People have treated us like rats, like dirt. But we're doing a job and people should know about it. (Blue Room 2009: 12)

This man is clearly aware of the 'whore stigma' associated with prostitution and clearly feels this keenly. Sibley (1995: 14) has argued that 'stereotypes play an important part in the configuration of social space because of the importance of distanciation on the behalf of social groups, that is, distancing from others who are represented negatively...group images and place images combine to create a landscape of exclusion'. This is evident in the fight to remain unnoticed and ambiguous when selling sex, and although many are successful at this it is within a landscape of exclusion that this practice takes place, crystallised in the language of dirt and degradation that the men use to describe their practices.

Where and for what purpose the men walk is thus a contributing factor to performing choreography. It is central to solicitation, and hence how the men ultimately commit this 'invisible crime'. They walk to pick up business; they walk to get away from the police, which for some, invokes feelings of shame and feelings of animalistic behaviour. The men also walk to remain more – or less invisible to the passerby oblivious to the fact that the man they have just passed has already walked that way 10 or 15 times in the past couple of hours. They walk to known patches to be identifiable, and walk routes around the beat to identify as commercially available to those 'in the know', and so those seeking to offer help or intervention can identify them. In essence walking is a key part of what it is to sell sex and is a major contributing factor to *how* the men solicit for business. We now move forward to consider the role of dress.

Dressing for sex: dressing for solicitation

Dress is a powerful mechanism for communicating identity, social allegiances and subjectivities which have long been explored in different contexts across the social sciences (Entwistle 2000). Ways of clothing the body are seen to have the power to communicate particular messages about different social groups, and social research on sexuality and methods of dressing prompt questions in terms of performing sex work.

Those men seeking business in both the Village and the Industry Street Area often dressed to convey and perform particular hyper-heterosexual, working-class 'rough and tough' masculinities. When discussing their involvement in sex work and other informal economies across the spaces (as for many of the men, sex work was just one way of 'grafting' to make money), the men commonly described themselves as 'scallys', or admitted that they often played up on what they imagined to be a 'scally' or 'chav' type identity. The scally represents a (usually) white, working-class, hyper-masculine, hyper-(hetero)sexed male, embodying a specific type of 'culturally burdensome whiteness' (Haylett 2001: 351). Undoubtedly portrayed as a socially excluded group, much media commentary around scally or chav culture has been offensive and derogatory (and rarely includes those labelled as such as active participants). The sexualisation of chav culture is one facet of this, and the symbol of the chav has been commoditised across heterogenous sex industry markets aimed at gay and straight men, including pornography, phone sex and escorting (see also Johnson 2008), hence it is not only those working the street that capitalise on this particular masculine performance. Performing this identity also allowed for the performance of an identity which was ambiguous or not noticeable to most, but key to attracting clients. Men interviewed spoke about clothing and how it was a key element of solicitation:

> If a lad is dressed up in trackys, a lot of punters will go for that lad. They like the straight-looking scally lads, you know that are always getting into trouble. (sex-work project participant)
>
> A lot of people dress in tracky bottoms and so yeah, they will get tagged with the other side of it [antisocial behaviour] you look like you're going out for trouble really…a bit rough and ready looking, scallified, it's just something to get their [the clients'] rocks off really. (sex-work project participant)

Entwistle (2000: 185) has written on the implicit links between clothing and sexuality, suggesting that 'body adornment can be linked to sexual acts, give sexual pleasure, send out sexual signals, mark out sexualised identities'. Clothing marks the men out as sexually available when in spaces of sex work, and draws on elements of the scally identity as erotic. The desirability of the body is enhanced through clothing, the sexual gendered and social identity of the person wearing it and crucially its antisocial connotations. Specific dress codes also allow the men to blend in with other non-sex-working people in their peer group using the area as a leisure space or for other informal and illicit economies. Some of the men expressed frustration that they were linked with other criminal activities ongoing in the area, with the presence of 'scallies' in the Village being seen as a threat associated with homophobia and violence (Moran 2000). Those selling sex, however, were able to subvert this identity, and transform a dangerous identity to one which is desired. As one man said:

> Yeah, it's more about control and aggression really, most of them, or just the thought of having like, a scally, you know somebody who's macho or something, doing what they want. (sex-work project participant)

Men therefore use dress to solicit:

> If you change your dress style, you wouldn't get as much money as you normally make you know, if you were wearing jeans. (sex-work project participant)

Indeed, the same man spoke of when he visited the Village not to sell sex but to accompany a peer who was sex-working at the time. He stressed the importance of dressing appropriately if you did not want to get approached by clients in cars:

> If I'm wearing jeans and shirt then no cars will follow me, because I look like I'm just a normal clubber. (sex-work project participant)

Methods of dressing also allowed outreach workers to 'spot' men who might want to access services; however, relying solely on dress to identify those selling sex can have unexpected consequences for clients. One female participant who was interviewed for the research who has short hair and often wore sports clothing described how she had been mistaken for a sex worker from behind several times and described how this made her feel:

> There's one guy who comes around and he's got an old fashioned car...and he's even followed me and I swear to you on three occasions...thinking that I might have been a boy because he followed me from the back and not from the front because we laugh about it....I was walking down that way and I could hear a car you know when a car slows down and I looked round and it was that car again.

Key to the performance of this particular choreography was that the men were at once able to mark themselves out as commercially available, but also blend in with the streetscape. As noted, this offered some affordances for men to protect their identities. They could be a 'scally' and perform a hyper, hetero-sexed machismo which enabled them to 'blend in' with their peer groups in the Village, while marking themselves out as offering sexual services at the same time.

Conclusion

This chapter has discussed solicitation by male sex workers as a type of 'invisible crime'. Central to the argument has been the practice of how men seek business through sexual choreographies, and how solicitation is performed in such a way to be visible to some but not others.

The signifying qualities of dress as a methodology employed by sex workers to represent themselves as commercially viable also allowed the men to trouble the hetero-homo binary with men performing 'rough' and 'hard' heterosexual masculine identities while catering to a male clientele. Indeed, those men selling sex spoke in interviews about how their clients would often want 'a straight looking lad', one who performs a particular type of working-class masculinity. Clients were also sometimes said to seek a particular type of sexual experience through the commercial transaction by paying for services with someone who could perform 'rough and hard' masculinities (and perhaps sex).

Elements of looking and walking were also considered key components of the choreography used by sex workers to solicit for business. The 'easily-missed-glance' as well as being 'in place' would be difficult to engage in discreetly if it were not for the vibrancy, buzz and affective properties of the Village and the known use of the Industry Street Area as a PSE. Key, however, to the conceptualisation of solicitation as a type of invisible crime is that the men were not engaging in obviously visible commercial sexual transactions. Place matters in street prostitution, and the Village and the Industry Street Area both offer particular affordances for discreet solicitation. As Turner (2003: 52) suggests in relation to cruising, it is '[t]he combination of an understanding of a specific place with an understanding of a specific urban practice [that] allows for – in fact, enables – cruising to take place'. Like the rambler then, who re-mapped the erotic topographies of the street in the pursuit of (mostly commercial) sexual pleasures, the men were able to re-shape the social and cultural contours of spaces to use them to meet their economic needs. Like the discussion of cruising offered by Brown (2008), they were able to 'manipulate' and 'play' with the features of the spaces; despite them often being infused with a politics of exclusion, they were able to mould it to fit their own purposes. Brown (2008) also contends that cruising for sex is not just a visual practice but one which is embodied, 'a set of accumulating, mutually reinforcing gestures, touches, stances and movements' (Brown 2008: 921) which is in essence what is described in this chapter. The practice of solicitation is an *embodied* one, and thus neatly fits into, and perhaps furthers, how we understand the invisible crime typology of *the body*.

In sum, the concept of sexual choreography in the context of paid sex is valuable for furthering criminological and geographical readings of sex work as it could be applied, not just to understandings of spaces of street working, but across a multiplicity of (sexualised) spaces. The data presented relates specifically to areas of street sex work and public sex in Manchester; however, as the literature on public sex indicates, the notion of sexual choreography has currency in a multiplicity of public sexual spaces in the city. Within this analysis, the architecture, ambiance and spaces of the city play a key role as they are shaped and manipulated by men and others for their own pleasure/leisure. As Turner (2003: 35) noted in his discussion of the flâneur (a much debated, peripatetic figure in the sexual, social sciences imagination): 'The city's passers-by, its loafers, its shoppers, its workers, its prostitutes, its cruisers – they all had their own way of moving and walking, of loitering with intent. All exist in a visual and spatial economy that is fundamentally uncertain and ambiguous.' In essence, it is this ambiguity that the men selling sex in the research drew on, and used to mask their sex-work practice. As Turner (2003) also reflects, the city is constituted of spaces which are ambiguous and contested, and these can be used to facilitate and engage in public sex practices and cultures while remaining 'relatively invisible'.

In some senses, this could be perceived as useful by the men, especially given that by the time the research had been completed (fieldwork ceased in 2008), not one had been charged with, or convicted of, a prostitution related offence. However, it could also be argued that their relative invisibility perpetuated their excluded status; their material invisibility meant they were often not considered in other policy and practice contexts. As outlined at the beginning of this chapter, representations of male and trans* individuals in sex-work policy and service provision is often limited; lack of visibility in the landscape only serves to compound this. Thus in the context of sex work and invisible crimes, perhaps future research within the typology of the body could not only consider the multiple and intersecting layers of invisibility as experienced by marginalised social groups such as sex workers, but also explore additional factors which serve to augment that invisibility. In the context of the data presented here – not only were those selling sex men, but they embodied an abject and excluded identity (the scally) which was seen to clash with the neoliberal, consumptive ideals of the Village by troubling normative representations of gender and sexualities. It is therefore important that future research considers the multiple facets of invisible criminality and its material manifestations.

Notes

1. Although see Ham and Gerard (2014) and their analysis of how sex workers engage in strategic management of their (in)visibility in different spaces and contexts; and Williams (2013) on how sex workers select locations for working using tactics of invisibilisation.
2. See https://uknswp.org/um/ for more information.

3. The data for this chapter is drawn from my original Ph.D. research which was conducted between September 2006 and September 2009 in Manchester, UK. The data set constitutes 31 interviews with 28 stakeholders, including sex workers, outreach workers, business owners, police officers and charity workers. In addition, I completed 600 hours of participant observation as a volunteer outreach worker with two local male sex-work projects (see Whowell 2010).
4. Lesbian, gay, bisexual, trans*, queer.
5. Although the Village is identified as a known space of sex work in this chapter, the street names have been given pseudonyms to offer an additional level of anonymity.

References

Atkins, M. (2007) *Objects That Look: How Is Ambiguity of Body and Self Maintained in the Public Sex Encounter?* Unpublished M.A. thesis. Manchester: University of Manchester.

Atkins, M. and Laing, M. (2012) 'Walking the Beat and Doing Business: Exploring Spaces of Male Sex Work and Public Sex', *Sexualities*, 15(5–6): 622–643.

Bell, D. and Jayne, M. (eds) (2004) *City of Quarters: Urban Villages in the Contemporary City*. Aldershot: Ashgate.

Bernstein, E. (2007) *Temporarily Yours: Intimacy, Authenticity, and the Commerce of Sex*. Chicago: University of Chicago Press.

Binnie, J. (2001) 'The Erotic Possibilities of the City', in D. Bell, J. Binnie, R. Holliday, R. Longhurst, and R. Peace (eds), *Pleasure Zones: Bodies, Cities, Spaces*. New York: Syracuse University Press, 103–130.

Blue Room (2009) *The Men's Room. A Strategic Plan for the Development of Holistic Services for 'Hard to Reach Men' in Manchester. Part Three: Evaluation and Findings of the Blue Room*. Working document. Manchester: The Blue Room.

Brickell, C. (2006) 'Sexology, the Homo/Hetero Binary, and the Complexities of Male Sexual History', *Sexualities*, 9(4): 423–447.

Brown, G. (2008) 'Ceramics, Clothing and Other Bodies: Affective Geographies of Homoerotic Cruising Encounters', *Social and Cultural Geography*, 9(8): 915–932.

Cresswell, T. (1996) *In Place/Out of Place: Geography, Ideology, and Transgression*. London: University of Minnesota Press.

Davies, P., Francis, P. and Jupp, V. (eds) (1999) *Invisible Crimes, Their Victims and Their Regulation*. Basingstoke: Palgrave Macmillan.

Davies, P., Francis, P. and Wyatt, T. (eds) (this volume) *Invisible Crimes and Social Harms*. Basingstoke and New York: Palgrave Macmillan.

Ditmore, M., Levy, A. and Wilman, A. (eds) (2010) *Sex Work Matters: Exploring Money, Power, and Intimacy in the Sex Industry*. London: Zed Books.

Dowsett, G.W. (1996) *Practicing Desire: Homosexual Sex in the Era of AIDS*. Stanford: Stanford University Press.

Entwistle, J. (2000) *The Fashioned Body*. Cambridge: Polity Press.

Gaffney, J. (2007) 'A Co-ordinated Prostitution Strategy and Response to Paying the Price – But What about the Men?' *Community Safety Journal*, 6(1): 27–33.

Ham, J. and Gerard, A. (2014) 'Strategic in/Visibility: Does Agency Make Sex Workers Invisible?', *Criminology and Criminla Justice*, 14(3): 298–313.

Haylett, C. (2001) 'Illegitimate Subjects? Abject Whites, Neoliberal Modernisation, and Middle-Class Multiculturalism', *Environment and Planning D: Society and Space*, 19(3): 351–370.

Home Office (2004) *Paying the Price: A Consultation Paper on Prostitution*. London: Home Office.

—— (2006) *A Co-ordinated Prostitution Strategy and Summary of Responses to 'Paying the Price'*. London: Home Office.

—— (2012) *A Review of Effective Practice in Responding to Prostitution*. London: Home Office.

Hubbard, P. (1999) *Sex and the City: Geographies of Prostitution in the Urban West*. Aldershot:Ashgate

—— (2012) *Cities and Sexualities*. London: Routledge.

Humphreys, L. (1970) *Tearoom Trade: Impersonal Sex in Public Places*. London: Aldine Transaction.

Ingold, T. (2000) *The Perception of the Environment*. London: Routledge.

Iveson, K. (2007) *Publics and the City*. Chichester: Wiley.

Johnson, P. (2008) 'Rude Boys: The Homosexual Eroticization of Class', *Sociology*, 42(1): 65–82.

Kingston, S. (2010) 'Intent to Criminalize: Men Who Buy Sex and Prostitution Policy in the UK', in T. Sanders, S. Kingston, and K. Hardy (eds), *New Sociologies of Sex Work*. Surrey: Ashgate, 23–38.

Laing, M. and Gaffney, J. (2014) 'Health and Wellness Services for Male Sex Workers', in V. Minichiello and J. Scott (eds), *Male Sex Work and Society*. New York: Harrington Park Press, 260–284.

Laing, M., Smith, N. and Pilcher, K. (eds) (forthcoming) *Queer Sex Work*. Oxon: Routledge.

Manchester City Council (2009) *Report for Information*. Manchester: Manchester City Council.

Minichiello, V. and Scott, J. (eds) (forthcoming) *Male Sex Work and Society*. New York: Harrington Park Press.

Mitchell, D. (2003) *The Right to the City*. London: Guildford Press.

Moran, L. (2000) 'Homophobic Violence: The Hidden Injuries of Class', in S. Munt (ed.), *Cultural Studies and the Working Class: Subject to Change*. London: Cassell, 206–218.

Morrison, T. and Whitehead, B. (eds) (2007) *Male Sex Work: A Business Doing Pleasure*. New York: The Haworth Press.

Rendell, R. (2000) 'Pursuits', in S. Pile and N. Thrift (eds), *City A–Z*. London: Routledge, 196–198.

Ross, B. (2010) 'Sex and (Evacuation from) the City: The Moral and Legal Regulation of Sex Workers in Vancouver's West End, 1975–1985', *Sexualities*, 13(2): 197–218.

Sanders, T. (2005) *Sex Work: A Risky Business*. Devon: Willan.

Sibley, D. (1995) *Geographies of Exclusion*. London: Routledge.

Smith, N. (2012) 'Body Issues: The Political Economy of Male Sex Work,' *Sexualities*, 15(5): 586–603.

Smith, N. and Laing, M. (2013) 'Working Outside the (Hetero)Norm? Lesbian, Gay, Bisexual, Transgender and Queer Sex Work', *Special Issue of Sexualities*, 15: 517–520.

Turner, M. (2003) *Backward Glances: Cruising the Queer Streets of New York and London*. London: Reaktion Books.

Whowell, M. (2010) 'Male Sex Work: Exploring Regulation in England and Wales', *Journal of Law and Society*, 37: 125–144.

Whowell, M. and Gaffney, J. (2009) 'Male Sex Work in the UK: Forms, Practices and Policy Implications', in J. Phoenix and J. Pearce (eds), *Regulating Sex For Sale: Prostitution Policy Reform in the UK*. Cambridge: Polity Press, 99–120.

Wilcox, A. and Christmann, K. (2008) 'Getting Paid for Sex Is My Kick: A Qualitative Study of Male Sex Workers', in G. Letherby, K. Williams, P. Birch and M. Cain (eds), *Sex As Crime*. Devon: Willan, 118–136.

Williams, L. (2013) 'Sex in the City: Why and How Street Workers Select Their Locations for Business', *Journal of Contemporary Ethnography*, October, online version.

Wunderlich, F.M. (2008) 'Walking and Rhythmicity: Sensing Urban Space', *Journal of Urban Design*, 13(1): 125–139.

8
Air Pollution and Invisible Violence
Reece Walters

Introduction

In recent years air pollution has been referred to as an 'invisible killer', and 'an invisible health crisis' (European Respiratory Society 2012). As other chapters in this collection have argued, the invisibility of crime is manifested through various lenses: lack of knowledge, lack of political and media attention, an absence of policing and regulatory focus, and an unwitting and ill-informed public. All such arguments pertain to air pollution; however, toxic emissions are also literally invisible from sight and consciousness, as are the associated consequences.

The devastating effects of toxic air are experienced at both a macro and micro level. As a toxic waste it is directly inhaled causing widespread individual injury, however, its broader social and environmental harm is experienced through the far-reaching destructive impacts 'of climate change. It is estimated that air pollution causes the annual premature death of two million people worldwide through respiratory infections, heart disease and lung cancer – all accelerated by, or the direct result of, poor air quality (Kinver 2013). In addition, air pollution as a key contributor to global warming threatens the very existence of low-lying Pacific nation states through unseasonal and unprecedented destructive climatic events. As a result, emissions cause damage and death on a global scale. Yet air pollution is not conceived of as violence or social harm. Its deleterious effects on climate change and air quality remain widely accepted as a necessary and unfortunate by-product of development, progress and capital accumulation (McGrath 2014). As a former leader of one of the world's smallest countries argues, 'If carbon emissions continue at the rate they are climbing today, my country will be underwater in seven years' (President Mohamed Nasheed, Maldives,

5 April 2012). The lifestyles and resulting greenhouse-gas emissions of advanced industrialised nations have perilous consequences for the very existence of non-polluting and smaller nations. Therefore it is the low-emission nations, such as the Maldives and Tuvalu, that are most at risk and thus officially recognised as 'extremely vulnerable' to environmental catastrophes (EVI 2011). The impetus for governments to address the dangers of air pollution are not, for example, driven by statistics of premature death, or the potential catastrophes experienced by climate change, but by the threats to commercial activities (Budds 2009).

The editors of this collection persuasively argue in the Introduction that this book's intention is to act as a speculum by shining light on previously unseen objects and making them visible. This chapter seeks to fulfil that ambition by challenging the priorities of global fiscal policies that prioritise trade and explore the political economy of air pollution. It draws on discourses of power, harm and violence to analyse air pollution within emerging frameworks of eco-crime (Walters 2010). In doing so, it identifies how criminology continues to push new boundaries by engaging with issues of both global and local concern.

Harm caused by air pollution

The world's biggest polluting nations are a combination of rapidly developing economies (China, India, Brazil, South Korea) as well as those with established advanced industrialised infrastructures (United States, Canada, Japan, Germany, United Kingdom) (AFOP 2013). It should be noted that when discussing air pollution it is the 'human-made' or secondary carbon emissions that are at issue (RCEP 2006). International protocols are not designed to monitor, regulate and set targets for 'primary pollutants' or natural pollution, such as carbon and sulphur produced from oceans, volcanoes and rain forests, but are focused on 'secondary pollutants', notably chemically created emissions from human activity.

There has been significant criminological scholarship devoted to discourses of harm, notably examinations of human activity and physical and psychological social harm (Hillyard et al. 2004). However, notions of environmental harm, within criminological studies, have been largely overlooked. The advent of Green Criminology, discussed further below, has sought to rectify the imbalance in understandings of crime-related harm. That said, the links between human and environmental harm from the rising rate of carbon emissions is well established.

The World Health Organisation recently reports that in 2012 alone, seven million people, mainly from Southeast Asia, died as a result of air pollution. The WHO director-general for family, children and women's health, Dr Flavia Bustreo, concluded, 'cleaning up the air we breathe prevents non-communicable diseases as well as reduces disease risks among women and vulnerable groups, including children and the elderly' (cited in Briggs 2014: 1). Exposure to air pollutants has been widely reported to affect pulmonary and lung dysfunction as well as a range of neurological and vascular disorders (Brook et al. 2004; Ghio and Devin 2001). It is also linked to bowel disease (Konkel 2013) and light birth weights (Smyth 2013) as well as lung and stomach cancer (ENS 2013). It is widely reported that diesel-propelled engines are the major cause of dangerous air pollution where almost half of all emissions result from road transport or industrial activities (Brisman 2005; LAEC 2009). The link between air pollution and premature death has been widely established (Jerrett et al. 2005; Walters 2012). People who live in less polluted cities will experience longer and healthier lives than those exposed to air pollutants such as SO_2 and PM10 (Pope et al. 2002). The particulate matter (PM10) is an atmospheric aerosol containing both solid and liquid matter 10 micrometers in diameter that damages human lungs (Department for the Environment 2014). It is estimated that twice as many people today suffer from lung disease and asthmatic conditions caused by air pollution than they did 20 years ago. In addition, it is now widely acknowledged that air pollution destroys habitats, compromises animal health and results in the loss of biodiversity (Defra 2013).

Moreover, as mentioned above, it is important to perceive of the harms created by air pollution in a broader global context. It is most often the poorest people that experience the worst effects of pollution. An estimated two-thirds of all annual deaths resulting from air pollution occur within the slums and poverty-stricken areas of developing countries (Cohen et al. 2005). As mentioned, the harms caused by air pollution also have a more pernicious reach, namely climate change that reportedly kills hundreds of thousands of people each year (WHO 2013; Pachauri and Reisinger 2007). Such deaths often result through the increasing rise of 'natural disasters' (UNISDR 2008), although, as UNESCO (2008: iv) reports, 'natural disasters are not entirely "natural", for people are agents of disasters'. The World Disasters Report identifies that devastating flooding in poor countries such as Bangladesh results from inter alia air pollution from affluent and industrialising nations (Muncie et al. 2009; Walters 2012). However, it is not only the world's poor who are experiencing pollution-induced climate change. In Australia the unprecedented October 2013 bush fires have been linked by UN officials to carbon emissions and climate change (Ireland 2013). In spite of UN expert Christiana Figueures's views, the recently elected Australian prime minister, a climate change sceptic, who in his first two months of office has already dismantled the climate change commission (Barbeler 2013), has suggested that the UN delegate is 'talking through her hat', arguing that the unprecedented and devastating spring bush fires are a natural part 'of the Australian experience' (Taylor 2013). This is all little comfort for the thousands of residents of New South Wales's Blue Mountains who have witnessed their homes and livelihoods burned to the ground.

In spite of sporadic examples of political denial and deflection, there is overwhelming acceptance from the international scientific community of the link between carbon emissions and deleterious climate change (Farrall et al. 2012). It is widely recognised that advancing technologies and the perpetuation of globalised trade have rapidly increased the amount of environmental harm (Heckenberg 2010). The rapid advancement of developing economies continues to create an indelible human footprint with both immediate and long-term environmental consequences (White 2011). As a result, discourses in environmental victimology (Williams 1996) continue to expand within criminological landscapes exploring the contexts and consequences of globalisation, climate change and carbon emissions (White 2013). Notwithstanding these important advances in socio-legal endeavour, the dominance of international trade law, and OECD and World Bank policies, ensures that air pollution remains tolerated within the priorities and imperatives of global fiscal growth. There is a normalisation of carbon emissions within the rhetoric of essential international trade, where the debate pivots on targets and thresholds, rather than alternative or greener energies.

Corporate power and the 'normalisation' of toxic air

The deaths of thousands of people and animals at Bhopal and the dioxin crises at Seveso and Baia Mare are all well-cited examples of toxic fumes resulting in widespread death, injury and destruction of the natural environment (White and Heckenberg 2014). However, such foreseeable acts of 'corporate violence' (discussed below) are often presented in media and political discourses as 'accidents' associated with high-risk commercial industries or natural disasters associated with unpredictable and volatile global weather systems. As I have written elsewhere (Walters 2012: 137)

> this categorisation serves to normalise and embed a discursive public consciousness about the origins, practices and outputs of 'necessary' industries. As a result, 'accidents', 'spills', 'leaks', and 'meltdowns' perpetuate a social and political tolerance that accepts environmental harm and human injury as an unfortunate by-product of essential capital enterprise. Such catastrophic events become part-and-parcel of industries that provide the essentials of our daily lives. As a result, both the industries and their actions assume a status of 'habitus' within individual lives; the acceptance of disaster and the enterprises that produce them become socialised within cultures of contemporary need. (Bourdieu 1999)

Destructive events caused by contaminated air are seen as the essential production of poisonous discharge and are widely held as a necessary outcome of modern development. The 'social harm' of air pollution is thus rendered invisible by those in positions of state and corporate power that construct it is an 'essential' by-product of contemporary 'progress' and technological development. Hence it is not only re-packaged as an inevitability of trade but a corporate necessity or, as Stretesky et al. (2014) argue, a deadly social harm concealed through the discourses of 'treadmill of production'. The treadmill of trade supersedes all other, and the granting of licences to corporations to 'legally pollute' serves to entrench the necessity of fiscal imperatives while minimising or demarcating issues of social harm and injury to the periphery of social and political consciousness. Moreover, the corporations that are non-compliant of state pollution permits and are responsible for 'exceedence', are regulated within a regime of partnership and not prosecution (Walters 2009a). When corporations exceed legal limits for air pollution emission, the language of crime or 'breach' is not used. Repeated exceedence in those countries with strict regulations, such as the United Kingdom, often results in warning letters (Walters 2010). There is a clear imbalance between non-compliance and prosecutions. It is very rare for an industry that repeatedly exceeds air pollution standards to be issued with court proceedings. The entire regulatory apparatuses are designed to enable corporate compliance and not prosecute malfeasance. In doing so, the corporate air pollution offenders are shrouded from public and political scrutiny through administrative mechanisms that do not publicly report non-compliance. Indeed, accessing information about air polluters in the United Kingdom, for example, is a very difficult task. In previously published works, I have identified how I was required to lodge complaints with the UK Information Commissioner after multiple Official Information requests from regulators were denied or delayed. The intervention of the Commissioner ensured that names and details of corporate polluters were released, but only after six months of appeals and re-submissions (see Walters 2009a). As Jupp et al. (1999) have accurately argued, 'knowledge' and information about certain forms of offending become invisible through state policies and processes of recording and reporting that serve to conceal and minimise harm. This is clearly the case with air pollution 'offenders'. It is extremely difficult to obtain details of corporations and individuals that violate air pollution laws. Moreover, just as too little publicly available information can conceal social harm, so can too much. The UK Air Quality Archive provides in-depth details of atmospheric conditions across all British counties (Defra 2014). That said, without qualifications in meteorology or environmental science, the endless amount of terms, statistics and graphs is impenetrable to the untrained eye. Yet this archive is designed to be the public portal for information and debate about air quality. However, with complex and convoluted data sets published online en masse without analysis or explanations, it is difficult to see how anyone can participate or meaningfully use the information for discussion. As a result, the voluminous and unexplained data provides a tangling web rather than an enabling bridge. Thus questions should be raised about the extent to which the public are genuinely informed and involved with government policies to enhance air quality.

As mentioned, the UK government's energy is devoted to an air pollutionindustry-led partnership model of compliance and regulation that includes support for international carbon-trading markets to reduce emissions. This commodification of air pollution allows high-polluting corporations to purchase carbon credits through the European Carbon Trading Scheme to reconcile emission targets with their host nations. This trading scheme, which will be introduced in Australasia in 2015, is a trade-oriented approach that utilises financial incentives to businesses to reduce emissions. In other words, corporations that come – in below their agreed-upon emission targets with their governments can on-sell their unused allowance for profit on the carbon market to those corporations who have exceeded their targets. This carbon approach has been widely condemned for its failure to reduce global emissions and permitting big polluters to buy their way out of responsible operation. Moreover, the trading scheme has revealed widespread frauds, scams and tax avoidance (Martin and Walters 2013). As a result, air pollution as a waste for capital production and distribution has also become an item of 'good' for global trade. It is not seen as a trade in poisonous gases but a financial exchange where big polluters can buy and sell 'carbon certificates' which grant a right to emit. The questions that then emerge are: How much air pollution from commercial and human activity is tolerable? When does the harm exceed the return of benefits of global trade? The answers to these important questions reflect a range of ideological positions regarding the relationship between humans, trade and nature. For liberal ecologists, technologies and lifestyles that cause environmental damage should be managed and monitored but not eradicated (DiZerega 1996). This is a human-centred position that accepts environmental harm in the interests of human progress, although recognising that efforts to minimise such harm should be undertaken. This position continues to remain centre stage in geopolitics and global trade. Interestingly, the level of acceptable damage not only depends on recognised experts but also the lived experiences and consequences of everyday people, often referred to as the 'scientific citizen' (Walters 2011). Within debates about air pollution, environmental harm is subject to risk assessments that include policies and practices aimed at reducing or managing activities that damage or destroy natural habitats. In this sense, environmental harm is seen as inevitable and unavoidable in the pursuit of greener and more efficient technologies, and in the interests of human progress.

Green criminology and eco-violence

Contemporary discourses in green criminology critique the corporate benefits of CO_2 emissions and their trade and refocuses the criminological lens on the ways in which environmental harm in general, and air pollution in particular, is relevant to issues of crime and justice (Brisman 2008; Halsey 2012; Kluin 2013). Green Criminology intersects diverse narratives in exploring the harms that people, states and corporations commit in the business of their everyday activities (Ruggiero and South 2013). The production of carbon emissions, as discussed above, is normalised as an essential of contemporary life. As mentioned above, most international and domestic air quality regulatory regimes prefer partnership models of compliance to prosecution, but some high-profile cases have resulted in large fines. Such cases remain small in number and are dealt with in civil and not criminal jurisdictions.

The Environmental Protection Agency in the United States, noted for its increasing prosecution of air-polluting corporations (Cartledge 2010), provides a list of the top ten fines in US courts for cases of environmental crimes. Two of the top ten involve 'air pollution offences'. For example, the EPA website indicates how, in 1998, the Louisiana Pacific Corporation, a timber mill, agreed to pay a '$31.5 million penalty for mail fraud and a $5.5 million fine for wilfully conspiring to violate the Clean Air Act' (Siegal 1998). The fines emphasised the fraud and not the pollution. In 2001, the Koch Petroleum Group was fined USD 20 million for deliberately covering up the disposal of toxic chemicals at its Texas oil refinery. This included the illegal release of ten tonnes of fumes from burning the highly dangerous and carcinogenic substance benzene (*The New York Times* 2001). In October 2008, Erler Industries was convicted for 'clean air crimes' and fined USD 1 million by the US District Court for the Northern District of Illinois for 'knowingly submitting false quarterly reports' (USEPA 2008). Within the context of a multi-trillion-dollar annual trade that contributes substantially to global air pollution, the prosecutions and the fines are minuscule, and tend to emphasise corporate 'fraud' and 'deception', rather than environmental criminality or misconduct. More recently, Shell has agreed to pay USD 1 million for air-quality violations resulting from oil-drilling activities in the Arctic waters near Alaska (Reuters 2013). It should be noted that while the language of 'crime' is used by the US regulatory authorities, most matters are settled outside courtrooms or as mentioned, within civil proceedings. For some criminologists, including Tombs and Whyte (2009: 143), criminal prosecutions for corporate polluters are in keeping with the severity of corporate harm where 'it can be assumed with confidence that the most deadly environmental pollution is caused directly by corporations'. This is not to say that criminal prosecutions are the only way forward for addressing large corporate polluters. If the end result is the reduction of carbon emissions and the enhancement of environmental sustainability, then Braithwaite (2002) suggests that restorative justice principles should play a key role in addressing corporate non-compliance. He calls for a non-punitive approach that inculcates business and market principles of self-regulation that seeks to facilitate 'corporate buy-in'. In this sense, corporate polluters see the commercial benefit of compliance and of being socially responsible. This alternative may return better results for the environment given the state's burdens of proof and the lengthy nature of corporate criminal trials. However, there remains an increasing push internationally to develop criminal proceedings for corporate environmental offenders.

The advent of international protocols and domestic environmental courts has provided an emerging space for serious corporate offenders to be pursued criminally (Walters and Westerhuis 2013). However, the ascendency and fixed place of trade within neoliberal economies continues to emphasise corporate environmental responsibility and industry self-regulation. There remains an ongoing tension and conflict between international environmental protection and trade law (Walters 2010). International targets to meet reductions in air pollutants are often met with mixed reactions. Corporations often report how regulatory requirements to be cleaner and greener will bring added costs to the consumer or, as Lukes (2005: 21) has observed, 'the securing of compliance through the threat of sanction'. In this case, rising consumer costs, reductions in productivity, and unemployment and loss of economic prosperity are all presented as the consequences of arduous air-pollution controls. This greenwashing of corporate activities, including the funding of conservation initiatives, also acts to neutralise criticism and deny responsibility or neglect (Cohen 2001). Here the polluting industries refute, deny or downplay claims that their operations are anything but a well-intended, scientifically based and progressive industry, meeting market needs, while ensuring consumer and environmental well-being. Interestingly, the world's worst polluter, namely China, is recognising that air pollution is causing deprivation and damage to humans and their living conditions. In an effort to improve air quality, China's Clean Air Action Plan seeks to invest USD 163 billion over the next five years to reduce air pollution by 25 per cent. This strategy coincides with increasing penalties for repeat offenders, as Ximeng (2013: 1) reports:

> Lawmakers in Beijing have strengthened the city's efforts to fight air pollution, removing the limits for fines on repeat polluters and giving citizens the right to seek compensation for pollution damage.... New rules to increase the fines for polluters – to levels that would exceed the potential profits of polluting.

This is a significant step forward by the Chinese authorities. Unlike most cities with poor air quality around the world, Beijing's smog is visible and frequent. Air pollution in Beijing has become a regular cause of disruption, shutting down roads, rails and airports (Shidon 2013). More importantly, a substantial study released in mid-2013 revealed that the lives of Chinese people are cut short by high and escalating levels of toxic air pollution (Dizikes 2013).

Air pollution as eco-violence

The harm caused by rapid industrial development is beginning to be recognised as not only disruption but as an economic fact that continues to compromise human life. The shortening of human life, and the injury and illness associated with exposure to dangerous levels of air pollutants, places emissions within a critique where air pollution can be conceived of as both aggressive and violent. Here we begin to see environmental harm as a form of violence. The theorisation of violence, however, has historically been dominated by psychological and behavioural scientific understandings of aggression and interpersonal conflict (Stanko 1990; Englander 2006), or what cultural theorists refer to as 'subjective violence'. This 'subject-to-subject' violence examines intentional physical and physiological damage by a perpetrator to a victim. Much of existing criminological discourse continues to define violence as intentional interpersonal 'force' and seeks answers through biosocial and psychological analyses (Galtung 1974; Hickey 2003; Wodarski et al. 2002). However, as Stanko (2013: 484) identifies, 'violence is rarely random and without a purposeful target'. This position supports the systematic and deliberate release of air pollution where places and populations who are targets of emissions are known in advance. It has long been recognised that to 'live on the wrong side of the tracks' was to be housed in the direction or side of the railway line worst affected by black smoke from passing coal-fired locomotives (Ananat 2011). The emergence and development of industrialised societies has witnessed the urban poor living alongside smokestacks, contaminated waterways and polluted air (Baker 2012). It is no coincidence that affluent areas in contemporary industrialised societies are not neighbouring the machinery of capitalism and the commitment pollution.

Of course, alternative discourses in violence have explored the ways in which states and corporations mediate violence through harmful actions or inactions (Salmi 2004). For Salmi (2004: 59), when people's lives are made insecure and denied 'physical, emotional, cultural and intellectual integrity', they are recipients of what he calls 'alienating violence'. Such views are consistent with Žižek (2009: 1), who expands upon earlier notions of structure and agency and refers to 'systemic violence' or 'the often catastrophic consequences of the smooth functioning of our economic and political systems'. The priorities of global trade, underpinned by a neoliberal politics of capital expansionism, continue to produce widespread consequences on a cartographic scale. As Bauman (1995) has argued that violence is an elusive phenomenon and able to wriggle out of all 'conceptual nets', Žižek (2009: 5) suggests that objective or systematic violence is the 'dark matter of physics, the counterpart to an all-too-invisible subjective violence'. The production of air pollution and the creation of devastating greenhouse-gas emissions have, as mentioned above, become normalised within the 'smooth' and productive operating of contemporary trade and democracy (Walters 2012). Yet, as Žižek notes, these institutionalised systems of trade and capital accumulation have a very real and violent edge resulting in widespread death and damage. As a result, Žižek (2011: 161) argues, when observing the world's natural disasters, and the tragedies of drought, famine, disease and war – often in distant locations – 'we should always take a self-reflexive turn and ask ourselves how we ourselves are implicated in it'. For the Canadian jurisprudence expert, Westra, this argument is consistent with what she calls eco-violence. Her work on eco-violence provides an analytical framework for 'eco-crime' that includes licensed or lawful acts of ecological degradation committed by states and corporations. For Westra (2004: 58), eco-crime is unprovoked aggression, 'committed in the pursuit of other goals and "necessities" such as economic advantage"'. In a similar fashion to Salmi, she suggests that harmful environmental actions committed in pursuit of free trade or progress is an 'attack on the human person' that deprives civilians of the social, cultural and economic benefits of their environment. Such a view, which should be extended to all living things, is important because it locates air pollution and environmental harm within broader notions of harm, power and justice (see Walters and Westerhuis 2013). This thinking questions the moral and ethical bases upon which contemporary laws permit air pollution, climate change, natural resource extraction and other exploitations of nature. In doing so, it critically examines the conditions in which coexistence and inter-species cooperation can be achieved. In that sense, air pollution becomes a subject of criminological inquiry that can draw upon different academic narratives such as law, science, sociology and development studies and enhance such understanding via engagement with social movements and citizen participation (Walters 2012). When air pollution is conceptualised within notions of violence, an intellectual space develops through which new forms of social harm and criminological inquiries emerge.

Air pollution and green justice

There remain substantial challenges to addressing acts of eco-violence caused by air pollution. Kibert (2001) has asserted that a 'green justice' should seek to redress the discrimination of ethnic and socially disadvantaged minorities who experience 'environmental racism and victimology' and the disproportionate effects of air pollution and advanced capitalism. As a concept, 'green justice' has been used by activists and left scholars to examine environmental injustice, namely, the plight of the poor and powerless at the hands of affluent industrial economies (Alier 2000). Others have used the phrase to discuss environmental law and policy and the use of court processes (Hoban and Brooks 1996). Therefore, the usage of green justice resonates in discourses of protest, resistance and anti-capitalism, but also within legal debates about the role of law. It has been interpreted thus far as an anthropocentric concept, influenced by liberal ecologists, to focus on human health and well-being, notably minorities and their victimisation.

Green justice has also emerged within philosophical and political science discourses, and, more specifically related to emissions and climate change, is the concept of atmospheric justice (Vanderheiden 2008). This position recognises that the vast majority of air pollution and greenhouse-gas emission is caused by fossil-fuel combustion, deforestation and the industrial activities of the world's most economically wealthy and powerful nations. This productivity continues to have devastating consequences for the world's lowest-emission-producing countries. The concept is based on principles of Rawlsian liberal egalitarian justice, as well as cosmopolitan justice and political realism. Vanderheiden proposes an international climate-change regulatory regime based on equity, responsibility and compensation. In essence he advocates the 'polluter pays principle' within a framework of 'fault-based liability' that includes historical emissions. He calls for internationally agreed-upon air-pollution targets with a system for compensating low-emitting nations for the environmental and human impacts of atmospheric injustices not of their doing. Unlike Kyoto and the carbon-credit system mentioned above, he asserts that a new international independent climate-change committee, with representatives from various nations, could collect and analyse air-quality data and policies from individual countries. This he refers to as 'environmental justice', a term that has sometimes been used within the green criminological lexicon as a human-centred or anthropocentric discourse with two dimensions (White and Heckenberg 2014). It assesses the equity of access and use of environmental resources across social and cultural divides. The imperatives of free trade create the unequal distribution of environmental harm, while limited access to environmental benefits threaten and compromise the ability of individuals to express their culture and reach their potential (see Walters 2012).

In addition, atmospheric justice must inculcate concepts of ecological justice that focus on the relationship or interaction between humans and the natural environment (White 2008). When humans develop the environment for material needs, this approach insists that such actions be assessed within the context of damage or harm to other living things. This position is often referred to as an 'ecocentric' understanding of human and nature interaction. Ecological justice argues that an environmentally centred perspective which upholds the importance of living creatures as well as inanimate and non-living objects (such as air, land and water) provides useful insights for guiding future economic and developmental decisions. It asserts the intrinsic value and equal status of nonhumans but explores the potential for sustainability while utilising environmental resources for fundamental human needs. The above notions of justice provide perspectives or theoretical parameters for underpinning policy and practice, or ways of mobilising alternative and new forms of justice (see Walters 2010).

Whatever shape a green justice may take, it will need to include transnational justice in a form that can assert a central place within criminological discourse across the globalised landscapes of contemporary organised, corporate and state crime (see Reichel 2005). International justice and transnational legal processes are emerging through protocols and interstate agreements that seek to regulate and prevent illicit corporate activity within the complex webs of global markets (Likosky 2002). As previously mentioned, environmental offences, including air pollution, are often seen as administrative matters rather than crimes. That said, the enforcement of international environmental protocols and treaties for both EU and non-EU countries may take place in the International Court of Justice. However, the costs and procedures governing access to the ICJ create barriers to justice. With increasing concerns about climate change, ecological degradation, ozone depletion, food and water security, and sustainable development, it is imperative that a legally constituted and representative system of justice be established to provide leadership in issues of global environmental concern (see Pirro 2002). Moreover, a range of innovative policing and prevention initiatives continue to emerge that harness the knowledges and experiences of environmental activists and local communities. Such endeavours seek to highlight the seriousness of air pollutants and provide novel ways to address emission reductions and regulation (Walters 2013; Spapens 2011).

Conclusion

An ability to engage with issues surrounding air pollution, violence and eco-crime requires green criminology to analyse the politics of power, harm and justice. The imperatives of commerce as presented by governments and corporations, the use of the WTO to enforce trade laws, the aggressive business policies of transnational corporations that pollute, government condemnations of anti-globalisation stances, and the monopolisation of industry-led regulatory arrangements within a context of little or no regard for environmental and cultural aspects of local economies, all serve to demonstrate what Bachrach and Baratz (1970: 8) referred to as the 'mobilisation of bias'. They describe this 'as a set of predominant values, beliefs, rituals, and institutional procedures ("rules of the games") that operate systematically and consistently to the benefit of certain persons and groups at the expense of others'. In relation to air pollution, industry operators are placed in a preferred position to defend and promote their vested interests (Walters 2012).

The ongoing challenge that existing international and national air pollution regimes face is that environmental concerns are grafted into a regulatory model that continually prioritises trade and economic prosperity. Existing systems of regulation and control are not founded on deterrence but on incentive, voluntary participation and partnership. As this chapter identifies, air pollution is both a major contributor to ozone depletion and climate change, as well as a direct influence on deleterious conditions affecting the health and well-being of human and non-human life. As such, corporate activities that result in air pollution must be seen as acts of violence. When air-pollution offences are viewed as acts of violence, it is likely that the severity of such acts will become subject to greater public, political and, subsequently, prosecutorial scrutiny.

References

Action for Our Planet (2013) 'Top 10 Polluting Countries'. Available at: http://www.actionforourplanet.com/#/top-10-polluting-countries/4541684868.

Alier, J. (2000) 'Retrospective Environmentalism and Environmental Justice Movements Today', *Capitalism, Nature, Socialism*, 11(4): 45–50.

Ananat, E. (2011) 'The Wrong Side(s) of the Tracks: The Casual Effects of Racial Segregation on Urban Poverty and Inequality', *American Economic Journal: Applied Economics*, 3(2): 34–66.

Bachrach, P. and Baratz, M. (1970) *Power and Poverty: Theory and Practice*. New York: Oxford University Press.

Baker, J. (2012) *Climate Change, Disaster Risk and the Urban Poor: Cities Building Resilience for a Changing World*. Washington, DC: The International Bank for Reconstruction and Development.

Barbeler, D. (2013) 'Abbott Abolishes Climate Commission', *The Sydney Morning Herald*. Available at: http://news.smh.com.au/breaking-news-national/abbott-abolishes-climate-commission-20130919-2u1c0.html. Accessed 19 September 2013.

Bauman, Z. (1995) *Life in Fragments: Essays in Postmodern Morality*. Oxford: Blackwell.

Bourdieu, P. (1999) *Language and Symbolic Power*. Cambridge, MA: Harvard University Press.

Braithwaite, J. (2002) *Restorative Justice and Responsive Regulation*. Oxford: Oxford University Press.

Briggs, H. (2014) 'Air Pollution Linked to Seven Million Deaths Globally', *BBC News*. Available at: www.bbc.com/news/health-26730178. Accessed 25 March 2014.

Brisman, A. (2005) 'The Aesthetics of Wind Energy Systems', *New York University Environmental Law Journal*, 13(1): 1–133.

—— (2008) 'Crime-Environment Relationships and Environmental Justice', *Seattle Journal for Social Justice*, 6(2): 727–817.

Brook, R., Franklin, B., Cascio, W., Hong, Y., Howard, G., Lipsett, M., Luepker, R., Mittleman, M., Samet, J., Smith, S. and Trager, I. (2004) 'Air Pollution and Cardiovascular Disease', *Circulation*, 109(21): 2655–2671.

Budds, J. (2009) 'Urbanisation: Social and Environmental Inequalities in Cities', in W. Brown, C. Aradau and J. Budds (eds), *Environmental Issues and Responses*. Walton Hall: The Open University: 99–139.

Cartledge, J. (2010) 'Biofuel Producer Hit with $176,000 Fine for Pollution Offences', *BioEnergy News*, 13 April 2010.

Cohen, S. (2001) *States of Denial: Knowing about Atrocities and Suffering*. Cambridge: Polity Press.

Cohen, A., Ross, A., Ostro, B., Pandey, K., Krzyanowski, M., Knzli, N., Gutschmidt, K., Pope, A., Romieu, I., Samet, J. and Smith, K. (2005) 'The Global Burden of Disease due to Outdoor Air Pollution', *Journal of Toxicology and Environmental Health*, 68(13–14): 9–23.

COMEAP (2009) *Long-Term Exposure to Air Pollution*. Available at: http://www.hpa.org.uk/webc/HPAwebFile/HPAweb_C/1317137012567. Accessed 30 June 2009.

Department for the Environment (2014) 'Particulate Matter (PM10 and PM2.5)', Australian Government. Available at: www.npi.gov.au/resource/particulate-matter-pm10-and-pm25. Accessed 27 March 2014.

Department for Environment, Food and Rural Affairs (2013) 'About Air Pollution'. Available at: http://uk-air.defra.gov.uk/air-pollution/.

—— (2013) 'Effects of Air Pollution'. Available at: http://uk-air.defra.gov.uk/air-pollution/effects. Accessed 23 December 2013.

—— (2014) 'UK-Air: Information Resource'. Available at: http://uk-air.defra.gov.uk/. Accessed 1 April 2014.

DiZerega, G. (1996) 'Deep Ecology and Liberalism: The Greener Implications of Evolutionary Liberal Theory', *The Review of Politics*, 4(58): 699–734.

Dizikes, P. (2013) 'Innovative Study Estimates Extent to which Air Pollution in China Shortens Human Lives', *Science Daily*. Available at: http://www.

sciencedaily.com/releases/2013/07/130708161941.htm. Accessed 8 July 2013.
Englander, E. (2006) *Understanding Violence*. 3rd edn. Mahway, NJ: Lawrence Erlbaum.
Environmental News Service (2013) 'Outdoor Air Pollution Declared a Human Carcinogen'. Available at: http://ens-newswire.com/2013/10/17/outdoor-air-pollution-declared-a-human-carcinogen/. Accessed 23 October 2013.
Environmental Vulnerability Index, EVI (2011) 'EVI Country Profiles'. Available at: www.vulnerabilityindex.net/EVI_Country_Profiles.htm.
European Respiratory Society (2012) 'Experts Call for Cleaner Air to Tackle Invisible Killer'. Available at: http://www.erscongress2011.org/eu-affairs/item/4502-experts-call-for-cleaner-air-to-tackle-invisible-killer.html. Accessed 1 March 2012.
Farrall, S., Ahmed, T. and French, D. (eds) (2012) *Criminological and Legal Consequences of Climate Change*. Oxford: Hart Publishing.
Galtung, J. (1974) *Peace, Violence and Imperialism*. Oslo: Dreyer.
Ghio, A. and Devlin, R. (2001) 'Inflammatory Lung Injury after Bronchial Instillation of Air Pollution Particles', *American Journal of Respiratory and Critical Care Medicine*, 164(4): 704–708.
Halsey, M. (2012) 'Defining Pollution Down: Forestry, Climate Change and the Dark Figure of Carbon Emissions', in S. Farrall, T. Ahmed and D. French (eds), *Criminological and Legal Consequences of Climate Change*. Oxford: Hart Publishing, 169–192.
Heckenberg, D. (2010) 'The Global Transference of Toxic Harms', in R. White (ed.), *Global Environmental Harm: Criminological Perspectives*. Willan: Devon, 37–61.
Hickey, E. (ed.) (2003) *Encyclopaedia of Murder and Violent Crime*. London: Sage.
Hillyard, P., Pantazis, C., Tombs, S. and Gordon, D. (eds) (2004) *Beyond Criminology: Taking Harm Seriously*. London: Pluto Press.
Hoban, T. and Brooks, R. (1996) *Green Justice: The Environment and the Courts*. 2nd edn. Boulder: Westview Press.
Ireland, J. (2013) 'Clear Link between Climate Change and Bushfires: UN Advisor Warns Tony Abbott', *The Sydney Morning Herald*. Available at: http://www.smh.com.au/federal-politics/political-news/clear-link-between-climate-change-and-bushfires-un-adviser-warns-tony-abbott-20131022-2vxs5.html. Accessed 22 October 2013.
Jerrett, M., Burnett, R., Ma, R., Pope, C., Newbold, B., Finkelstein, N., Shie, Y., Krawski, D., Thurston, G., Calle, E. and Thun, M. (2005) 'Spatial Analysis of Air Pollution and Mortality in Los Angelos', *Epidemiology*, 16: 726–736.
Jupp, V., Davies, P. and Francis, P. (1999) 'The Features of Invisible Crimes', in P. Davies, F. Francis and V. Jupp (eds), *Invisible Crimes Their Victims and Their Regulation*. Basingstoke: Macmillan, 3–28.
Kibert, N. (2001) 'Green Justice: A Holistic Approach to Environmental Injustice', *Journal of Land Use and Environmental Law*, 17(1): 169–182.
Kinver, M. (2013) 'Air Pollution Kills Millions Each Year, Says Study', *BBC News Science and Environment*. Available at: http://www.bbc.co.uk/news/science-environment-23315781. Accessed 15 July 2013.

Kluin, M. (2013) 'Environmental Regulation in Chemical Corporations', in R. Walters, D. Westerhuis, and T. Wyatt (eds), *Emerging Issues in Green Criminology: Exploring Power, Justice and Harm*. London: Palgrave, 145–172.

Konkel, L. (2013) 'Air Pollution and the Gut: Are Fine Particles Linked to Bowel Disease', *Environmental Health News*. Available at: http://www.environmentalhealthnews.org/ehs/news/2013/air-pollution-and-the-gut. Accessed 20 September 2013.

Likosky, M. (ed.) (2002) *Transnational Legal Processes: Globalisation and Power Disparities*. London: Butterworths.

London Assembly Environment Committee (2009) *Every Breathe You Take: An Investigation into Air Quality in London*. May 2009. Available at: https://www.london.gov.uk/mayor-assembly/london-assembly/publications/every-breath-you-take-investigation-air. Accessed 22 October 2013.

Lukes, S. (2005) *Power: A Radical View*. 2nd edn. Basinstoke: Palgrave.

Martin, P. and Walters, R. (2013) 'Fraud Risk and the Visibility of Carbon', *International Journal for Crime, Justice and Social Democracy*, 2(2): 27–42.

McGrath, M. (2014) 'Climate Impacts "Overwhelming" – UN', *BBC News Science and Environment*, 31 March 2014. Available at: www.bbc.com/news/science-environment-26810559. Accessed 1 April 2014.

Muncie, J., Talbot, D. and Walters, R. (2009) (eds) *Crime: Local and Global*. Devon: Willan.

Nasheed, M. (2012) quoted in *Voyager*. Available at: http://www.voyagermagazine.com.au/gallery/yellowstone-national-park. Accessed 19 October 2013.

The New York Times (2001) 'Company News: Koch Petroleum Fined $20 Million in Pollution Case', *The New York Times*, 10 April 2001.

Pachauri, R. and Reisinger, A. (eds) (2007) *Contribution of Working Groups I, II and III to the Fourth Assessment Report of the Intergovernmental Panel on Climate Change*. Geneva: IPCC.

Pirro, D. (2002) *Project for an International Court of the Environment – Origins and Development*. Available at: www.biopolitics.gr/HTML/PUBS/VOL8/html/Pirro.htm. Accessed 18 October 2013.

Pope, C., Burnett, R., Thun, M., Calle, E., Krewski, D., Ito, K. and Thurston, G. (2002) 'Lung Cancer Cardiopulmonary Mortality and Long-Term Exposure to Fine Particulate Air Pollution', *JAMA*, 287: 1132–1141.

Reichel, P. (ed.) (2005) *Handbook of Transnational Crime and Justice*. London: Sage.

Reuters (2013) 'Shell to Pay $1.1 Million in Fines for Arctic Air-Quality Violations'. Available at: http://www.reuters.com/article/2013/09/06/us-shell-alaska-fines-idUSBRE9850UM20130906. Accessed 6 September 2013.

Royal Commission on Environmental Pollution (2006) 'What is the Royal Commission on Environmental Pollution?' Available at: www.rcep.org.uk/about.htm#(1). Accessed 18 November 2013.

Ruggiero, V. and South, N. (eds) (2010) Special Issue on Green Criminology. *Critical Criminology – An International Journal*, 18(4).

—— (2013) 'Toxic State-Corporate Crimes, Neo-liberalism and Green Criminology: The Hazards and Legacies of the Oil, Chemical and Mineral Industries', *The International Journal of Crime, Justice and Social Democracy*, 2(2): 12–26.

Salmi, J. (2004) 'Violence in Democratic Societies: Towards an Analytical Framework', in P. Hillyard, C. Pantazis, S. Tombs and D. Gordon (eds), *Beyond Criminology: Taking Harm Seriously*. London: Pluto Press.

Shidon, Z. (2013) 'China Reopens Beijing Roads, Airports After Smog Shutdown', *Bloomberg News*. Available at: http://www.bloomberg.com/news/2013-10-07/beijing-smog-closes-highways-as-travelers-return-after-holiday.html. Accessed 7 October 2013.

Siegal, N. (1998) '"If I Believed in Hell, This Could Be No Worse": Louisiana-Pacific Corp. Sued over Environmental Crimes', *The Progressive*. Available at: www.findarticles.com/p/articles/ml_m1295/is_1998_Dec/ai_53281653. Accessed 25 October 2013.

Smyth, C. (2013) 'Pollution at Rush Hour Roads Linked to Underweight Babies', *The Times*. Available at: http://www.thetimes.co.uk/tto/health/child-health/article3894682.ece. Accessed 22 September 2013.

Spapens, T. (2011) 'Cross-Border Police Cooperation in Tackling Environmental Crime', INECE Conference Proceedings: 237–299, reprinted in R. White (ed.) (2013), *Transnational Environmental Crime*. Surrey: Ashgate.

Stanko, E. (1990) *Everyday Violence*. London: Pandora.

—— (2013) 'Violence', in E. McLaughlin and J. Muncie (eds), *The Sage Dictionary of Criminology*. 3rd edn. London: Sage, 483–486.

Stretesky, P., Long, M. and Lynch, M. (2014) *The Treadmill of Crime: Political Economy and Green Criminology*. London: Routledge.

Taylor, L. (2013) 'Tony Abbott Says UN Climate Head Is "Talking through Her Hat" about Fires', *The Guardian*. Available at: http://www.theguardian.com/world/2013/oct/23/abbott-figueres-talking-hat-bushfires. Accessed 23 October 2013.

Tombs, S. and Whyte, D. (2009) 'Crime, Harm and Corporate Power', in J. Muncie, D. Talbot and R. Walters (eds), *Crime: Local and Global*. Devon: Willan, 137–172.

United Nations International Strategy for Disaster Reduction (UNISDR) (2008) *Disaster Figures for 2007: Asia Continues to Be Hit Hardest by Disasters*. UN/ISDR 2008/01. Available at: www.unisdr.org/eng/media-room/press-release/2008/pr-2000-01-disaster-figures-2007.pdf. Accessed 22 October 2013.

—— (2008) *Disaster Risk Reduction*. Available at: http://portal.unesco.org/science/en/ev.php-URL_ID=6003&URL_DO=DO_TOPIC&URL_SECTION=201.html.

United States Environmental Protection Agency (2008) 'October 2008 Enforcement Action Summaries'. Available at: http://www.epa.gov/oecaerth/resources/publications/data/planning/priorities/fy2008prioritycwacafo.pdf. Accessed 20 October 2013.

—— (2009) 'EPA Fugitives'. Available at: www.epa.gov/fugitives/. Accessed 21 October 2013.

Vanderheiden, S. (2008) *Atmospheric Justice: A Political Theory of Climate Change*. Oxford: Oxford University Press.

Walters, R. (2009a) *Crime Is in the Air: Air Pollution Control and Regulation in the UK*. London: CCJS.

—— (2009b) 'Environmental Law and Environmental Crime', in W. Brown, C. Aradau and J. Budds (eds), *Environmental Issues and Responses*. Walton Hall: The Open University Press.

—— (2010) 'Toxic Atmospheres: Air Pollution and the Politics of Regulation', *Critical Criminology: An International Journal*, 18(4): 307–323.
—— (2011) *Eco Crime and Genetically Modified Food*. London: Routledge.
—— (2012) 'Air Crime and Atmospheric Justice', in N. South and A. Brisman (eds), *Routledge International Handbook of Green Criminology*. London: Routledge, 134–149.
—— (2013) 'Eco Mafia and Environmental Crime', in K. Carrington, M. Ball, E. O'Brien, and J. Tauri (eds), *Crime, Justice and Social Democracy: International Perspectives*. London: Palgrave, 281–294.
Walters, R. and Westerhuis, D. (2013) 'Green Crime and the Role of Environmental Courts', *Crime, Law and Social Change*, 59(3): 279–290.
Westra, L. (2004) *Eco Violence and the Law: Supranational Normative Foundations of Ecocrime*. Ardsley, NY: Transnational Publishers Inc.
White, R. (2008) *Crimes Against Nature: Environmental Criminology and Ecological Justice*. Devon: Willan.
—— (2011) *Towards an Eco–Global Criminology*. London: Routledge.
—— (ed.) (2013) *Transnational Environmental Crime*. Surrey: Ashgate.
White, T. and Heckenberg, D. (2014) *Green Criminology: An Introduction to the Study of Environmental Harm*. London: Routledge.
Williams, C. (1996) 'An Environmental Victimology', *Social Science*, 23(1): 16–40.
Wodarski, J., Rapp, P. and Roberts, A. (eds) (2002) *Handbook of Violence*. New York: Wiley.
World Health Organisation (2013) 'Deaths from Climate Change'. Available at: http://www.who.int/mediacentre/factsheets/fs266/en/. Accessed 22 September 2013.
Ximeng, C. (2013) 'Beijing Boosts Air Pollution Penalties', *Global Times*. Available at: http://www.globaltimes.cn/content/814346.shtml. Accessed 26 September 2013.
Žižek, S. (2009) *Violence: Six Sideways Reflections*. London: Profile Books.
—— (2011) *Living in the End Times*. London; Verso.

9
Invisible Pillaging: The Hidden Harm of Corporate Biopiracy

Tanya Wyatt

Introduction

Social and economic harm caused by corporations has been a topic of concern for decades. This is currently the case with multiple highly publicised instances of corporate practices contributing to the global economic crisis, such as the Libor scandal in the United Kingdom. Many harmful actions undertaken by corporations receive even less attention than those witnessed during and since the global recession. This chapter explores the invisible nature and power dynamics of the pillaging and theft of natural resources by corporations which is known as biopiracy. The global South contains areas that are some of the richest in biodiversity and therefore biological materials. Generations of indigenous people have relied upon and cultivated the different plants and non-human animals that are the source of this diversity for use as medicine, food and ornamentation. Western corporations, seeing the possibility for potential new products and financial reward, hunt out biological materials that hold commercial promise in these regions. At times, without consent or permission, the corporations patent and claim ownership over their new 'discoveries'.

These new products fall into two categories: medicine and horticulture. Through two case studies, the harm and exploitation of this hidden pillaging by transnational corporations will be explored. The first case study is the patenting of the active ingredient in the African plant *Hoodia* by a British biotechnology firm. The second is the patent, again by a British company, of a hybridised variety of the Busy Lizzie plant, popular in many British gardens as well as gardens around the world. Both examples will demonstrate the economic and social impacts of the biopiracy of the knowledge and environment that pit marginalised indigenous people against the rich Western companies' claims of ownership and their powerful intellectual property regimes.

What is biopiracy?

Companies, as part of their development of new products, search for naturally occurring compounds or organisms that they can use in medicines or other commercial applications (US Department of the Interior 2009). This legitimate practice is called bioprospecting; in other words, the exploration of natural resources in order to find commercially viable products, most likely pharmaceuticals. Related to this, but widely regarded as illegitimate, is biopiracy. The term was coined by a worker in the Canadian non-governmental organisation (NGO) Rural Advancement Foundation International (Robinson 2010). It stemmed from the frustration of the 'appropriation and monopolisation of long-held medicinal and agricultural knowledge about nature, as well as the related physical resources (plants, animals and their components)' (Robinson 2010: 39). The 'appropriation' is the pillaging or theft of the knowledge without recognition of or compensation to the indigenous communities from which the knowledge was taken. The 'monopolisation', as will be demonstrated, is the exclusive ownership of the products created from that knowledge that is made possible because of the power of the corporations.

Bioprospecting is not a new phenomenon as such exploration for new products and pillaging of knowledge can be seen in the exploitation of indigenous knowledge during the colonial period (Crosby 1993). What biopiracy specifically captures is the dominance of modern technological and institutional structures which have created and encouraged new inequities between those seeking the knowledge (corporations rather than colonisers [South 2007]) and indigenous people (Robinson 2010). The inequities stem from corporations' access to legal redress and protection and to being heard by national governments and inter-governmental agencies, such as the WTO, whereas indigenous communities have none of these, resulting in their lack of power. Reid (2010: 77) defines biopiracy as the 'process of taking indigenous people's knowledge without compensation'. For Shiva (2001: 49) 'biopiracy refers to the use of intellectual property systems to legitimise the exclusive ownership and control over biological resources and biological products and processes that have been used over centuries in non-industrialised cultures'. Additionally, there is the dynamic of the 'asymmetrical and unrequited movement of plants and TKUP [traditional knowledge of the uses of plants] from the South to the North through the processes of the international institutions and the patent system' (Mgbeoji 2006: 13).

Integral then to the conceptualisation and understanding of biopiracy is the presence of modern Western institutions that ensure the monopolisation of processes and practices derived from indigenous knowledge and that legitimate the pillaging of traditional knowledge through the legal system. Central to this occurring is the unequal power balance between those for whom the use of natural resources, in particular traditional medicines, has a long cultural and social tradition and those Western multinational corporations that seek to profit from this knowledge and utilise the Western legal system to protect their interests.

Bioprospecting and biopiracy are frequently focused on traditional medicines (Reid 2010). Traditional medicine 'refers to the knowledge, skills and practices based on the theories, beliefs and experiences indigenous to different cultures, used in the maintenance of health and in the prevention, diagnosis, improvement or treatment of physical and mental illness' (WHO 2013). For instance, Colgate Palmolive was given a patent on the use of red iron oxide in toothpaste by the United States (US) Patent Office but, as Indian officials pointed out, people in India have been using this sort of tooth powder since antiquity (Blakely 2010). Similarly, arguments have arisen over patents being given for an antifungal extract from the neem tree, which has been used in India for centuries, and for turmeric, which has wound-healing properties (Vidal 2000; Blakely 2010). These examples begin to uncover the unequal power balance evident in biopiracy. In these illustrations the powerful US intellectual property regime expressed through the US Patent Office is pitted against the less influential Indian government representing people with centuries of traditional knowledge.

As mentioned, medicine is one of the areas of biopiracy. The other is horticulture, which may involve agricultural products, such as the controversy over the patenting of basmati rice. In this case, the US Patent Office granted the company RiceTec Incorporated a patent for 'basmati' rice, which is a variety of rice with a particular starch structure and which undergoes a unique drying process that was developed decades ago in India and Pakistan (Trade and Environment Database (TED) n.d.). By allowing the rice grown in the United States to be called 'basmati', the US Patent Office was not only ignoring or denying years of cultural heritage and traditional knowledge of the Himalayan region, but it was also potentially damaging the economies of both India and Pakistan, which export a significant amount of basmati rice to the United States and the European Union (TED n.d.). Again, in this example, a powerful nation, the United States, and a large US corporation capable of cheaply producing and exporting rice, have used their own legal system to protect the corporation's 'invention'. This means that the less influential governments of India and Pakistan, along with the smaller rice-producing companies with less financial capital than RiceTec Incorporated, are burdened with challenging the threat and alleged theft of their traditional knowledge. This highlights the power dynamics that will be explored further.

Drahos (2000) argued that a vast majority of the indigenous knowledge that has been employed in creating medicines in particular has not resulted in new products. Furthermore, traditional knowledge is mostly an input to other research, which makes it difficult to attach monetary value to it (Drahos 2004). Some claim that biopiracy is a myth and patenting of knowledge as currently taking place is legally acceptable (Chen 2006; Heald 2003; Oxley 2005). Others argue that making claims of biopiracy hurts indigenous communities because such allegations scare away corporations and therefore possible economic benefits for the local people (Nash 2001). Nash (2001) suggests that it is lawyers who benefit most from biopiracy because of the complicated and lengthy legal battles that ensue. He also argues that charities benefit from biopiracy claims because of the campaigns against it and that the financial rewards those indigenous communities would gain from having intellectual property rights over their knowledge are exaggerated (Nash 2001).

Yet the potential of chemical compounds in plants is known by indigenous people and makes the identification of potential sources of new medicines much more efficient and cheaper for the pharmaceutical companies that are conducting experiments (Reid 2010). In the case of pharmaceuticals, indigenous people who have helped researchers locate the biological resources to make new medicines have received less than .001 per cent of the profits from those drugs (Coombes 1998). Similarly for horticultural products, 'uses by local peoples have been the starting point for all major Floras Kew [Gardens] has produced over the last 150 years' (Grenville 1989: 209) though there is no evidence of compensation. Additionally, 'the inclusion in patents (or other IP [intellectual property]) protection requirements on life forms clearly neglects to adequately consider the moral and cultural norms of many societies, to both the technologies involved and the monopolisation of life forms' (Robinson 2010: 42). In other words, just because something is legal does not mean that it is socially or morally acceptable or that it does not cause harm. Slavery is an obvious example of historical practice that was within the bounds of the law yet was clearly harmful and its unacceptability eventually acknowledged publicly. As Robinson (2010) argues, the result in regard to biopiracy is the power elites imposing their standards on the world. Control of indigenous knowledge is given to the multinational corporations through a system that they themselves have helped create. As will be evidenced below, this, despite claims to the contrary, deprives communities of economic benefits, depletes access to natural resources and medicines in the areas where the biodiversity is taken from, and robs indigenous people of their traditions and cultures without compensation (Liang 2011). Corporations are able to keep the harm and injustice they have caused invisible by controlling the dissemination of the knowledge of their actions and by controlling the regulatory system itself through their powerful influence. Two more detailed examples of biopiracy in indigenous communities are explored in the case studies below; these will then be used to illustrate the injury caused by this invisible harm.

Hoodia: patenting its active ingredient

The San (Bushmen) of the Kalahari Desert in South Africa have been ingesting the hoodia plant for generations to stave off hunger when out hunting (Barnett 2006). The South African governmental research centre, the Council for Scientific and Industrial Research (CSIR), undertook years of research into the nutritional value of such bush foods (van Heerden et al. 2007). In 1983, CSIR researchers discovered that hoodia species contained a compound that was an appetite suppressant (van Heerden et al. 2007). They patented the compound as P57 (Reynolds 2004) and sold it to a pharmaceutical company without consulting the San and ignoring the needs of the indigenous community (Liang 2011). The patented compound appears to have been used by various companies in their drugs made for weight loss. Reynolds (2004) reported that the British pharmaceutical company, Phytopharm, was conducting trials in 1997 that confirmed P57's appetite suppressant property and used it in anti-obesity and diet drugs. It was also reported that a sub-licence was given to Pfizer, another major pharmaceutical multinational corporation, for these drugs for £13 million (Reynolds 2004). Also involving Phytopharm, but with other multinational corporations involved, Barnett (2006) reported that Phytopharm patented the active ingredient in hoodia. Phytopharm is linked to the multinational company Unilever, which apparently claimed that the San from whom the knowledge originated were extinct (Barnett 2006). This created a public outcry in 2001

(Barnett 2006). It has been reported that the San heard from a charity that hoodia had been appropriated by these Western companies and that they were making considerable profits from the diet drugs derived from the San's knowledge (Reynolds 2004).

Once the San became aware of drugs made from hoodia, efforts were made on their behalf to challenge the patents and the intellectual property rights of the multinational corporations regarding the ownership and origin of this knowledge. With the help of charities, and in a rare victory for indigenous people, the San have been given some of the profits from these products (Barnett 2006). Additionally, in 2004 CSIR signed a memorandum of understanding with the San acknowledging their rights in regard to hoodia as the custodians of such traditional knowledge (Reynolds 2004). The agreement also recognised the role that CSIR had in isolating the particular property in hoodia and identifying the active ingredient causing appetite suppression that was then used in drugs to assist with weight loss (Reynolds 2004).

The multinational corporations did not admit to biopiracy and argue against the very concept. As Phytopharm spokespeople have indicated, it is thought that it is impossible to discover who 'owns' plants which are growing in various regions of the world and have been used by different groups of people (Barnett 2006). Furthermore, patents are essential to incentivise pharmaceutical companies to engage in new product research. This is because creating a new drug costs between £100 and £250 million to produce and without patents, which provide a monopoly for a limited time (Vahabi 2009), financially it would not be worth developing new drugs (Barnett 2006). Additionally, Phytopharm claims that without efforts such as theirs, traditional knowledge would die out completely with the extinction of indigenous people or the loss of their cultures due to Westernisation (Barnett 2006). Ironically then, the multinational corporations champion themselves as the protectors of endangered knowledge.

Busy Lizzie: patenting hybridised varieties

The Busy Lizzie or *Impatiens wallerina* is one of the most popular plants in British gardens (Barnett 2006) and in other parts of the world. It, like hoodia, has been part of an international row over patenting and intellectual property. Similarly, this row raises concerns over multinational corporations' exploitation of the poor and possible human rights violations (Barnett 2006). In the case of the Busy Lizzie, a new hybridised variety that 'trails' or hangs from planters was 'invented' by the multinational biotechnology company Syngenta to great (financial) success (Barnett 2006). They did so by crossing the *Impatiens wallerina* with a rare variety of impatiens, the *Impatiens usambarensis*. The latter variety grows in isolated areas of Tanzania and had been categorised by Syngenta as 'commercially insignificant' (Barnett 2006). Hybrids of these two varieties of impatiens occur naturally in Tanzania and Syngenta has admitted this (Barnett 2006). Their innovation stems from taking seeds of the *Impatiens usambarensis* from the Royal Botanical Garden in Edinburgh, which had originally obtained the seeds from London's Kew Gardens in 1982 (Barnett 2006). Syngenta then crossed the *Impatiens usambarensis* seeds with seeds from the common *Impatiens wallerina*. The claims of biopiracy arise through dispute around the 'natural' or 'invented' nature of the plant: how can something be 'invented' when it already occurs in nature? Additionally, the original seed collector (thief?) did not pay for taking the seeds of the rare *Impatiens usambarensis* from the indigenous community in Tanzania where they are found (Barnett 2006). Therefore, the indigenous people in Tanzania have received no compensation and shared in none of the profits from a highly profitable horticultural product which originated in their community.

Syngenta appears not to agree with the claims of biopiracy. This is partly due to the timing of their acquisition. The Convention on Biodiversity (CBD), which Britain became a member of in 1994, has a clause that recognises the property rights of developing countries and within this is the recommendation that agreements should be made to share the commercial benefits of products developed from indigenous and/or traditional knowledge (Barnett 2006). These seeds were obtained before the CBD, so one argument is that its recommendations do not apply. Biopiracy of horticulture is different from that of medicinal knowledge in that the corporations presumably do not have to dedicate as much time or effort into research, such as isolating active ingredients. In the case of basmati rice or in this instance of the Busy Lizzie, the plant itself is acquired and minimal modification is done to make the 'new' product that the multinational corporations sell.

Both of these incidents raise the issue of whether living organisms can be and should be patentable. Does a kind of rice belong to a particular people? Does an ornamental plant belong to particular people because it is found within their country? Should a company have exclusive rights over a particular kind of life and profit from selling it? The US Patent Office and the British equivalent gave corporations from their respective countries exclusive rights and ownership over plants that are not found within their territory and are only known about because of the knowledge of people in the original habitats. The harms this creates will be explored shortly, but first a discussion of the mechanisms that keep biopiracy from being visible though this kind of pillaging of knowledge may happen frequently.

How biopiracy remains invisible

The Brazilian ambassador to the United Kingdom in 2004 was quoted as calling biopiracy a 'silent disease' as it is an elusive activity often abetted by well-known multinational corporations (Barnett 2006). But why is it that something that is known about can still be invisible? What are the factors that keep certain harms hidden? In the case of biopiracy, it takes place at a nexus of power, isolation and marginalisation that form the foundation on which injustices can be rendered invisible.

The power is witnessed in the influence and financial strength of multinational corporations and connects to the lack of knowledge, statistics and control which make up the features of invisibility proposed by Jupp et al. in 1999 and revisited in Chapter 1 of this book. There is arguably widespread knowledge that corporations search, for example, for cures for cancer and other new medicines in highly diverse environments. What is kept hidden by the corporations is the role that indigenous communities play in this search and that successful 'discoveries' do not include or compensate them.

As proposed, power manifests in the influence and financial prowess of the multinational corporations, which are perpetually looking for new ways to make money. Their influence in particular enables them to control knowledge of biopiracy. Instances of biopiracy and other white-collar and green crimes go unrecorded and/or unacknowledged because the public relations departments of multinational corporations are able to manipulate the messages that are in the media (South 2007), so the role of indigenous people in the development of medicines and new products is purposefully kept invisible. It is also hidden because it does not attract the media attention like other green or environmental crimes. For instance, deforestation and pollution is covered in the news much more readily (Barnett 2006). Presumably this is connected to the location of the harm – far away and out of sight – and the victim – unknown and/or marginalised indigenous communities. This essentially means that there are no wider knowledge and no official statistics.

Multinational corporations' influence and power are also extremely evident in the contents of international law, especially in relation to intellectual property. Even though patents must be novel in order to be granted and cannot be knowledge from the public domain (*The Herald* 2004; Vahabi 2009; Reid 2010), these powerful companies are given ownership over 'discoveries' that have been known to indigenous peoples for generations (South 2007). This creates a conundrum for indigenous people because in order to avoid being exploited by colonisers and corporations they are secretive and protective of their traditional knowledge (*The Herald* 2004). This contributes to why there is little or no recorded evidence of indigenous knowledge.

Exploitation in part stems from the Trade-Related Aspects of Intellectual Property Rights Agreement (TRIPS), a section of the World Trade Organisation (WTO) agreement. It is a charter designed in such a way that Northern knowledge is protected and those countries are given secure control over knowledge as well as over markets (McCoy 2005). This is in the interest of not only multinational corporations, but also the governments where these companies work and apply for their patents (Reid 2010). TRIPS often forms a section of the bilateral trade agreements between nations (White 2009). It has been documented that some of these bilateral agreements between industrialised nations and less developed countries like Vietnam and Nicaragua have required the ability to patent plants and animals (White 2009). Furthermore, invisibility of these harms is maintained through confidential negotiations of these agreements where parliaments and the public are never consulted (White 2009).

Such intellectual property regimes disadvantage and undervalue indigenous knowledge because to be recognised knowledge it must be recorded (Reid 2010). In the United States this means it must be published; in the European Union (EU), oral tradition is recognised (Reid 2010). The patent system is also disadvantageous to indigenous communities because they frequently lack the resources to be able to apply for patents (Reid 2010). So even if they were aware that they should record and protect their traditional practices, it might be beyond their capacity to do so. Since indigenous communities fundamentally view nature in a different capacity from corporations, indigenous communities sometimes avoid or refuse to implement intellectual property regimes outlined in the WTO (Liang 2011). By not engaging with the dominant system, this limits their access to the legal rights that would supposedly be given to them under the system (Liang 2011).

Further power over knowledge is seen in international law preferencing certain kinds of knowledge over others; this too originates in international law being constructed by the powerful developed North. Multinational corporations wielding their considerable economic power are able to draw upon greater professional and highly regarded expert opinion to sustain long complicated defences of legal rights and claims which are required to prove ownership (South 2007). In contrast, indigenous communities' knowledge is founded on centuries of tradition that is likely to be passed down orally from generation to generation rather than having been peer-reviewed or defended in a courtroom. This gives them very limited bargaining power when conflict arises (Reid 2010). They also often do not have the legal experience or financial capital to challenge corporations' claims of ownership. The offender – the multinational corporation – has nearly complete control over the knowledge of the harm, the definition of what harm is and what knowledge is deemed valuable. The indigenous community – as victim – is rendered powerless with little ability to control their knowledge of the plants and non-human animals which are products susceptible to biopiracy.

As mentioned, the theft of traditional knowledge is taking place in regions of the world that are frequently isolated from the public gaze and media coverage. This amplifies the lack of knowledge. It also limits indigenous people's knowledge of the theft and of the legal system governing intellectual property because they may have infrequent information and/or contact with people outside of their communities. In some of the examples given, the indigenous people would not have known they were victims of biopiracy if an international charity or NGO had not intervened. Isolation may also inhibit indigenous people's access to legal and financial aid to fight for the right to their intellectual property. If injustices such as biopiracy are not publicly and legally challenged they can easily remain hidden as knowledge about their existence is not created. Isolation intersects with power. Employees of multinational corporations may be able to control the information about isolated indigenous groups; for instance, in the case of the hoodia plant, one of the companies involved claimed that the group from which the knowledge was taken was extinct. If not for international charities, this misinformation may have decided the challenge to the patent.

Linked to the preferencing of certain knowledges are particular gendered and racist underpinnings which further illustrate the disregard for non-Western–generated uses of nature (Mgbeoji 2006). As mentioned, the scientific or Western development of knowledge, is often viewed as the only legitimate form of knowledge whereas traditional developments are considered inferior (Mgbeoji 2006). Mgbeoji (2006) argues that the cultural context of the legal framework that allows biopiracy to occur is grounded in a persistent denigration of the intellectual worth of traditional knowledge and the people who have developed it. This tends to be local women farmers (Mgbeoji 2006). Even though indigenous people are victimised when biopiracy takes place, as with other green crimes they are excluded from methods to gain redress and from ways to protest (Lynch and Stretesky 2001). Most importantly, indigenous people are only sometimes 'consulted' rather than being key stakeholders in the decision-making processes that affect the use of their knowledge and the health of their environment (White 2009: 158). Marginalised knowledge coming from already marginalised people leads to invisible victims.

Academia has not helped to uncover this hidden harm and injustice. The protection of indigenous lands, culture and folklore has been neglected in criminology and ineffectively affirmed in national and international law (Orkin 2003). South (2007) agrees that criminology has been essentially silent on biopiracy though the debates of power, isolation and marginalisation proposed here are central debates of the discipline. This reflects the Western hegemony of criminology as a discipline where there too voices of the South and East remain largely unheard.

While biopiracy is a social harm that remains invisible to the criminological community and to the public to a large degree, it is also a practice that is largely invisible to economists (Vahabi 2009). Vahabi (2009: 355) argues that markets that are coordinated through 'intimidation, threat and use of non-institutionalised coercive means', which he calls 'destructive coordination', are invisible within the discipline. 'Appropriation through piracy, confiscation and so on connotes ownership of resources by disregarding, violating, annihilating or excluding the property rights of others' (Vahabi 2009). Such occurrences, which biopiracy is clearly categorised as, are neglected in mainstream economics (Vahabi 2009). They are, however, engrained within international trade regimes. For instance, TRIPS gives corporations with private ownership rights of discoveries and inventions the limited monopoly referred to earlier (Vahabi 2009). Biopiracy 'institutionalises private property through the abolition of property rights' (Vahabi 2009: 373). The origin of this private property is colonialism, piracy or other violent means (Vahabi 2009). The only reason that intellectual property and private property of this kind are included in TRIPS and the WTO is because of direct pressure from US pharmaceutical and agricultural companies (Correa 2000).

Without the interest of the academic community, which is surprising given the multi- and interdisciplinary claims of criminology in particular, more of the features of invisibility emerge, such as 'no research' and 'no theory'. These, combined with the power of the corporations, the remote locations of biopiracy and the marginalised status of the victims, create the conditions for biopiracy to stay hidden and the victims of corporate pillaging to frequently go unnoticed and unassisted.

Impacts of biopiracy, invisibility and intellectual property regimes

Just because the harm of biopiracy is invisible does not mean that it does not impact upon the victims. The invisibility itself also has negative impacts as do the intellectual property regimes that contribute to the continuation of biopiracy. The pillaging and theft of culture and knowledge have negative consequences in the communities where they take place. Whereas the theft of culture may have more intangible impacts, such as the violation of a human right, the theft of knowledge has real financial and environmental consequences.

Biopiracy is responsible for the loss of economic opportunity. By pirating these products, multinational corporations are robbing developing nations of the means to finance important sustainable development projects (Barnett 2006). For instance, the people of Tanzania could potentially grow trailing Busy Lizzies and sell them to Western consumers, but with Syngenta being given a patent on the Tanzanians' naturally occurring flora, this is no longer an economic opportunity for them. This reasoning applies to red iron oxide toothpaste and to basmati rice. Since Western corporations have been given the monopoly over these products, the Indian and Pakistani people who have been cultivating and using these products for centuries no longer can compete on the global market, thus potentially suffering significant financial loss. After the fact, profits from the products made from the active ingredient in hoodia are being shared with the San. Yet the possibility for them to cultivate hoodia on their own and sell it are probably now limited because a patent has been issued. With corporate ownership being located in the West, indigenous communities lose control over their natural resources (Wyatt 2012). This also happens because multinational corporations may replicate and synthesise genetic materials that at one time may only have been found in the South (Wyatt 2012). Therefore there may be no market for cultivated crops from indigenous communities (Wyatt 2012), which is another loss of potential income.

Biopiracy also creates a disincentive to conserve biodiversity as the value of that diversity is not shared with the local people (Barnett 2006); this can lead to environmental harm and degradation. An elite few decide that nature is a commodity and rather than the environment being shared for the greater good of the community – for treating the sick, for feeding the people – it is reduced to its genetic components, which are only given instrumental value determined by and given to corporations (Robinson 2010). Since indigenous communities are precluded from a global governance system reliant on market forces and independent government agencies, there is no incentive for those communities closest to the natural resources to conserve them (Liang 2011). Ironically, the environment in developing countries that could be a source of new medicines, horticultural products and economic opportunities becomes depleted because those living in the closest proximity to it cannot or will not preserve the environment due to the theft of their knowledge of it.

Beyond the harm caused to indigenous communities, biopiracy also challenges the sovereignty of nations (Vidal 2000). This is clearly seen in the cases mentioned earlier of the neem tree and basmati rice, where India and Pakistan are forced to challenge the laws of another country (the United States) for decisions that dictate what is allowed with the knowledge and agriculture developed and originating from within their own countries. Sovereignty is brought under pressure by imposing the commoditisation of nature on nations, typically developing, but clearly not always, through intellectual property regimes which do not recognise other knowledges (Wyatt 2012). This can be viewed as a violation of the rights and obligations of nations to care for and govern their own people.

Invisibility also has its own impacts. By remaining hidden, biopiracy goes unchallenged and therefore continues and spreads with more indigenous communities being victimised and having their culture and knowledge pillaged. They, too, may then lose out on potential income from the traditions that they have long practised. Corporations are strengthened even further and their power firmly cemented. This does not create the conditions that would then promote partnerships between what Drahos (2000: 245) describes as the most unequal relationship of 'globalised and hypermodern companies seeking deals with some of the world's most local and traditional people'. The San receiving some compensation for their knowledge of hoodia appears to be the exception rather than the rule. In fact, at the time it was one of seven claims of biopiracy in Africa by British firms (Barnett 2006). These are just the ones that are known about and only takes into account the United Kingdom, not other European countries or the United States, which are also engaged in activities largely regarded as biopiracy. Additionally, these are the claims in Africa alone. There are undoubtedly similar practices in South and Latin America as well as parts of Asia. Furthermore, hoodia cannot be considered a partnership as the San had to fight for recognition of their traditional knowledge. Indigenous communities then continue to be marginalised, to have their knowledge taken for the gain of Western companies and to struggle with poverty and economic exclusion, all largely hidden and invisible.

The intellectual property regimes, mostly set out in TRIPS of the WTO, seem partly responsible for creating conditions for biopiracy and for its invisibility. Western capitalist beliefs that commoditise nature are engrained in this international trade system that dominates the globe. The consideration of nature as a commodity has become hegemonic in that it is also embedded in the CBD. A convention that is designed to conserve the biodiversity of the planet advocates, as mentioned, for sharing the commercial benefits from traditional knowledge and genetic resources (Wynberg and Chennells 2009). This is seen in the Nagoya Protocol on Access to Genetic Resources and the Fair and Equitable Sharing of Benefits Arising from their Utilisation (Liang 2011). This clearly engrains nature as a genetic resource into conservation efforts. This creates conflict and marginalises certain peoples as not all cultures and nations subscribe to such definitions and appropriations of nature. As described above, many of the world's people, including indigenous cultures, conceptualise nature as a common good and a common heritage of humankind (Robinson 2010). The idea then that life can be patented, owned and monopolised by one company is not a universally held belief, but one that is forced upon societies through powerful multinational corporations profiting from this system. On the one hand, TRIPS and the CBD do not recognise nature as a public good as a valid belief. On the other hand, indigenous communities do not recognise intellectual property regimes. The consequence is that indigenous people are then left unprotected either because the regimes do not recognise the situated knowledges of indigenous cultures or indigenous cultures do not engage with the intellectual property regimes to gain protection. Either way, there is further marginalisation and lack of protection – a perpetuating cycle that allows for invisible harm and continuation of biopiracy.

Conclusion

The transnational mobility of corporations and property laws has reshaped the basis of rights and indigenous concepts of nature (South 2007). As discussed, this reshaping to where nature is regarded as a genetic resource is a very Euro-American viewpoint and in conflict with other cosmologies (Robinson 2010). Haraway (1991) argues that feminist critiques of universal objectivities can be applied to the intellectual property regimes that have perpetuated this belief. Rather than feminist knowledges, in this case universal objectivities are imposed upon material processes that maintain 'scientific and technological, late industrial, militarized, racist and male dominant societies' (Haraway 1991: 188). The result is that a 'newborn culture of specific economic protectionism trumped a plethora of long-held and widely dispersed moral and cultural norms about the treatment of nature' (Robinson 2010: 42). The dominant cultural paradigm that nature is a commodified genetic resource undervalues and ignores centuries of traditional knowledge and marginalises and disadvantages indigenous people who often are already suffering from discrimination and poverty. Biopiracy is a poignant example of the power of corporations to keep their harmful actions hidden. By controlling knowledge, information and the governance system surrounding the production process, they keep invisible the pillaging they perpetrate, which inflicts harm and injustice on indigenous communities.

In order to combat this hidden injury, the Western hegemonic intellectual property system that is expressed through TRIPS and national patent systems must be further researched and challenged. This task may well fall to international NGOs and charities whose role in this complex struggle also warrants further exploration. Strategies to recognise and value other forms of knowledge need to be championed by governments and academics in order to prevent further biopiracy and harmful pillaging.

References

Barnett, A. (2006) *Special report:* 'The New Piracy: How the West "Steals" Africa's Plants'. Swiss and British firms are accused of using the scientific properties of plants from the developing world to make huge profits while giving nothing to the people there, *The Observer*. 27 August.

Blakely, R. (2010) '"Thousand-Year-Old" Toothpaste Leads to Accusations of Biopiracy; India'. *The Times*. 21 October, 1st edn, Ireland.

Chen, J. (2006) 'There Is No Such Thing as Biopiracy...It's a Good Thing Too', *McGeorge Law Review*, 37: 1–32.

Coombes, R. (1998) 'Intellectual Property, Human Rights and Sovereignty: New Dilemmas in International Law Posed by the Recognition of Indigenous Knowledge in the Convention on Biodiversity', *Indiana Journal of Global Legal Studies*, 6: 59–116.

Correa, C. (2000) *Intellectual Property Rights, the WTO and Developing Countries: The TRIPS Agreement and Policy Options*. London: Zed Books.

Crosby, A. (1993) *Ecological Imperialism: The Biological Expansion of Europe, 900–1900*. Cambridge: Cambridge University Press.

Drahos, P. (2000) 'Indigenous Knowledge, Intellectual Property and Biopiracy: Is a Global Biocollecting Society the Answer', *European Intellectual Property Review*, 22(6): 245–250.

—— (2004) 'Towards an International Framework for the Protection of Traditional Group Knowledge and Practice', UNCTAD-Commonwealth Secretariat Workshop on Elements of National *Sui Generis* Systems for the Preservation, Protection and Promotion of Traditional Knowledge, Innovations and Practices and Options for an International Framework. Geneva.

Grenville, L. (1989) 'Plant Collecting and Conservation', in F.N. Hepper (ed.), *Plant Hunting for Kew*. London: HMSO, 209–211.

Haraway, D. (1991) *Simians, Cyborgs and Women: The Reinvention of Nature*. London: Routledge.

Heald, P.J. (2003) 'Rhetoric of Biopiracy', *Cardozo Journal of International and Comparative Law*, 11: 519–546.

Jupp, V., Davies, P. and Francis, P. (1999) 'The Features of Invisible Crimes', in P. Davies, P. Francis and V. Jupp (eds), *Invisible Crimes: Their Victims and Their Regulation*. Basingstoke: Macmillan, 3–28.

Liang, B. (2011) 'Global Governance: Promoting Biodiversity and Protecting Indigenous Communities against Biopiracy', *Journal of Commercial Biotechnology*, 17(3): 248–253.

Lynch, M. and Stretesky, P. (2001) 'Toxic Crimes: Examining Corporate Victimisation of the General Public Employing Medical and Epidemiological Evidence', *Critical Criminology*, 10(3): 153–172.

McCoy, D. (2005) 'Strong Medicine', *RSA Journal*, June: 48–53.

Mgbeoji, I. (2006) *Global Biopiracy: Patents, Plants and Indigenous Knowledge*. Vancouver: UBC Press.

Nash, R. (2001) 'Who Benefits from Biopiracy?' *Phytochemistry*, 56(5): 403–405.

Orkin, A. (2003) 'When the Law Breaks Down: Aboriginal Peoples in Canada and Governmental Defiance of the Rule of Law', *Osgood Hall Law Journal*, 41(2 and 3): 445–462.

Oxley, A. (2005) *Retarding Development: Compulsory Disclosure in IP Law of Ownership and Use of Biological or Genetic Resources*. Australian Asia–Pacific Economic Cooperation Study Centre. Melbourne: Monash University City.

Reid, J. (2010) 'Biopiracy: The Struggle for Traditional Knowledge Rights', *American Indian Law Review*, 34: 77–98.

Reynolds, J. (2004) 'Fighting the Pirates of the Natural World', *The Scotsman*, 5 April.

Robinson, D. (2010) 'Locating Biopiracy: Geographically and Culturally Situated Knowledges', *Environment and Planning*, 42: 38–56.

Shiva, V. (2001) *Protect or Plunder? Understanding Intellectual Property Rights*. London: Zed Books.

South, N. (2007) 'The "Corporate Colonisation of Nature": Bio-Prospecting, Bio-Piracy and the Development of Green Criminology', in P. Bierne, and N. South, *Issues in Green Criminology: Confronting Harms Against Environments, Humanity and Other Animals*. Devon: Willan, 230–247.

The Herald (2004) 'Briefing: Biopiracy', *The Herald* (Glasgow). February 20.

Trade and Environment Database (TED) (n.d.) 'Basmati Case Study', *TED Case Studies*. Available at: http://www1.american.edu/ted/basmati.htm. Accessed 16 August 2013.

US Department of the Interior (2009) 'Benefits-Sharing in the National Parks. Environmental Impact Statement: What Is Bioprospecting?' Available at: http://www.nature.nps.gov/benefitssharing/whatis.cfm. Accessed 16 August 2013.

Vahabi, M. (2009) 'An Introduction to Destructive Coordination', *American Journal of Economics and Sociology*, 68(2): 353–386.

Van Heerden, F., Horak, R., Maharaj, V., Vleggaar, R., Senabe, J. and Gunning, P. (2007) 'An Appetite Suppressant from *Hoodia* Species', *Phytochemistry*, 68(20): 2545–2553.

Vidal, J. (2000) 'Biopirates Who Seek the Greatest Prizes', *The Guardian*. 15 November.

White, R. (2009) *Crimes against Nature: Environmental Criminology and Ecological Justice*. Devon: Willan.

World Health Organisation (WHO) (2013) 'Traditional Medicines'. Available at: http://www.who.int/topics/traditional_medicine/en/. Accessed 12 August 2013.

Wyatt, T. (2012) 'Biopiracy', in M. Beare (ed.), *Encyclopedia of Transnational Crime & Justice*. London: Sage, 29–30.

Wynberg, R. and Chennells, R. (2009) 'Green Diamonds of the South: An Overview of the Sans-*Hoodia* Case', in Wynberg, R., Schroeder, D. and Chennells, R. (eds), *Indigenous Peoples, Consent and Benefit Sharing: Lessons from the San-Hoodia Case*. London: Springer, 89–124.

10
War and Normative Visibility: Interactions in the Nomos

Wayne Morrison

Look around – behold thousands of slain, thousands of wounded, writhing with anguish and groaning with agony and despair. ... Here again lie headless trunks, and bodies torn and struck down by cannon shot; such death is sudden, horrid. ... Some readers will call this scene romantic: others disgusting; no matter; it is faithful; and it would be well for Kings, politicians and generals, if, while they talk of victories with exaltation, and defeats with philosophical indifference, they allow their fancies to wander to the theatre of war, and the field of carnage. (Sherer 1824, surveying the field of Albuera after battle)

We have waged war in the most ferocious and ruthless way that has ever been waged. We waged it against fierce and ruthless enemies that it was necessary to destroy. Now we have destroyed one of our enemies and forced the capitulation of the other. For the moment, we [the United States] are the strongest power in the world. It is very important that we do not become the most hated. ... We need to study and understand certain basic problems ... and remember that no weapon has ever settled a moral problem. It can impose a solution, but it cannot guarantee it to be a just one. An aggressive war is the great crime against everything good in the world. A defensive war, which must necessarily turn aggressive at the earliest moment, is the great counter crime. ... We must never think that war, no matter how necessary, nor how justified, is not a crime. Ask the infantry and the dead. (Hemingway 1946)

Introduction: making the invisible of war visible

I must confess to some ambivalence in writing this chapter. The invitation from the editors laid out the project: even in our globalised world there remain major crimes, social harms and injustices taking place hidden from view, occupying 'spaces' of invisibility. Such injustice can be countered by a normative project or performance that strips away powers of concealment and exposes to scrutiny a reality otherwise unknown or distorted. Having made the invisible visible we can then turn to regulation and criminalisation.

War, however, is particularly challenging for that agenda. First there is a post-Enlightenment project of exposing the horrors of war that sought to take control of the presentation of war from the elites to the democratic masses. Our question may be why has this seemingly had so little effect. The reality of human suffering in the conflicts in Spain and Portugal in the early 1800s is the subject of my first quotation above from Moyle Sherer surveying the field of Albuera after the battle of 16 May 1811. This had left around 7,000 dead or wounded on both sides; after receiving a factual account of it the Duke of Wellington exclaimed that the account must be rewritten as a Victory for England. Whereas Sherer portrays what she saw, an Internet search gives many more traditional images of heroic cavalry charges, valiant defenders and finely toned bodies in resplendent uniforms. Unless unavoidably present few could see or care to relate the impact of war on common soldiers or civilians. Dempsey (2008) relates that the newspapers only gave the names of the officers killed while the NCOs and privates were simply numbers. He also recounts Jane Austin's response: 'How horrible it is to have so many people killed! And what a blessing that one cares for none of them!' In 1815 the young surgeon and academic Charles Bell, desperate for practical experience, and hearing of the Battle of Waterloo, took off to Belgium to work with the wounded and sketch the wounds and forms of death as illustrations for his professional lectures. After eight horrific and exhausting days cutting and sawing limbs off the wounded he visited the field of battle. There, 'the gallant stories, the charges, the individual instance of enterprise and valour recalled me to the sense the world has of victory and Waterloo'. But this was a 'transient' feeling, for 'a gloomy, uncomfortable view of human nature' seemed 'the inevitable consequence of looking upon the whole' (letter of July 1815; Bell 1870: 245). These accounts were essentially private: in 1844, however, the *Westminster Review* published one of the great anti-war articles by William R Greg. The *Westminster Review* was founded by people around Jeremy Bentham (who is noted in criminology for his writings on punishment but whose anti-war position is wholly neglected) and the article – which quotes from Bell's letters at length – is structured by the belief that the initiative and good sense of the people would detest war when their 'vision' of war was freed from the shackles of power (Greg 1844: 192 ff.). Greg saw the Enlightenment principles of liberty and fraternity as dimmed by the realities of war, but he looked forward with optimism: given greater public knowledge of the excesses of war the populace would demand a better future where individuals would not be asked to sell their souls and engage in activities that would be censured as grave sins and crimes if undertaken domestically.

My second quotation evidences the futility of that optimism. For World War I and the wars of and against the totalitarian regimes of World War II gave an industrial scale and techniques to killing in which the individual seemed subjected to a bio-power in which the main lesson was the total dispensability of the naked person. Out of that experience comes a self-congratulatory narrative that holds we are now in a period where a new global legal order is being established with a lingua franca of human rights and substantive international criminal law slowly being enforced by an array of tribunals such as the International Criminal Court (*War Crimes Law Comes of Age*, to quote the title of a book by Meron, 1998). This order develops from the response to World War II, with the tribunals at Nuremberg and Tokyo and the international covenants (such as the Genocide Convention) promulgated by a new body, the United Nations. In 1946 at the International Military Tribunal at Nuremberg it was proclaimed that the greatest crime was waging aggressive war. Nuremberg *outlawed war*, except, of course, it did not; war endures, changes, technologies intensify risk. I will comment on the image of war and the horrors of war presented at Nuremberg in a later section and note the difficulty inherent in using (liberal) criminal law to tame war. Second, war is anything but invisible; images of it assail us from the media, history and the entertainment industry. For most individuals their knowledge of war is mediated and representational. Such multiplicity of visions and indeterminacy in meaning undercut our ability to focus and may constitute a form of invisibility. In what follows I will link war and vision in various ways. I certainly accept Judith Butler's (2010) argument that war cannot operate without partnership with the materiality of the image, and this partnership involves all of us. At the most intimate, the image is that which the soldier has of the other, an image held in one's sights, in the focal point of the artillery or bombsight, and the camera image of the drone; that is to say, the focusing on the target. At a more general level we need to understand better how the public sphere is constituted by the visual technologies of war, and what kinds of public emerge, how today personhood (both of the participant and of the bystander) is constituted and de- constituted within the field of war and how the boundaries of 'war' have become so diffuse that it is difficult to see where war is different from policing.

There are many complex issues and in one chapter I can only be brief and hint at complexity and possibilities; herein my central term is nomos. Nomos derives from the Greek νόμος, nómos (pl. νόμοι, nómoi) which means 'law', but also 'pasture, field; division, distribution; district, province'. The German legal theorist Carl Schmitt (*The Nomos of the Earth* [1950] 2006) used the term to evoke a structuring of space and time throughout the globe; wherever we are in the world we inhabit nomos and he sought to show that there was an objectivity to our diverse positioning (if only somehow one could see the world from outside) which is also a subjectivity, a personal positioning that also gives an existential living of the acceptable and unacceptable. If to be human – to live, rather than merely exist – is to act, to make, to be creative in personal action and social interaction, humans do this in circumstances prefigured; from birth we are positioned 'normatively' by powers discursive, constitutive, disciplining and enabling, powers that purport to make our particularity (our locality) and our world visible and powers that make aspects hidden. As Cover (1983: 31) interprets it, 'a nomos is a present world constituted by a system of tensions between reality and vision', it is 'an integrated world of obligation and reality *from which the rest of the world is perceived*'. This is an epistemological grid. Each human inhabits a certain nomos of the world and in this chapter I will first work through my own positioning; I will then confront aspects of globalisation, provide a discussion of some particular instances of the visibility/invisibility mix with crime and war and, finally, suggest that globalisation places an ethical responsibility on all to grasp the normativity of our individual positioning and that such a project may lead to understandings that reduce the harms of war.

Excursus: turning Black Africans into floppies

Nomos refers to our location in spatiality: I grew up as a Pakeha (a white person from the heritage of European – predominately British and Irish – settlers) in New Zealand, that most faithful of the old Empire/Commonwealth. In the twentieth century New Zealand provided soldiers in more conflicts than any other nation (from the Boer War, through the World War I where New Zealand had over 20 per cent of its male population in uniform and suffered 58 per cent of those enrolled either killed or wounded, the highest casualty rate on the Allied side, to Afghanistan). My father had, like many others, volunteered for service in

World War II and, I am certain, had the best years of his life in the navy. For most of the rest of his life he was probably bored and in employment that never stretched him. And, of course, the one topic that could never be talked about was war. This was common for my generation – the children of those who went but did not talk when they returned, whatever their experiences.

What vision of the world did my father hold, what resources was he presented with to see, when in 1939 he volunteered for service? Since the advent of 'democratic' armies in the nineteenth century (started by Bonaparte), the call of war was increasingly the 'call of duty', of service to nation, to state (and, in this case, Empire. My father had a large ashtray at the head of which was a lion and an inscription that read 'The Sun Always Shines on the British Empire'). What would he have known of the sights of war? In every town in New Zealand stood memorials to World War I, the Great War, which, in the disaster beneath the cliffs of Gallipoli (now called ANZAC cove, where due to a navigational error, the forces landed rather than the gentle slopes a mile south), Australian, New Zealand and other Commonwealth forces under British command forged a common identity in a particular act of sacrifice and remembering. Each subsequent year, on April 25, ANZAC day, throughout New Zealand processions would be held going to the cenotaph – empty since the deaths occurred in distance lands, although adorned usually with a list of names of those killed who had gone from the town. These are stylised memorials (the cenotaph in front of the Auckland War Memorial Museum is virtually identical to the cenotaph in Whitehall, London, denoting a common or universal struggle for right, civilised interests) evoking but avoiding any 'shocking sights of woe'.

At school my loves were sport, poetry (James K. Baxter) and accounts of war, in particular the valiant wars by which we Westerners spread civilisation to the New World (Westerns, John Wayne and so forth) and Vietnam. My understanding of war was through a limited range of media, which was clearly now what I would regard as verging on, if not wholly, propaganda. (I accepted, of course, that whatever 'wars' white settlers waged against the native Maori were unquestionably good, in service of opening the country up for trade and settlement). In my first year at university I joined with others to give due deference to a lecturer who always lectured in a black gown and about whom it was said he had been a public prosecutor in Kenya during the Mau Mau emergency (as related in Geary et al. 2009, chapters 1 and 6; I only later understood the judicial killings, concentration camps and torture involved in that 'state of exception', that defence of civilised values). In my second year

I joined the (Territorial) Army training to be an infantry officer which entailed spending three and a half months, first in intensive basic and then in advanced training, theoretical (yes, lectures on tactics) and practical. During the early part of the second period at a camp in the North Island I was introduced to another world: a somewhat older fellow trainee, who had recently emigrated from South Africa and who claimed to have served in South African forces (in particular the covert operations in Angola) was witness to our Maori sergeant (with whom I had a hate–love relationship) verbally castigating me face to face as I stood to attention (yes, the films are true): I stood there: 'Yes, sergeant, yes' After the sergeant left the fellow trainee came up to me and, misreading my deference to the sergeant, put one arm over my shoulder and said:

> 'Don't worry, really he is just a floppy....'
>
> 'What's a floppy?' I asked.
>
> 'Ah! A floppy is the way a black looks when you fill them full of the magazine, they just flop around as the bullets hit them....'
>
> 'What ...?'
>
> 'Yea, mate, a floppy ...floppies are what we turn them into. I've done a few, and don't worry.... Once you get a taste for turning them into floppies you'll fucking love it.'

I stood still, not reacting, and, taking that as acquiescence, he moved off.

And that, in that existential moment, I did not know what to do – that I did not find eloquent words to cut him down, that I did not raise a fist and punch him – haunts me still.

Visualising the 'crimes of war' in the nomos of the world

So I listened. I was subject to a recounting in which blacks were turned into floppies and it was assumed that I was an appreciative audience. A learned mode of behaviour in 'covert operations' in Angola was transferred into a space that the narrator assumed was still his, still a product of the regimes of power that gave him a technology of transformation (a machine gun) and a freedom from accountability. He assumed I shared his world view; my feeling of guilt for my (shocked) silence a later realisation that one does not need to actively share or be a participant, but that the acquiescence of passivity also upholds those regimes of power.

For war to be waged 'subjects' must be willing to acquiesce. In war some must be willing to die, or at least to kill, while others, perhaps far more numerous, support or remain silent. Both groups inhabit normative frameworks that constitute them in opposition to others seen as the 'enemy' in a mutual conflict, a presumptive antagonism. It is helpful that the other is put at a moral distance and (legitimate) authority reassures that it is vital to a cause that the other is not treated as morally equivalent to oneself and that violence done to the other is justified.

In retrospect it is not difficult to reconstruct the nomos that my father inhabited and in slightly changed form I inherited. Schmitt ([1950] 2006) provides a magisterial account of the development of a Eurocentric global order, constituted in the discovery and colonialisation of the New World, at its peak in the late nineteenth century and undercut in the world wars of the twentieth century. European power created the first truly global order of international law, opening the world to trade through maritime power, contracts and the device of the Company (as in the East India Company that allowed British domination in the Indian subcontinent). The New World first appeared 'as free space, as an area open to European occupation and expansion'; the seizure of land is the first move to establish a new nomos, but the process of expanding into and occupying these spaces led to internal political struggle within Europe that eventually balanced naval power that could control the sea (British navy) and contrasting power that controlled land. Europe could become ordered but outside was a rather anomic other/new world. Order and anomie coexist or, rather, the prospect of anomie resurfacing is the threat that energises the political acts that structure space. In Schmitt's view, following Hobbes, the Leviathan, or the powerful European sovereign state not answerable to normative constraints other than those founded on its existence (the self-sufficiency of sovereignty), was the greatest achievement of Occidental rationalism; in becoming the principal agency of secularisation, the European state created the modern age.

Notable in Schmitt's discussion of the rise and decline of the European epoch of world history is the role played by the New World, which he sees as ultimately replacing the Old World as the centre of the Earth and becoming the arbiter in European and world politics. According to Schmitt, the United States's internal conflicts between economic presence and political absence, between isolationism and interventionism, are global problems which continued, at least in 1950, to hamper the creation of a new world order. But however critical Schmitt is of American actions at the turn of the twentieth century and after World

War I, by 1950 he considered the United States to be the only political entity capable of resolving the crisis of global order.

Writing in 2014 – against a background of an ever increasing despair at the consequences of the 'war on terror', the 2003 invasion of Iraqi and subsequent attempts by the United States and others to 'spread democracy', which generally appears an abject failure other than in generating a rise in Islamic militancy – Schmitt's concept of nomos gains greater relevancy. As Schmitt relates, in the creation of the contemporary, what the European powers would recognise as legitimate outside of Europe was what served their purposes: the wars of the other, wars of resistance, were not truly wars but terrorist resistance (and it is noted that in the exchange above the South African military forces in Angola were essentially fighting a colonial war, white masters against recalcitrant blacks). What happened in the colonies stayed there: war was, or should have been, inconceivable in Europe. This, in Schmitt's view, was unhinged when Belgium took over responsibility of the Congo Free State given to King Leopold of Belgium by the Berlin Treaty of 1885 in 1908, not on the basis that they took over the responsibilities of the Treaty, but merely the right of effective occupation. This reopened the nomos to the power of occupation; a new form of war was inevitable and it would now be global. As Schmitt declares: 'the transition to a new, no longer Eurocentric world order began from Asia with the inclusion of an East Asian Great Power [Japan]' (2006: 191).The Pacific war ended the British Empire, although in New Zealand, unlike India and Southeast Asia, that took time to be realised. The racist depiction of the Japanese, essential to fuel that war, contributed to a drastic underestimation of Japan's power and, certainly in the first year of that war, meant that the United States and United Kingdom (along with allies/current and ex-colonies) were substantially behind. We now know of the power of ideology and structured vision in shaping the existential form of that war (see Dower 1986). Japan's enormous effort (it would suffer some 2.5 million casualties, but inflict substantially more on its targets, in particular some 15 million on China) was maintained by a substantial control over domestic opinion, a control that has continued in only weakened form since. This is exemplified by the almost total lack of subsequent review of activities such as Unit 731's medical experiments (the concealment of the Japanese experiments, more widespread than the Nazis', is in large part due to the fact that US officials wanted to take the results). In my upbringing knowledge of World War II was often obtained through comics (and not of the quality of Art Spiegelman's *Maus: A Survivor's Tale*); I had a vague understanding of Hiroshima but none of Auschwitz. The message of Bruno Bettelheim, now common to our understanding of modernity, was to be read in my European future:

> In World War II Auschwitz and Hiroshima showed that progress through technology has escalated man's destructive impulses into more precise and incredibly more devastating form.... Progress not only failed to preserve life, but it deprived millions of their lives more effectively than had been possible ever before. (Bettelheim 1979: 21)

The nomos my father existed in and in changed form I grew up in gave relatively few possibilities for radical reflexivity. That 'should', in most of the world, be no longer possible: whether we think of it in quasi-romantic terms of a human cosmopolitanism or a relentless spread of a market that devours and spits out all in its path, globalisation is now our context. This has many consequences: certainly globalisation means that the pursuit of social justice is no longer a question internal to the Westphalia nation state but global. The proliferation of high technology, an increase in scholarship, knowledge creation and dissemination, mass communication, the digitalisation of archives, destroys regimes of common sense and reveals the world as it has never been seen before; complicating, confusing, turning common sense (i.e., local ways of thinking) into cascades of relativity. Information and images become open, transferable (the thumb-drive memory stick makes Wikileaks possible and inevitable), developing awareness, and thus constitutes a new world (Nancy 2007) and makes feeling at home a huge challenge: never before has so much been written, so much made visible, and yet so many people feel impotent and state-authority-diminished. Are we on the verge of breaking the grip of modernity – with its cult of the nexus of sovereignty and power elites and the clear demarcation of political organisation from religious belief – or is modernity collapsing upon us?

Visualising the harms of war in the contemporary nomos

Since the early 1980s I have lived in London, capital of the United Kingdom. For a great deal of this time I have fought my private battles aimed, perhaps, at overcoming the lack of reflexivity inherent in the nomos I grew up in. 'Develop a global consciousness', may be a nicely phrased mantra, but joined with a modicum of reflexivity, also a dispiriting one. In the empiricist ethical tradition of Adam Smith and David Hume our common sociality is dependent upon 'sympathy'. Sympathy is a fellow feeling plus (dis)approbation; it is not enough simply to observe and be affected by emotion, nor to communicate that affect; to sympathise with means to align with an estimation of right and wrong. But how to achieve this is the problematic of a post-modern global ethics. Certainly we are now open to being at least quasi global spectators assailed by images of forms of 'war', pain and suffering. Yet how do we move beyond their 'affects' into an ethical consideration of a progressive political and intellectual stance? Consider images provided by Shaam News Network on Thursday, 22 August 2013, that show dead bodies after an attack on Ghouta, Syria on Wednesday, 21 August 2013. The report relays that the early-morning barrage against rebel-held areas around the Syrian capital, Damascus, immediately seemed different: the rockets made a strange, whistling noise. Seconds after one hit near his home, Qusai Zakarya says he couldn't breathe, and he desperately punched himself in the chest to get air. Hundreds of suffocating, twitching victims flooded into hospitals. Others were later found dead in their homes, towels still on their faces from their last moments trying to protect themselves from gas. Doctors and survivors recount scenes of horror from the alleged chemical attack a week ago. (AP Photo/Shaam News Network, File) (AP/Shaam News Network; CBS News, 30 August 2013, 4:50 p.m. Syria chemical weapons attack blamed on Assad, but where's the evidence?)

These images occasioned calls for intervention by the United States and others. In the United Kingdom, Parliament refused to back the Prime Minister's motion which would have lead to air strikes and military action against the Assad Government. Consequently no direct military action was taken but increased military aid to the groups fighting the Assad government. Fast forward to August 2014 where one of the groups fighting Assad, ISIS, a radical Islamic militant group now number 70,000 plus and controls a significant section of Syria and Iraq. The images now are of the suffering of the Catholic Yazidi sect, with reports claiming hundreds, if not thousands, massacred for refusing to convert to Islam (for example 'Mount Sinjar: Iraq's mountain of death', *Telegraph*, Wednesday, 13 August 2014). Social media sites show systematic executions reminiscent of the destruction of the Jews in occupied Eastern Europe in 1941. A number of responses occur. One is to note complicity, that the invasion of Iraq in 2003 has fuelled sectarian militancy and brought extremely violent chaos. Another is a form of resignation: to accept that Sontag was right when she said 'Look ...this is what it's like.... This is what war does. And that, that is what it does too. War tears, rends. War rips open, eviscerates. War scorches. War dismembers. War ruins.' (Sontag 2003: 8). But this is accompanied by a feeling of powerlessness and, for many, helplessness countered by an urge to go shopping (as a friend communicated to me). What intellectually, as criminologists, can we make of this? My brief reading that follows prioritises Hobbes as the foundational framer for modernity. Hobbes continues to structure the frame; Judith Butler (2004, 2010), for example, draws a distinction between grievable and ungrievable populations and the constitution of 'the sovereign subject' that directly re-presents Hobbes.

Constituting the frame: the legacy of Hobbes's *Leviathan*

Criminology has always been a particularly visual 'science'. This has been a constrained visuality which can be traced back to the frontispiece of Hobbes's *Leviathan* (1651), where the sovereign, the representative (and representation) of the people, he who determines the distinction between 'crimes' as acts internal to the protected territory of the sovereign, and 'war' as the acts of the sovereign directed towards external 'enemies', gazes outwards, while the subjects gaze inwards. The concerns of the sovereign-subjects (the public) are with personal and group security, 'law and order', and with the pursuit of material goods (what Hobbes calls felicity), and crime is what our representative the sovereign (the state) calls it. War is waged to protect the internal 'we' from external threats, or, in the case of the colonial encounter, to subdue the native other so that trade and civilised modes of life may be extended globally. The 'peace' of a civilised world is the end, the telos, and that telos is written through the inscription of Western (military) power and the subjects' conformity.

The basic concept for Hobbes is the threat to life of all in the natural condition which is remedied by the giving up of natural rights to a 'sovereign', a mortal God, and this common power overawes enemies. The sovereign-subject is thus protected by the power. While commentators rightly point to the use Hobbes makes of the notion of the natural condition of mankind as a state of war (warre) of every man, against every man, and the epistemic control Hobbes gives to the sovereign, the dialectics of the visibility of actual harms of war is not commented upon. Hobbes's state of nature was no hypothetical device but a reflection of the wars of Europe brought out so clearly in Callot's 'The Miseries and Misfortunes of War', usually claimed as the first 'anti-war art' (Brandon 2007: 26, although Brandon oversimplifies neglecting, for example, the anti war nature of Durer's Four Horsemen of the Apocalypse). The frontispiece of *Leviathan* was engraved by the Frenchman Abraham Bosse in cooperation with Hobbes; Bosse had met Callot in Paris in 1630 and was deeply influenced and declared he would take Callot's techniques to a new level.

My claim is that Hobbes's frontispiece is a direct response to the making visible of the horrors of war and a technique for subduing their effect. The atrocities involved in the Spanish conquest of the Americas was brought home in the writing of Bartolomé de Las Casas and then turned into pictorial representations in the etchings of Theodore De Bry that accompanied the English translations of Las Casas.[1] They spawned an almost pornographic concern in the horrors of, particularly, Spanish soldiers against Protestant areas of Europe. But etchings, such as of the capture of Brill (1572) and the conquest of Oudewate (1575), where most of the inhabitants were massacred, along with the occasional oil of Spanish attacks on Flemish towns and villages, were occasional and not part of any coherent narrative positioning. This changed with the extraordinary set of etchings by Jacques Callot in 1633. Europe at the time was ravaged by the Eighty Years' War and the Thirty Years' War,, Catholic against Protestant and Protestant against Protestant. Callot's 'Miseries' are not propaganda, nor is there any obvious emotive condemnation (Goya's *The Disasters of War*, 1810–1812, is different); we have prints characterised by clear daylight, wide-angle perspective, meticulous drawing, and figures who display little emotion. But there is certainly a narrative: abuses of power. The title – 'Miseries and Misfortunes of War' – would be enough, but we have a story, very unheroic, from the enrolment of men as mercenaries in a war in which they did not believe or need to believe in any cause for, to a scene of battle and then pillage (sackings of villages and towns were rewards for poorly paid soldiers) and onwards in a story line of lack of discipline and distorted processes that result in men perpetrating all kinds of depravities. Lacking any bias, Callot's '*Misères*' indicate no specific conflict, site, army or politics (Wolfthal 1977: 224). As a result, they are open to explore humanistic concerns regarding the value of the individual as they show complete destruction applying to both sides of the war, but the message is clear: all are precarious.

For Hobbes the state solves the issue of precariousness through a reordering of space around the figure of the sovereign. The territory is civilised, and in putting legitimate violence in the hands of the sovereign, violent opposition to society is off limits: war on society (civil war) is criminalised, interstate war is legalised, or, more aptly, it will be subject to the growth of customs. This works on the basis of a boundary that includes and excludes; this is still with us and lacking an idea of itself as a society, wars against international society remained inconceivable.

The vision of Nuremberg

The German colonial genocide in what is now Namibia followed the nomos of Hobbesian Westphalian sovereignty, that is, it aroused some concern elsewhere but was not subject to any form of sanction. Post-World War I the German state was deemed virtually a criminal state and subjected to a punitive treaty (namely, Versailles in 1919). Anger at the terms of the treaty and the dysfunction of the Weimar Republic enabled the Nazi party to come to power. The Nazi state, seeking Lebensraum (living space for expansion) but prevented from overseas colonies, turned eastward. Obeying the injunction of sovereignty, Hitler launched a campaign of 'social hygiene' and racial engineering in order to biologically reorder Europe (and then the world). We now see the Holocaust at the centre of Nazi 'crimes' and Omer Bartov reminds us that

> our main difficulty in confronting the Holocaust is due not only to the immense scale of the killing, nor even to the manner in which it was carried out, but also to the way in which it combined the most primitive human brutality, hatred and prejudice, with the most modern achievements in science, technology, organisation, and administration. It is not the brutal SS man with his truncheon whom we cannot comprehend; we have seen his likes throughout history. It is the commander of a killing squad with a Ph.D. in law from a distinguished university in charge of organising mass shootings of naked women and children whose figure frightens us. It is not the disease and famine in the ghettos, reminiscent perhaps of ancient sieges, but the systematic transportation, selection, dispossession, killing, and distribution of requisitioned personal effects that leaves us uncomprehending, not for the facts but their implications for our own society and for human psychology. Not only the 'scientific' killing and its bureaucratic administration; not only the sadism; but rather the incredible mixture of detachment and brutality, distance and cruelty, pleasure and indifference. (Bartov 1996: 67)

But this complexity is a later view and still not widely shared. There is a myth about the Nazi era that prevents us from visualising the complexity of the crimes involved. The myth is that Nuremberg (and in particular the trial of the Justices) put lawlessness on trial; that at Nuremberg a new path for war crimes was forged when the major war criminals were put in trial, that individual responsibility flowed from the fact that a group of international brigands (essentially pirates) had seized the reins of power in an otherwise advanced Western state and through terror coerced an otherwise blameless population into following orders and committing mass atrocities in breach of the laws of land warfare and of the sea.² To reinforce this narrative a particular act of rendering the invisible visible was undertaken. Early in the trial a film, *Nazi Concentration Camps*, with searing images of the horrors that the camp liberators found, was shown. Here was a set of images that exposed events that seemed almost beyond the concept of 'crime', turning the viewer into shocked silence. Several days later another film, *The Nazi Plan*, purported to show a general conspiracy by the leader to wage aggressive war (see Hartouni 2012, for the best treatment of visualising atrocity at Nuremberg and at the trial of Eichmann). But were the men in the dock really the causal agents? The tactics of making visible brought forth human subjects but rendered invisible the whole supporting structure (which included, we may note, the scientific edifice that criminology was constitute within [Morrison 2006]). But this could not be shown, for this was not simple victor's justice but a tribunal called on behalf of 'civilisation' itself (as Justice Jackson put it in his opening address) and that meant a widening, but not discarding, of the included/excluded division of Hobbes. Civilisation could not put civilisation on trial.

Some of us today see the Holocaust as the culmination of many factors of modernity (see, for example, Bauman 1989; Fraser 2005). Beyond the men tried, for example, two professions made the Holocaust: the lawyer and the doctor. They were essential to construct a system of legalised barbarism; they worked with forms to legitimate the medical killings, to define the Jew, and a scientific gaze that calmly surveyed the materials for the eugenic reorganisation of history. The euthanasia of the mentally ill and physically handicapped worked on lives deemed unworthy (scientifically) of life, then the Jews, the subhuman criminals, were brought within a modern anti-Semitism that is distinguished from traditional anti-Semitism by its combination of biological and legal definitions. As a political system National Socialism worked on the foundation of the legal machinery of the state and when it went beyond their jurisprudence, new forms of the Fuhrer principle and of a system founded on a homogenous Volk, the doctors sanctioned murder and the lawyers legalised killings, which in turn required other lawyers and victors' courts to turn into 'crime'. Crimes that took place in a special place outside of normal operation: the 'foundational' genocide for the contemporary was positioned in an interpretive frame that shows it always happens 'elsewhere', 'outside international pacts, systems and rules of law rather than as an effect of them' (Hartouni 2012: 124).

'Unwatchable: Is your phone rape free?': trying to break the boundaries (September 2011)

The film is short, just over six minutes. It starts as if in a dream world of civilised space: a beautiful young blond girl is picking flowers in the grounds of a stunning English country house; inside her beautiful (also blond) mother is washing dishes; her older sister (a blond teenager) walks inside talking on her mobile telephone; outside her father is washing the car. A large helicopter comes into view in the clear blue sky; the girl looks up and waves, welcomingly, but as the helicopter comes down to land flares are thrown, the glasses in the house start to shake, the mother looks out the window wondering what is happening. The father backs away as disembarked soldiers rush forward, one violently clubbing him with a rifle butt. Next are four horrific minutes: the teenage daughter is raped on the table with the mother forced to watch; the father, having been dragged inside to watch and be beaten, is now dragged outside, shot dead and has his penis cut off and pushed into the mother's mouth; she is left alive prostrate over her husband's corpse while the young girl flees (hopefully to safety) but as the film fades we see other soldiers are in her path across the trees.

Unwatchable is a viral video made on behalf of the Save the Congo NGO and released in September 2011.[3] It aims to arouse, to cut through polite rational discourse and shock Western consumers into ethical accountability in the trade in conflict minerals and, the makers argue, the mass rapes and extreme brutality it fuels. We are asked to transpose ourselves as viewers, to be witnesses, to see in this representation of horror and bestiality brought on the beautiful (our beautiful) and to feel, to experience angst, hurt and frustration while we understand that this is an attack on a family by militiamen, an all-too-common occurrence in eastern Congo. We are asked to break the boundaries of civilised space and recognise ourselves in the frame. The makers explained that *Unwatchable* was 'not as shocking as the truth', then asked us to imagine 'that this is not an isolated case of some out of control soldiers drugged out of their minds. This is part of systematic raping.... This is driven by the trade in "blood" minerals that end up in our mobile phones.' But why show a white middle-class family in England 'being destroyed'? Their response is that we have received so many images of atrocity that they do not affect us anymore. 'So to locate the film in England poses the question – if we find this so unacceptable that this would happen here, we should also find it unacceptable it being perpetrated "over there".' It is simple. ('Why we made this', at www.unwatachable.cc/the-true-story/why-we-made-this/, accessed 11 October 2011.)

So the real – the actual story of the human victims in the eastern Congo – no longer holds us, instead it is the unreal, the simulation, that is called into action. We are 'Africa'd out', reality is a hierarchy of victimhood. As with the civilian deaths in the Iraq and Afghan campaigns, or the thousands still living in a reduced human state in the Palestinian refugee camps, human vulnerability occupies a social geography.

Reactions to images of atrocity have become almost overdetermined. Consider the reception of the publication by the Rolling Stones Magazine of the photos made by the so-called 'Kill Team'. One stands out: it expresses how upset the blog poster was 'that *Rolling Stone* published this article in its magazine without so much as a warning about the graphic content that was about to be displayed'. But for me the key complaint of the poster was the question: what would have been the impact if a child had picked up the copy of the magazine 'after seeing their favourite Pop star on the front cover, then opening up the page to see all this horrible mutilation and brutality. I understand that these images are real-life situations, but I don't think the general public who wanted to read an article about musicians or actors should have been subjected immediately to it because they wanted to leaf through these pages.' (Blog comment posted 12 April 2011 on the decision by *Rolling Stone* magazine to publish an article on 'The Kill Team' alongside images and videos that the soldiers had made. This related how a group of US soldiers in Afghanistan decided to kill a number of innocent Afghani civilians for their own fun and record the events on camera. (accessible at http://www.rollingstone.com/politics/news/the-kill-team-20110327). So the defence of the right to go about the everyday and not know: in 1809 Charles Bell made his first acquaintance with the suffering of war going to Portsmouth to attend to the wounded (and with his real motive to gather examples of injuries for his lectures); in a letter of 3 February he relates that he should have written giving his first 'sensations' on seeing the wounded which he hoped were 'as any good man should feel', but these have been 'blunted by repetition' and he feels guilt at 'being what I am – so mere a creature like the rest, going about my common affairs'(Bell 1870: 139).

Another contrasting account is produced by a professional photographer, showing an American soldier photographing a dead body of an Iraqi clearly killed by a head shot from the amount of blood that has seeped on the ground around the head. The photo credit is Ashley Gilbertson, Iraq, who gives the following explanation: 'American soldiers rarely get a chance to study a dead Mahdi Army fighter. The insurgents usually duck in and out of soldiers' lines of sight. The soldiers are curious to see the human face of their enemy, especially when they're dead. In accordance with army policy, dead are left on the street for Iraqis to recover and bury. "They clean up their own," said one soldier.' The image was displayed in the Brighton Photo Biennial 2008, *Iraq through the Lens of Vietnam, Memory of Fire – The War of Images and Images of War*. On the Flickr pages were the following blog comments: 1. *** says: I want to vomit – the man on the ground he could be my friend. 2. Powerful, tense, imagery, *** says: I love this pic!! I wish all those bastard insurgents would die sooner!! 3. *** says: Hi, I'm an admin for a group ... and we'd love to have this added to the group!

They clean up their own. ... US soldiers in the post-invasion period were aliens in the traditional sense: 'an alien could enter the radius of physical proximity only in one of three capacities: either as an enemy to be fought and expelled, or as an admittedly temporary guest to be confined to special quarters and rendered harmless by strict observance of the isolating ritual, or as a neighbour-to-be, in which case he had to be made like a neighbour, that is to behave like the neighbours do' (Bauman 1993: 150). The invasion of Iraq was justified in part by the imposition of distance: for US President Bush Iraq 'was the central front in the war on terror' and it was better to fight them over there than at home; if the United States pulled out 'terrorists will follow us here'. Pace Bauman, in part this allows an abrogation of the moral status and responsibility of human subjectivity: 'responsibility is silenced once proximity is eroded; it may eventually be replaced with resentment once the fellow human subject is transformed into an "other"' (Bauman 1989: 184). Bush's (pace Hobbes, pace Schmitt) sovereign invocation of the power to define (this is a 'war on terror', not a campaign to deal with a form of crime) and invoke distance, of boundaries as a defence, is doomed to tragic consequences.

Conclusion: where to ground ethical responsibility in a new nomos

> A lie is a lie. Just because they write it down and call it history doesn't make it the truth. We live in a world where seeing is not believing; when only a few know what really happened. We live in a world where everything you know ... is wrong.
>
> ... You will move without boundaries; you will act above the Law; you will use whatever means are necessary to stop the wars that are hidden from the world; and if you succeed, you will do so without recognition. Because you do not exist.

(Voiceover to *Call of Duty Black Ops*, full uncut trailer, by Treyarch, Activision, released for US and Europe sales on 9 November 2010; trailer viewed by 5,631,375 on YouTube as of 10 November 2010)

> Sick glorification of war in a way that it is not even fought. Fucken sick, just like the phychopathic society that glorifies it. (Chexxxx)
>
> Hey shut up fuckass [response to above] just play. (doxxxx)
>
> This is not only a game, they have political ideologies, the game is repugnant but the graphics are so cool. (elmxxxx)
>
> This is fucking fun as hell. (jusxxxx) (Selection from comments trail to *Call of Duty Blacks Ops*, YouTube, accessed 10 November 2010; identities amended)

Judith Butler (2010: introduction) calls upon us to avoid being 'conscripted [as supporters] into the trajectory of the bullet or missile', and instead 'to apprehend the precarious conditions of life as imposing an ethical obligation on us' to 'refuse the target as frame ...and to insist on an ethical connection to the populations being "depicted" in this way'. In a similar fashion, Tarik Kochi (2009) implies that legal judgement, even in the new order, exists in a dialectic of political and legal violence. The vision of war crimes that new tribunals work with is pre-structured by political power. Subjects change: if war between sovereign states tends to reduce, asymmetrical wars involving 'partisans' (often manipulated and for causes they falsely comprehend) has increased. Such partisans are refusing the ordered nomos of the past; our responses risk inflaming and creating even more opponents. Kochi advises our judgements need to be guided by an effort to recognise the ethics of the other's position and demands. I would endorse such inter-subjectivity; what other path is there that offers any hope for reducing the horrors of war in a globalised world where the divisions that Hobbes helped create continue? My final question concerns, however, the position in a changing nomos in which this might take place.

Am I being realistic or pessimistic when I note that Butler's text was not a big seller; currently listed at number 486,706 on the Barnes & Noble list; on amazon.com she fared slightly better at number 271,660 (18 March 2014). So how are the public in the civilised space of the West engaging with the ethics of war? *Modern Warfare: Call of Duty* series, launched in 2003, has sold over 120 million copies. *Call of Duty: Black Ops II* was released on November 2012. More than 2.5 million people queued at 16,000 shops in the United States and United Kingdom alone, with 7.5 million copies sold on launch day. It was the fourth year in a row that the *Call of Duty/Modern Warfare* series had broken the sales record for video/computer games (an estimated 40 million people worldwide are playing the game at any one time!).

As globalisation intensifies, space changes, the world of cyberspace opens up. What effect does this have on nomos? Computer or video games have broken through a barrier and become immersive. In *Call of Duty: Black Ops*, a first person shooter – you – becomes the main character; you cannot but invest something of yourself in the game. 'So you have this experience of all this is happening to you ... when you are playing the game you feel like you are in that world, you feel like you are on those black ops missions, like you are in the midst of all this danger and mayhem' (writer David Goyer, advisor to production of *Black Ops*, interviewed, Snider 2010).

The technology of war is increasingly robotic; the human element moved to a control room while actual soldiers play shooter games such as *Modern Warfare* and *Call of Duty*. Many worry about the effect on 'real' war.[4] For Hall, referring more generally to film and TV, 'combat related entertainment is a major thoroughfare for the transmission of the ideology of militarised imperialism into the bodies and emotions of individual subjects, training citizens in what the power of the nation should feel like in their bodies' (Hall 2007: 99). In neo-Hobbesian terms she suggests that those who consume war entertainment are trained to expect that any harm done to the United States or its interests 'will be answered with swift and awesome force against any and all perceived as the enemy'. The distance at which US consumers learn to experience war 'trains them to watch that others do the dirty work of killing'. I am not so sure, but certainly this needs empirical research. There is a wide range of media and the triumphant and vengeful movies can, in part, be countered by the more thoughtful presentations of *Taxi to the Dark Side* or *Why We Wage War*. I draw everyone and anyone's attention to *The Act of Killing* (2013), but cannot understand why it did not get the Academy Award for best documentary. However, for all the changes, some things are (un)reassuringly similar: the opening sequence of *Call of Duty: Black Ops II* was a (one-sided) battle where the player guns down fleeing Black African 'rebels', only this time they not so much 'flopped about' as disintegrated. Thankfully, this did not go without criticism.

Notes

1. Bartolome de Las Casas, educated at the University of Salamanca, sailed for Hispaniola in 1502. At first he participated in the colonial practices of the

conquest but sickened of the treatment of the natives and campaigned for rights for them. He became a Dominican priest, devoting himself to alleviating the sufferings of the Indians. In 1542 he was made bishop of Chiapas, and in 1549 he returned to Spain.In 1552 Las Casas published a short treatise, *Brevissima Relacion de la Destruycion de las Indias*, indicting the Spanish conquerors for their cruelties to the Indians. Originally printed in Madrid, it was quickly translated into several languages. The first of nine tracts on this subject, the work was seen by Europeans as a horrible example of Spanish colonial policy and Catholicism at work. The engraver De Bry provided horrific illustrations for his 1598 Latin edition. Subsequently it was republished throughout the seventeenth century under various titles, such as 'Tears of the Indians' or 'Popery', proof of the evil of the Catholic Spanish.

2. In his report to the US President, Justice Jackson set out the assumptions underlying the plan to prosecute: in Durkheimean terms these lay in explaining what had offended the sense of justice of the American and other civilised peoples. 'They came to view the Nazis as a band of brigands, set on subverting within Germany every vestige of a rule of law which would entitle an aggregation of people to be looked upon collectively as a member of the family of nations. ... Once these international brigands, the top leaders of the Nazi party, the S.S., and the Gestapo, had firmly established themselves within Germany by terrorism and crime, they immediately set out on a course of international pillage. ... They flagrantly violated the obligations which states, including their own, have undertaken by convention or tradition as a part of the rules of land warfare, and of the law of the sea.'

3. *Unwatchable: Is your phone rape free?* At http://www.unwatchable.cc/.

4. 'Equally discomfiting is the "PlayStation mentality" that surrounds drone killings. Young military personnel raised on a diet of video games now kill real people remotely using joysticks. Far removed from the human consequences of their actions, how will this generation of fighters value the right to life? How will commanders and policymakers keep themselves immune from the deceptively antiseptic nature of drone killings? Will killing be a more attractive option than capture? Will the standards for intelligence-gathering to justify a killing slip? Will the number of acceptable "collateral" civilian deaths increase?' ('A killer above the law?', Philip Alston and Hina Shamsi, Guardian.co.uk. 2 August 2010)

References

Bartov, O. (1996) *Murder in Our Midst: The Holocaust, Industrial Killing, and Representation*. Oxford: Oxford University Press.
Bauman, Z. (1989) *Modernity and the Holocaust*. Cambridge: Polity Press.
—— (1993) *Postmodern Ethics*. Oxford: Blackwell.
Bell, C. (1870) *Letters*, selected by George J. Bell. London: John Murray.
Bettelheim, B. (1979) *Surviving the Holocaust and Other Essays*. New York: Knopf.
Branden, L. (2007) *Art and War*. London and New York: I.B. Taurus.
Butler, J. (2004) *Precarious Life: The Powers of Mourning and Violence*. London and New York: Verso.
—— (2009/2010) *Frames of War: When is Life Grievable?* London and New York: Verso.

Dempsey, G. (2008) *Albuera 1811: The Bloodiest Battle of the Peninsular War*. Barnsley: Frontline Books.
Dower, J.W. (1986) *War Without Mercy: Race and Power in the Pacific War*. New York: Pantheon Books.
Fraser, D. (2005) *Law after Auschwitz*. Durham, NC: Carolina Academic Press.
Geary, A., Morrison, W. and Jago, R. (2013) *The Politics of the Common Law*. Milton Park, Oxon: Routledge.
Greg, W.R. (1844) 'Review of Alison's *History of Europe*', *The Westminster Review*, 41–42, available online as a Google ebook.
Hall, K. (2007) 'False Witness: Combat Entertainment and Citizen Training in the US', in F. Guerin and R. Hallas (eds), *The Image and the Witness: Trauma, Memory and Visual Culture*. London: Wallflower Press.
Hartouni, V. (2012) *Visualising Atrocity: Arendt, Evil, and the Optics of Thoughtlessness*. New York and London: New York University Press.
Hemingway, E. (1946) 'Introduction' to *Treasury for the Free World*. New York: Ben Raeburn.
Kochi, T. (2009) *The Other's War: Recognition and the Violence of Ethics*. Oxford: The Birkbeck Law Press.
Meron, T. (1998) *War Crimes Law Comes of Age*. Oxford: Clarendon Press.
Morrison, W. (2006) *Criminology, Civilization and the New World Order*. Abingdon, Oxon: Routledge-Cavendish.
Nancy, J.-L. (2007) *The Creation of the World or Globalization*. Albany: State University of New York Press.
Schmitt, C. (2006) *The Nomos of the Earth in the International Law of Jus Publicum Europaeum*. Candor. NY: Telos Press Publishing.
Sherer, M. (1824) *Recollections of the Peninsula*. London: Longman, Hurst, Rees, Orme, and Brown.
Sontag, S. (2003) *Regarding the Pain of Others*. New York: Farrar, Straus and Giroux.
Snider, M. (2010) 'Q&A: Screenwriter David Goyer on "Call of Duty: Black Ops"', *USA Today*, November 26.
Wolfthal, D. (1977) 'Jacques Callot's *Miseries of War*', *Art Bulletin*, 59.

11
Health and Safety 'Crimes' in Britain: The Great Disappearing Act

Steve Tombs

Introduction

This chapter provides an (empirically informed) reminder of the fact that for politicians, the media, the wider public and, indeed, some academics, some crimes are less visible than others. Moreover, as will be demonstrated, this relative lack of visibility is not static, but dynamic, while at the same time it is always subject to contest and struggle.

The focus here is on the regulation and enforcement of occupational health and safety in workplaces in the United Kingdom,[1] with a particular emphasis upon developments since the turn of the century. The chapter sets out the wider policy context for these considerations before turning to its central task: a presentation of various forms of data relating to trends in enforcement over the first decade of this millennium. It then examines the extent to which such trends are likely to continue or indeed be intensified under the Coalition Government. Finally, the chapter will note what appears to be a development that sits in tension with the general picture of decriminalisation which this chapter will paint: namely, the introduction in 2008 of a new criminal offence of corporate manslaughter. Prior to these tasks, it is worth turning to a brief consideration of the scale of the problem of 'health and safety'.

Occupational death and injury as a social problem

The scale of health and safety harms associated with British workplaces is significant, although, as with much corporate harm, relatively obscured. Indeed, in obscuring the scale of this social – and, potentially, crime – problem, the main national regulator in this sphere, the Health and Safety Executive, plays a crucial role; as we shall see, through its approaches to enforcement, investigation, and use of formal sanctions, not least prosecution, it acts as a key filter through which harm is separated from potential or actual crime. Indeed, this institutional framing of the problem of health and safety at work – one in which the 'problem' is consistently minimised – takes place even in its recording and presentation of officially collected data.

Thus, each year the Health and Safety Executive (HSE) releases a statistical bulletin that is press-released with a figure for work fatalities; the most recent such release stated that provisional data for April 2012 to March 2013 (2012/2013) shows '148 workers fatally injured – down from 171 the previous year' (Health and Safety Executive 2013a). But this 'headline' figure is highly misleading. It excludes deaths of members of the public which are recorded by HSE, and included in their detailed statistical bulletin; in 2012/2013 there were 423 deaths to members of the public recorded by HSE (Health and Safety Executive 2013c: 4). But even this augmented figure, including members of the public, reflects a fraction of occupational deaths caused by fatal injury: the annual total is some five to seven times greater than the 'headline', so that the actual figure is likely to be somewhere between 1,300–1,400 fatal occupational injuries per annum, albeit that many of these are recorded by government bodies other than HSE (Tombs and Whyte 2008).

If occupational fatality data, then, is problematic, it is at least in principle amenable to reconstruction. Much more difficult is any effort adequately to capture the toll of death as a result of occupational illness. The HSE does not report an annual figure for such deaths, but its latest (2013) statement notes that 'There are currently around 13,000 deaths each year from work-related diseases' (Health and Safety Executive 2013b: 5). Again, this is an underestimate. For example, Hämäläinen et al. (2009: 137) calculate almost 21,000 deaths per annum in the United Kingdom from work-related fatal diseases, while accepting both that such data 'might still be an under-estimation' and that work-related diseases are 'increasing' (Hämäläinen et al. 2009: 132). O'Neill et al. (2007) produce a UK estimate of up to 40,000 annual deaths caused by work-related cancers alone. And long-term research by the Hazards movement, drawing upon a range of estimates derived from studies (some commissioned by HSE) of occupational and environmental cancers, the percentages of heart-disease deaths which have a work-related cause, as well as percentage estimates of other diseases to which work can be a contributory cause, produces a lower-end estimate of up to 50,000 deaths from work-related illness in the United Kingdom each year, or more than four times the HSE estimate (Palmer 2008). This annual total ranks high in comparison with virtually all other recorded causes of premature death in the United Kingdom (Rogers 2011).

Unfortunately, and despite the employer's legal duty to report injuries, each category of *non*-fatal injury data is subject to significant under-reporting, a point to which we return below. Knowledge of this had prompted, since 1990, the collection of self-report data as part of the Labour Force Survey (LFS). The most recent LFS injury data records 212,000 injuries leading to at least three days' absence from work (Health and Safety Executive 2012b: 1), with about a quarter of these requiring more than seven days' absence (Health and Safety Executive 2012b: 9). Labour Force Surveys also collate occupational health data, and again this indicates levels of illness far in excess of those officially recorded; in 2011/2012, there were 1.1 million people 'suffering from an illness (long-standing as well as new cases) they believed was caused or made worse by their current or past work' as well as a further 0.7 million 'former workers (who last worked over 12 months ago)...suffering from' such an illness (Health and Safety Executive 2012b: 1). Thus, in 2011/2012, there were 22.7 million days lost due to work-related ill health and a further 4.3 million lost due to workplace injury. Such levels of work-caused absenteeism carry with them significant economic costs: as HSE has estimated, 'Workplace injuries and ill health (excluding cancer) cost society an estimated £13.4 billion in 2010/11' (Health and Safety Executive 2012b: 1).

So, we can conclude both that the scale of death, injury and illness is virtually impossible to quantify, but also that it is a significant social problem. Yet understanding the proportion of these which are attributable to violations of law on the part of employers – that is, those which we might legitimately term health and safety *crimes* – is an even more difficult task. In general this is a product of the fact that crime is a function of those acts to which the state responds and processes through a legal system, – of which, more below. For now, however, what we can say is that there is good evidence to believe that – at least in the context of workplace *fatalities* – there is a criminal case to answer in up to two-thirds of these (Tombs and Whyte 2007: 103–105). On this basis, however sketchy and provisional, many workplaces might be considered crime scenes – albeit unlikely ever to feature in any TV drama where investigating police officers and forensic scientists scour for evidence.

Some wider contexts

There are two broader, albeit related, contexts within which the enforcement trends – and the 'disappearing act' to which the subtitle of this chapter alludes – are to be placed.

One is with the emergence of a broader phenomenon of actuarial justice, as well as with the explicit shift towards risk-based targeting in the context of business regulation, not least with respect to health and safety in the United Kingdom. It became commonplace in the context of traditional forms of criminal justice to highlight trends towards actuarial justice from the 1980s onward. In the spheres of business regulation in general – and not least in government efforts to improve standards of occupational health and safety in particular – approaches centred around risk management has always been central (Braithwaite 2000). Risk-based approaches rest on the idea that risks can be scientifically managed out of industrial systems by the application of technologies such as probability analysis, safety management systems and so on.

What did become pronounced in the United Kingdom from the early 2000s, however, was a shift towards a very explicitly formulated risk-based rationale that argued for the targeting of limited enforcement resources on risk-based criteria so that, in effect, risk-targeting for the few meant non-enforcement for most of the 'regulated' population, a consequence emphasised by the empirical data presented below.

Risk-based forms of regulation are now ubiquitous across UK regulatory bodies, indeed, the 'risk regulation' coupling has established itself conceptually in the past decade as a key element of the new common sense regarding the nature and limits of regulation. Within the very coupling of the words 'risk regulation' are the simultaneous ideas that *some* level of risk is ubiquitous, that regulation always needs to be balanced against risk, and that determining this balance is not necessarily even the task of government or regulatory agencies per se. Thus, 'Risk regulation refers to the governance, accountability and processing of risks, both within organisations as part of their risk management and compliance functions, and also at the level of regulatory and other agencies that constitute "risk regulation regimes"'.[2] Regulation extends beyond and indeed is 'de-centred' from the state (Black 2002) to various non-state bodies within the economic sphere, not least operating through market-based relationships, and through civil society (Hutter 2006). 'At a minimum', determining the risk regulation balance entails 'the use of technical *risk-based tools*, emerging out of economics (cost–benefit approaches), and science (risk assessment techniques)' (Hutter 2005: 3, emphasis in original).

Shifting to a broader political and economic register, risk-based approaches couched in the above terms are entirely compatible with political agendas that are explicitly pro-business. In a pro-business climate, governments can reinforce their commitment to boosting profits by offering 'risk-based' strategies *as an alternative to* enforcement strategies. Thus the risk-based approach to regulation coheres with dominant ways of thinking about the role of the state which gained ground with the entrenchment – in the United Kingdom but also, of course, beyond – of varieties of neo-liberalism. Thus, several assumptions about regulation served to strengthen the trajectory towards a risk-based approach (Tombs and Whyte 2013a, 2013b).

First, it has widely been accepted both in a variety of political circles as well as across much social science itself, that state capacity has dwindled with respect to private actors and 'the market', while state resources are not and never will be sufficient for the task of overseeing compliance with regulation. If the latter has generally been so, the former renders this fact less problematic than might otherwise have been the case in the sense of lending a sense of inevitability to state impotence vis-à-vis the business world.

Second, and in any case, not least on grounds of efficiency, the preferred regulatory option is to leave the management of risks to institutions beyond the state – notably to business organisations and their managements themselves, but also to other private actors, including trade associations, insurers and investors, so that corporations should be encouraged to act as responsibilised, self-managing, risk-mitigating organisations. Hence, and in fact, there are symbiotic relationships between risk-based approaches to regulation and a whole plethora of political and indeed academic claims for variations of self- or responsive forms of regulatory strategy.

Third, forms of self-regulation are both feasible and indeed desirable because, somehow, anthropomorphised corporations can and do have moral commitments to preventing and mitigating risks: they are not artificial entities, legally constructed as profit-driven, amoral calculators, which in fact will routinely kill, injure, poison, lie, cheat and steal based upon (accurate or erroneous) cost–benefit analyses. Thus it is not unsurprising to see that the era of risk-based discourse has been accompanied by a resurgence of popular, academic and political interest in claims around corporate social responsibility.

It is also worth emphasising here that the idea of 'risk-based regulation' has 'several broad meanings' (Black 2010: 187), is operationalised by different regulatory agencies in differing ways (passim), and has a variety of external and internal political motivations (Black 2010). Moreover, risk-based regulation is both central to the 'Better Regulation' agenda (Black 2010: 186, 189, 210; Hutter and Amodu 2008: para 24) – at both UK and European levels – and to which, in both contexts, the Hampton Report, below, was central. At the same time, risk-based regulation is as much a 'legitimating device' *for regulatory agencies themselves* (Black 2010: 188) as it is a series of techniques for regulatory practice. Moreover, as Black has noted, this 'framing of the regulatory task...has the potential to have more than a rhetorical effect: it imports particular conceptions of the problem at hand, and leads to the framing of a solution in a particular way' (Black 2010: 188). In what follows I examine briefly how the specific issue of risk-based targeting has impacted upon the UK regulatory landscape in respect to occupational health and safety enforcement.

And so the second context for the discussion of enforcement data in this is a more specific one. As we shall see in the next section, the Labour administrations of the first decade of this millennium accelerated a withdrawal from enforcement of health and safety law, while the subsequent Coalition Government has continued this while also embarking upon a formal process of deregulation. But there is a longer-term context for these trends which can be traced back to the Thatcher governments of the 1980s.

As a life peer at the heart of Thatcher's government, Lord Young had, in the mid-1980s, overseen two deregulatory White Papers: *Lifting the Burden* (Cmnd. 9571) and *Building Business – Not Barriers* (Cmnd. 9794). While these ultimately had little practical effects upon health and safety regulation and enforcement, not least through the resistance of, then, a relatively strong labour movement, they did begin to establish the language of regulation as a 'burden' on business, holding back profit-making enterprise (Tombs 1996). Then, the Major government's Deregulation and Contracting Out Act 1994 was passed, an open-ended law designed 'to remove or reduce certain burdens affecting persons in the carrying on of trades, businesses or professions or otherwise, and for other deregulatory purposes'.[3] While not ostensibly nor actually even to any great extent targeted at health and safety law, its effects were twofold. First, it placed at the heart of government an institutional mechanism designed to maintain a deregulatory impetus and indeed to deliver deregulatory reforms (James and Walters 2005). Second, it represented a key moment in the unfolding of a discursive, now more or less cultural, initiative that has resulted in health and safety protection in particular at best being ubiquitously ridiculed, at worst synonymous with the term 'burdens' borne by business, and thus anathema to entrepreneurialism and healthy risk-taking.

More than a decade after Major's initial legislative initiative and following a series of legislative and policy reforms that extended the measures introduced in the 1994 Act, the then Chancellor of the Exchequer Gordon Brown could have been reading from the same script as the Major government when announcing the Hampton Review of regulation and enforcement. This was to do away with the 'old regulatory model' according to which, 'for more than one hundred years', the principle, 'from health and safety to the administration of tax and financial services has been, irrespective of known risks or past results, 100 per cent inspection whether it be premises, procedures or practices' (Brown 2005).

The subsequent Hampton Report, *Reducing Administrative Burdens: Effective Inspection and Enforcement* (Hampton 2005), called for more focused inspections, greater emphasis on advice and education and, in general, for removing the 'burden' of inspection from most premises. Most fundamentally, inspections were to be cut by a third across some 60-plus regulators, equating to one million fewer inspections. Regulators were to make much more 'use of advice' to business. Moreover, 'Regulators should recognise that a key element of their activity will be to allow, or even encourage, economic progress and only to intervene when there is a clear case for protection' (Hampton 2005: 7). A year later, on the implementation of Hampton's proposals in the November 2006 Legislative and Regulatory Reform Act, the Cabinet Office pronounced its aim to 'cut the burden of regulation and embed a light touch, risk-based approach to regulation...to improve our status as one of the world's most attractive places to do business' (Cabinet Office 2006).

To sum up on the wider policy contexts: the approach described is typical of the risk-oriented nature of justice more generally, albeit, in the context of business regulation, with an increasingly explicit bias towards and assumption regarding the necessary freedoms of business to do business. In the case of the HSE, this new risk-based approach is based upon the assumption that the most likely offenders can be clearly identified via an evidence base and risk calculus. But herein lies a major contradiction. The Hampton Report's first recommendation is that 'all regulatory activity should be on the basis of a clear, comprehensive risk assessment' which should be based upon 'past performance and potential future risk'. It is conceded at this point that regulation should include 'a small element of random inspection' (Hampton 2005: 33) – even if Hampton tellingly declined to indicate the level of inspection that might be credible (Vickers 2008: 226). This logic begs a rather fundamental question: how might the past performance of businesses central to risk calculus be measured in a system where, as we shall see, there is a diminishing chance of the business having been inspected? Hampton's strategy becomes self-defeating. It seeks a reduction in the types of activity most likely to gather useful data for targeted intervention, so that regulation can be based upon targeted intervention.

The Health and Safety Executive: a disappearing act

In the first decade of this millennium a series of initiatives within HSE had placed targeted enforcement, based upon a risk-based model, on an ever more formalised basis. In fact, HSE provided Hampton with something of a model regulator. We have discussed these initiatives and this process extensively elsewhere (James et al. 2013; Tombs and Whyte 2010, 2013a, 2013b). The effect of these was quite simple and quite stark: on almost every indicator, HSE, as the chief regulator, seemed to disappear from more and more workplaces.[4]

The decline of inspections

It is an obviousness – albeit one that needs emphasis – that the corollary of targeting is the assumption that, for the most part, most businesses can be left, safely, with minimal or no intervention. And, indeed, we find not just low but declining levels of inspection coverage during the 2000s and beyond. In terms of the absolute data, in 1999/2000, there were 75,272 'inspection records', compared with 27,849 in 2012/2013. Thus, during this period, there was a 63 per cent decline in inspections. This long-term trend is due, according to the HSE, to changes in 'strategies, intervention targeting, internal procedures, guidance and operational information systems'.[5] In particular, the HSE notes that as the method of undertaking and recording inspections changed from 2004/2005, then data before and after this change are not strictly compatible. However, if we break the period at 2005/2006, when the method of recording changed, we still find steep falls in inspections on either side of this apparent watershed: whatever changes have been made to the logging of inspection activity, a downward trend since the start of the last decade is very clear.

Further, if the decline in the absolute number of inspections is, as the HSE has argued, a product of targeting, it is also important to recognise that this trend in fact makes targeting less feasible. Indeed, the very premise upon which this 'strategy' was based has been questioned in a Better Regulation Executive and National Audit Office (Better Regulation Executive / National Audit Office 2008) report. The report rated the HSE 'highly' in terms of its working within the 'Hampton principles', endorsing the fact that it 'works well with business, including recognising the need to minimise burdens on business' (Better Regulation Executive / National Audit Office 2008: 5, 12). However, this assessment of the HSE's enforcement activities revealed the fundamental contradiction at the heart of a targeting strategy. The report's central criticism of HSE practice was that it should make 'better use of intelligence' in order to 'improve its targeting of business' (Better Regulation Executive / National Audit Office 2008: 7). The three reasons revealed for the intelligence deficit are significant.

First, the report noted the failure of many businesses even to register their existence with the HSE, leaving the regulator to expend resources trying to identify premises before their risk could be assessed. What is not mentioned is that the requirement to register is a legal one. So what we have here is a targeting strategy, premised on the assumption (above) that most businesses are compliant with law, undermined by the fact that many business premises remain unregistered – that is, are violating the law.

Second, the report found that the strategy for targeting was being undermined by the focus on high-risk issues, rather than duty-holders' 'past performance and other factors', which it stated were inadequately taken into account (BRE/NAO 2008: 21). This was explicitly attributed to the relative lack of inspections (Better Regulation Executive / National Audit Office 2008: 23).

Third, the BRE/NAO report bemoaned the level of injury reporting,[6] again something that significantly undermines its intelligence base. In fact, employers' under-reporting of injuries and illness at work is a longstanding issue – one of widespread non-compliance with law, in fact – highlighted over 40 years ago by the Robens Committee[7] (Robens 1972: 135, and chapter 1). Despite various attempts to improve reporting levels, they remain low, perhaps even as low as 30 per cent (Davies et al. 2007: v).[8]

Finally, it is worth stating the obvious – that the decline of inspectorial activity means that workplace harms are less likely to be detected, and thus less likely to form part of any offence, or 'crime', data (see below).

The decline of investigations

By definition, the investigation of a workplace death, injury or, indeed, 'near-miss' is an integral part of any occupational health and safety regulatory system, in the United Kingdom as elsewhere. For it is only on the basis of investigation that any form of accountability for incidents can, in principle, be determined. Further, such investigations have a significant preventative role in that they may uncover factors that can be eradicated to minimise the likelihood of future, repeat incidents. And of course investigation of incidents is the sine qua non of any of these being processed as offences.

During the 2000s, the proportion of incidents reported to HSE that have been investigated by HSE has fallen significantly: between 1999/2000 and 2008/2009, there was a 63 per cent decline in numbers of HSE investigations; this is a decline from 11,462 in 1999/2000 to 4,272 in 2008/2009. Data on RIDDOR reports in this section is available up to and including 2008/2009 only. But there is no reason to believe that the trends – the general decline – in investigations have changed since that end point.

This sharp decline is replicated in further detail in the data on investigation *type*. The HSE continues to investigate 100 per cent of *employee* fatalities reported to it, a constant over the past decade (these are the fatalities that make up the 'headline' figure; see above). However, since 1999/2000, we also find that investigations of reported major injuries declined by 55 per cent; of over-three-day injuries by 83 per cent; and of dangerous occurrences by 37 per cent. By 2008/2009, less than 1 per cent of over-three-day injuries that were reported to the HSE were actually investigated. Less than 1 in 10 (8%) of reported major injuries were actually investigated, and by 2012 this ratio was less than 1 in 20 (O'Neill 2012). In 2008/2009, the HSE did *not* investigate the following:

- 66 per cent of amputations;
- 84 per cent of major fractures;
- 96 per cent of major dislocations;
- 84 per cent of major concussions and internal injuries;
- 90 per cent of major lacerations and open wounds;
- 83 per cent of major contusions;
- 75 per cent of major burns;
- and 66 per cent of major poisonings and gassings.

It is hard to imagine any Chief Constable in the United Kingdom being able to defend to their Police Commissioner such low levels of investigation of serious injury and, thus, potentially serious crime. But even in HSE's own terms, it is hardly a basis for sound intelligence about offending behaviour. Generally, then, in the absence of either robust historic intelligence or the ability to maintain existing levels of intelligence regarding safety and health performance as a function of a dwindling inspectorial resource, it is difficult to see how a risk-based model or any coherent programme of targeted inspections/interventions can be sustained.

The decline of formal enforcement

If we now shift from HSE investigation to other formal enforcement action, we again find consistent declines in levels of activity since 1999/2000.[9] This is the clearest conclusion to be reached from an examination of data for all forms of enforcement notice, as well as prosecutions of both offences and 'duty holders' (employers).

Thus, on enforcement notices, we find:

- Total notices issued by HSE declined from 11,144 in 1999/2000 to 8,480 in 2011/2012 – a decline of 24 per cent
- Improvement notices – the least serious form of notice – declined from 6,972 in 1999/2000 to 5,350 in 2011/2012 – a decline of 23 per cent
- All Prohibition notices – the most serious form of notice – declined from 4,368 in 1999/2000 to 3,130 in 2011/2012 – a decline of 28 per cent

On prosecutions of *offences*, we find that both the number of offences prosecuted, and thus the number of convictions, declined from between 1999/2000 to 2011/2012. Thus,

- Prosecutions of offences fell from 2,115 in 1999/2000 to 969 in 2011/2012, a decline of 54 per cent
- Convictions for offences fell from 1,616 in 1999/2000 to 780 in 2011/2012, a decline of 52 per cent

And, finally, on prosecution of *duty holders*,[10] we find that both the number of duty holders prosecuted, and thus the number of convictions, declined from between 1999/2000 to 2011/2012. Thus,

- Prosecutions of duty holders fell from 991 in 1999/2000 to 584 in 2011/2012, a decline of 41 per cent
- Convictions of duty holders fell from 965 in 1999/2000 to 537 in 2011/2012, a decline of 43 per cent

Taking the above data together, we find that, during the period under examination, while all forms of formal activity declined – by between one-half and one-quarter, there is a direct correlation between the higher declines being in the more serious forms of enforcement response. Thus the greatest declines during this period were for prosecutions; then, within overall notices, we find that the greatest declines were in the more serious forms of notice, prohibition notices, than for the least serious form, improvement notices. Finally, it is also worth noting, as revealed by the two sets of prosecutions data, that the fall in prosecutions for *offences* is some 20 per cent sharper than is the fall for prosecutions of *duty holders* – indicating that while fewer duty holders are being prosecuted, they are also being prosecuted, on average, for fewer offences.

There are of course variations within these overall trends that require analysis, which I have undertaken, with Whyte, elsewhere (Tombs and Whyte 2010). At the same time, what is remarkable, taking all these data together, is the common trend across them: one of declining activity on the part of the regulator. And the net effect of all of these processes is to render harms relatively invisible, and to filter them out, systematically, from any recorded offence data: the 'disappearance' of enforcement means the disappearance of crime.

The institutionalisation of 'low-risk'

These data indicating generalised declines in HSE activity all relate mostly to the *last* decade. Remarkably, and subsequently, on its formation in 2010, the new Coalition moved quickly to reduce further the 'burden' of health and safety regulation and enforcement. We turn to some of these attempts in the rest of this subsection. But prior to doing so it is worth noting an even more remarkable aspect of this specific shift towards further deregulation: for it occurred in the wake of financial crisis which, for all the disagreement on the detail of its antecedents, is at least widely recognised as having one of its causes in the nature and level of regulation of financial services in most of the major economies across the globe. In other words, even as the new government was embarking upon further initiatives against health and safety regulation in the United Kingdom, both there and more broadly one might have expected the neo-liberal idea of regulation of business to be under greater social and political questioning or scrutiny than had hitherto been the case.

If this questioning did occur, then it occurred variously across different nation states; in general, however, the critical scrutiny to which the neo-liberal idea of regulation was subject was relatively short-lived, and of little apparent import. While there are significant national-state specifics in understanding why this has proven to be the case, there are also general characteristics of neo-liberalism as a set of ideas that make it comprehensible. In a recent review of the 'resilience' of such ideas across Europe in the wake of the financial crisis (Schmidt and Thatcher 2013a), Schmidt and Thatcher highlight five characteristics that have combined to protect the ideological dominance of neo-liberalism in general, and its commitment to 'reducing regulation' in particular: namely, its diversity and adaptability; the gap between rhetoric and reality, which always creates a space for the promise of 'real' neo-liberalism to be fulfilled; the relative absence or weaknesses of alternative ways of seeing the world; the powerful interests that are served by the prevalence of such ideas; and the institutional embeddedness of these ideas over the course of 30-plus years, both at national levels and also through supranational institutions such as the European Union (Schmidt and Thatcher 2013b).

Indeed, in the United Kingdom, as in some other jurisdictions where neo-liberal ideas had become especially dominant, governmental responses to the crisis – reframed as state overspending – were to further arguments for 'deregulation'. Thus, all three major political parties that fought the General Election in 2010 were committed to *reducing* regulation: regulation in general was inherently burdensome and only to be an option of last resort, a minimalist necessary evil; and, in any case, regulation entailed costs for both the state and for business, costs that had to be restricted in the new 'Age of Austerity'. Thus regulatory costs had to be minimised on the one hand as part of the overall attempt to tackle the new fiscal crisis of the state, and on the other hand to reduce the costs for the private sector, which was seen as the only vehicle for economic recovery.

It was in such a context that, three weeks into the new Coalition Government, Vince Cable, as Business Secretary, established a Reducing Regulation Committee to put an ''end to the excessive regulation that is stifling business growth' (Department for Business, Innovation and Skills 2010).

Days later, Lord Young was appointed to investigate 'concerns over the application and perception of health and safety legislation' (Hope 2010). Young's appointment was of no little significance – it was he who had overseen the Thatcher government's unsuccessful deregulatory initiative some 25 years earlier. His report, *Common Sense, Common Safety*, published in October 2010, made a series of recommendations aimed 'to free businesses from unnecessary bureaucratic burdens' (Young 2010: 9). Most significantly, the removal of the burden of regulation from 'low-risk' workplaces featured centrally in the report (Young 2010: 16–17).

Following the Young Report, there were a series of policy interventions conforming to and extending the same agenda. In March 2011, the Department for Work and Pensions launched its *Good Health and Safety, Good for Everyone*, which announced that 'HSE will reduce its proactive inspections by one third, around 11,000 inspections per year' by ending preventative inspections to lower-risk areas (Department for Work and Pensions 2011a: 9), now enacted within HSE as policy (Health and Safety Executive and Local Government Group 2011). A further government report, published in November 2011, proposed to review all regulators, 'to make sure each one is making the fullest possible use of the range of alternatives to conventional enforcement models. ... We will expect to see a significant reduction in state-led enforcement activity' (Department for Business, Innovation and Skills 2011: 6). It urged a 'transparent and light-touch risk-based system' (Department for Business, Innovation and Skills 2011: 7).

In June 2011, the government had also launched its 'Red Tape Challenge', which Employment Minister Grayling called 'an opportunity that every beleaguered business leader, incredulous community group or outraged newspaper reader has been waiting for – a chance to directly change the laws underpinning Britain's health and safety culture' (Health and Safety Executive 2011). And the Department for Business, Innovation and Skills introduced a 'One In, One Out' policy which aimed to ensure that any new regulation that imposes costs on business must first 'identify and remove existing regulations with an equivalent value' (HM Government 2011: 3).[11]

Perhaps most significant of all, however, was the Löfstedt Review, established by the Prime Minister in March 2011. This was to review 'health and safety regulations to identify opportunities to simplify the rules' and thus reduce 'the burden of health and safety regulation on business' (Department for Work and Pensions 2011b). And it was the Löfstedt Report (Löfstedt 2011) that was to be pivotal in the consolidation of 'low-risk'. The Löfstedt Report in fact uses the phrase 'low-risk' in four senses: 'low-risk' work activities, 'low-risk' businesses, 'low-risk' sectors and 'low-risk' workplaces. Now, although the report notes the difficulty of defining what constitutes 'low-risk' (Löfstedt 2011: 36), none of these concepts is actually defined in any useful sense (James et al. 2013). Unfortunately, such a lack of precision is highly useful for a government that wishes to use a vague, flexible concept of 'low-risk' to justify regulatory withdrawal. For example, *before* the review was published, the Department for Work and Pensions had applied a very wide-ranging use of the concept, to include low-risk manufacturing (for example, textiles, clothing, footwear, light engineering, electrical engineering), the transport sector (air, road haulage and docks), local authority–administered education provision, electricity generation, and the postal and courier services (Department for Work and Pensions 2011a: 9). The classification of docks as low-risk, for example, simply cannot withstand scrutiny: official data records the fatality rate therein currently running at between five to twenty times[12] the all-industries average (O'Neill 2012). More generally, one recent analysis of worker fatalities shows that, from April 2011 to October 2012, over half were in 'low-risk' sectors (O'Neill 2013). This is not even to mention 'hidden' problems of fatal exposures which are prevalent in many so-called 'low-risk' sectors; witness, for example, the increasingly apparent problem of asbestos in schools, universities and offices.[13]

Thus the 'concept' of 'low-risk' workplaces may be best understood as a legitimation for regulatory disengagement, and, indeed, since the publication of the Report, Löfstedt has raised concerns in public about the reduction in numbers of inspections (Hyde 2012). Yet the formal position for HSE now is that the majority of employers will be effectively left to self-regulate, only even potentially coming into contact with the regulator when a death, injury or incident is reported (Taylor 2012).

The anomalous emergence of corporate manslaughter?

Within this context of the general *decriminalisation* of health and safety, one development stands out as entirely anomalous: namely, the passage of the Corporate Manslaughter and Corporate Homicide Act 2007, an explicitly pro-criminalisation development. However, this anomaly may be more apparent than real, and it is worth exploring this in a little more detail. On 8 December 1994, OLL Ltd, a very small company, had become the first company in English legal history to be convicted of homicide after three schoolchildren were killed while canoeing in the 'care' of the company. A handful of further convictions for corporate manslaughter followed, all of small organisations (Matthewson 2012). The fact of these all being against small companies highlighted a key problem in applying the common law on manslaughter to a larger corporate entity: its legal test required identifying a company's acts and omissions with those of one or more controlling minds, corporate guilt being dependent on the guilt of one or more senior individuals. Thus, the very size and complexity of organisations such as P&O Ferries, Great Western Trains, Occidental Petroleum, or Railtrack had not simply been a key factor in producing large-scale fatalities following which a case of manslaughter has been considered, but were the same features that had rendered such charges almost bound to fail.

In 1996, the Law Commission published a fully developed set of proposals for a new criminal offence of corporate manslaughter (Law Commission 1996). But these were not simply a response to problems of law, but also to changes in popular discourse and sentiment: the term 'corporate manslaughter' had slowly but surely entered popular vocabulary, not least following a long series of high-profile disasters, and victims' campaigns in response to these (BBC News 2002; Tombs and Whyte 2003). Even set against this backdrop, the path to the passage of the 2007 Act was characterised by dead ends, controversies and broken promises. Several rounds of formal and informal consultation were undertaken, and only when proposals to include legal duties upon individual directors were dropped did key employers' organisations become reconciled to any new law (Tombs 2013). When the Act was finally passed in 2007, changes to the law had been so significant during this long period of contestation that many of those pro-regulatory organisations that had initially campaigned most vehemently for it were scathing of it when it was ultimately passed (Tombs 2013). It is perhaps unsurprising, then, that the result is 'conservative in form and is unlikely fundamentally to change' efforts to hold corporations legally to account for workplace killing (Almond and Colover 2012: 1000).

Since the Act came into force on 6 April 2008, there have been three convictions under it, all against small companies of the kind that could have been prosecuted under the old, common law offence of manslaughter. And, since no large organisation has yet been prosecuted, the extent to which the Act can do that which was originally intended remains untested in court. Such a test will, eventually, come: in October 2012, the Crown Prosecution Service stated that there were at that time 74 cases under review under this Act, while, since April 2008, 152 such cases had been referred to the CPS.[14]

Even as presently under-utilised, the existence of the Act still sits in tension with the more general trends towards the decriminalisation of health and safety offending, outlined above. Yet it is possible to see the latter – the increasingly obvious inefficacy of safety and health regulation and enforcement – as generating a *greater* likelihood in the use of occasional, symbolic criminal prosecutions under the new law. Almond (2013: 158–159) has recently claimed that there is an international trend towards the criminalisation of workplace deaths – one which represents a turn to the criminal law for a symbolic effect which regulatory law per se is unable to achieve – and that this trend is most pronounced in those neo-liberal political contexts where the instrumental potential of regulatory law has been most thoroughly undermined (not least the United Kingdom). In other words, corporate manslaughter prosecutions may mitigate the *political* risks of the manifest failures of regulatory law, so that the Act steers a path between the symbolic need to do something about 'companies that kill' (Almond 2013: 32) while not unduly harming business interests (Almond 2013: 33).

Certainly the Corporate Manslaughter and Corporate Homicide Act was never intended to revolutionise corporate accountability for workplace deaths, not least since its ambit is:

> restricted to one statistically minor (in terms of its incidence although clearly not in terms of the seriousness of the harm caused) dimension of a much more complex problem – injuries and deaths caused by an organisation's blatant disregard for the safety and welfare of employees, consumers and members of the public. (Gobert 2008: 414)

In fact, in its Regulatory Impact Assessment of the proposed legislation prior to its passage into law, the Home Office had estimated that 'the proposals would lead to a possible 10–13' prosecutions per year (Home Office 2006: 13). Nor would these represent *additional* prosecutions, but would *replace* charges which would in any case have been brought under health and safety legislation (Home Office 2005: para 39). The ambition of the law is, to say the least, modest. It is perhaps best viewed, as Almond has intimated, as a political response to the political risks of a risk-based system of health and safety regulation and enforcement.

Conclusion

Almost 15 years ago, I wrote of the various ways in which health and safety crimes were rendered *relatively* invisible (Tombs 1999), focusing upon a series of mutually reinforcing processes, none in themselves remarkable, but all with mutually reinforcing effects. This chapter has focused on two of these processes – regulation and enforcement. We have seen how trends in each have served to remove workplace harms from the register of crime, through legal 'reform', as well as reductions in inspection, investigation and prosecution. It should go without saying that regulation and enforcement never exist in an economic, political or social vacuum as this chapter has sought to indicate. But the clearest conclusion of this contribution is that, in the context of health and safety crimes, the United Kingdom has seen no penal or punitive turn, no culture of control, no surveillance society, nor any net-widening. In fact, as HSE activity has declined significantly, health and safety crimes have declined also. Each is disappearing further from view, notwithstanding the ongoing, routine and widespread harm generated by working for a living.

Acknowledgements

This chapter draws extensively on my ongoing collaborative research work with David Whyte, and any merit it may have owes a great deal to that work.

Notes

1. The Health and Safety Executive enforces law in *British* workplaces only; however, the wider regulatory contexts at issue in this chapter emanate from HM Government and thus apply across the United Kingdom.
2. http://www.lse.ac.uk/collections/CARR/aboutUs/Default.htm.
3. See http://www.legislation.gov.uk/ukpga/1994/40/introduction?view=plain. Accessed 1 November 2013.
4. For technical reasons relating to the consistency and availability of data, *most* of the data used in this chapter is from 1999/2000 only, to the latest year in which each form of data is available.
5. *Freedom of Information Request Reference No. p2010020046*, 12 April 2010, page 7 of 8.
6. Regulations (RIDDOR) require employers to report to HSE specific classes of injury and incident.
7. The Robens Committee Report led to the establishment of the Health and Safety at Work Act 1974 and the Health and Safety Executive.
8. Two changes in the law, in 2102 and 2013, removed many of the requirements upon employers to report both 'minor' and 'major' injuries.
9. Sources for data presented in this section are: *Freedom of Information Request Reference No. 2010020046*; *Enforcement action taken by enforcing authorities in Great Britain where region is known, 2001/02 – 2009/10p*; and *Enforcement action taken by enforcing authorities in Great Britain where region is known 2007/08 – 2011/12p*; and Health and Safety Executive, 2012a.
10. That is, cases resulting in conviction for at least one offence.
11. Later to be superseded by a 'One In, *Two* Out' initiative, to take effect from January 2013 (Department for Business, Innovation and Skills 2012).

12. Depending upon which employment figure is used as the denominator.
13. For example, the Department of Education estimates that over 75 per cent of schools contain asbestos (The Asbestos in Schools Group 2011).
14. Request under the Freedom of Information Act 2000, CPS, Ref: 3539.

References

Almond, P. (2013) *Corporate Manslaughter and Regulatory Reform*. London: Palgrave Macmillan.

Almond, P. and Colover, S. (2012) 'Communication and Social Regulation: The Criminalization of Work-Related Death', *British Journal of Criminology*, 52(5): 997–1016.

Asbestos in Schools Group (2011) *Asbestos in Schools: The Scale of the Problem and the Implications* [online]. Available at: http://www.asbestosexposureschools.co.uk/pdfnewslinks/AiSreportonASBESTOSINSCHOOLS.pdf. Accessed 1 February 2012.

BBC News (2002) *Chronology of Rail Crashes*, 10 May 2002 [online]. Available at: http://news.bbc.co.uk/1/hi/uk/465475.stm. Accessed 31 January 2013.

Better Regulation Executive/National Audit Office (2008) *Effective Inspection and Enforcement: Implementing the Hampton Vision in the Health and Safety Executive*. London: Better Regulation Executive.

Black, J. (2002) *Critical Reflections on Regulation. CARR discussion paper, 4*. London: Centre for Analysis of Risk and Regulation, London School of Economics and Political Science.

—— (2010) 'Risk-Based Regulation: Choices, Practices and Lessons Being Learnt', in G. Bounds and N. Malyshev (eds), *Risk and Regulation Policy: Improving the Governance of Risk*. Paris: OECD.

Braithwaite, J. (2000) 'The New Regulatory State and the Transformation of Criminology', in D. Garland and R. Sparks (eds), *Criminology and Social Theory*. Oxford: Oxford University Press.

Brown, G. (2005) 'A Plan to Lighten the Regulatory Burden on Business', *Financial Times*, 23 May.

Cabinet Office (2006) *New Bill to Enable Delivery of Swift and Efficient Regulatory Reform to Cut Red Tape – Jim Murphy, Cabinet Office News Release, 12 January*. London: Cabinet Office Press Office [online]. Available at: http://www.egov-monitor.com/node/4164. Accessed 5 August 2007.

Davies, J., Kemp, G. and Frostick, S. (2007) *An Investigation of Reporting of Workplace Accidents under RIDDOR Using the Merseyside Accident Information Model. Research Report RR528*. Norwich: HSE Books.

Department for Business, Innovation and Skills (2010) *Action Plan Announced to End Excessive Regulation. Press Release, 2 June* [online]. Available at: http://news.bis.gov.uk/Press-Releases/Action-plan-announced-to-end-excessive-regulation-64fb4.aspx. Accessed 30 June 2010.

—— (2011) *Transforming Regulatory Enforcement: Government Response to the Consultation on Transforming Regulatory Enforcement*. London: Department for Business, Innovation and Skills.

—— (2012) *'One-in, Two-out': Government to Go Further and Faster to Reduce Burdens on Business and Help Britain Compete in the Global Race. Press Release, 19*

November [online]. Available at: http://news.bis.gov.uk/Press-Releases/-One-in-two-out-Government-to-go-further-and-faster-to-reduce-burdens-on-business-and-help-Britai-6838c.aspx. Accessed 10 January 2013.

Department for Work and Pensions (2011a) *Good Health and Safety: Good for Everyone. The Next Steps in the Government's Plans for Reform of the Health and Safety System in Britain* [online]. Available at: http://www.dwp.gov.uk/docs/good-health-and-safety.pdf. Accessed 21 January 2012.

―― (2011b) *Press Release, 20 April 2011. Scope of Löfstedt Review into Health and Safety Set Out* [online]. Available at: http://www.dwp.gov.uk/newsroom/press-releases/2011/apr-2011/dwp042–11.shtm. Accessed 1 February 2012.

Gobert, J. (2008) 'The Corporate Manslaughter and Corporate Homicide Act 2007: Thirteen Years in the Making but Was It Worth the Wait?' *Modern Law Review*, 71(3): 413–433.

Hämäläinen, P., Saarela, K. and Takala, J. (2009) 'Global Trend According to Estimated Number of Occupational Accidents and Fatal Work-Related Diseases at Region and Country Level', *Journal of Safety Research*, 40: 125–139.

Hampton, P. (2005) *Reducing Administrative Burdens: Effective Inspection and Enforcement.* London: HM Treasury/HMSO.

Health and Safety Executive (2011) *National Press Release. Public Urged to 'Restore Sanity' to Health and Safety Rulebook, 27 June* [online]. Available at: http://www.hse.gov.uk/press/2011/hse-redtapechallenge.htm. Accessed 15 September 2011.

―― (2012a) *Prosecutions (2011/12p). Enforcement Action Taken by HSE, Local Authorities and, in Scotland, the Crown Office and Procurator Fiscal Service (2011/12p)* [online]. Available at: http://www.hse.gov.uk/statistics/prosecutions.pdf. Accessed 10 July 2013.

―― (2012b) *Statistics on Fatal Injuries in the Workplace 2011/12* [online]. Available at: http://www.hse.gov.uk/statistics/pdf/fatalinjuries.pdf. Accessed 1 September 2012.

―― (2013a) *Workplace Major Injuries Hit an All Time Low for 2012/13. Press Release, 30 October 2013* [online]. Available at http://press.hse.gov.uk/2013/workplace-major-injuries-hit-an-all-time-low-for-201213/?eban=govdel-press-release&cr=30-Oct-2013. Accessed 3 November 2013.

―― (2013b) *Health and Safety Statistics 2012/13. Annual Statistical Report for Great Britain* [online]. Available at http://www.hse.gov.uk/statistics/overall/hssh1213.pdf. Accessed 3 November 2013.

―― (2013c) *Statistics on Fatal Injuries in the Workplace in Great Britain 2013. Full-year Details and Technical Notes* [online]. Available at: http://www.hse.gov.uk/statistics/pdf/fatalinjuries.pdf. Accessed 3 November 2013.

Health and Safety Executive and Local Government Group (2011) *Joint Guidance for Reduced Proactive Inspections* [online]. Available at: http://www.hse.gov.uk/lau/pdfs/reducedproactive-inspections.pdf. Accessed 1 February 2012.

HM Government (2011) *One In, One Out (OIOO) Methodology.* London: Department for Business, Innovation and Skills.

Home Office (2005) *Corporate Manslaughter: A Regulatory Impact Assessment of the Government's Draft Bill.* London: The Home Office.

―― (2006) *Corporate Manslaughter and Corporate Homicide: A Regulatory Impact Assessment of the Government's Bill.* London: The Home Office.

Hope, C. (2010) 'Health and Safety Rules Should Be Removed from Offices, Says David Cameron Adviser', *The Telegraph*, 10 June [online]. Available at: http://www.telegraph.co.uk/news/politics/7826183. Accessed 15 January 2011.

Hutter, B. (2005) *The Attractions of Risk-based Regulation: Accounting for the Emergence of Risk Ideas in Regulation. CARR discussion paper 33*. London: Centre for Analysis of Risk and Regulation.

—— (2006) *The Role of Non-State Actors in Regulation. CARR discussion paper 37*. London: Centre for Analysis of Risk and Regulation.

Hutter, B. and Amodu, T. (2008) *Risk Regulation and Compliance: Food Safety in the UK*. London: LSE.

Hyde, J. (2012) 'Health and Safety Guru Warns of Political Misuse', *The Law Society Gazette*, 18 January [online]. Available at: http://www.lawgazette.co.uk/news/health-and-safety-guru-warns-political-misuse. Accessed 1 March 2012.

James, P., Tombs, S. and Whyte, D. (2013) 'An Independent Review of British Health and Safety Regulation? From Common Sense to Non-sense', *Policy Studies*, 34(1): 36–52.

James, P. and Walters, D. (2005) *Regulating Health and Safety at Work: An Agenda for Change?* London: Institute of Employment Rights.

Law Commission (1996) *Legislating the Criminal Code: Involuntary Manslaughter: Item 11 of the Sixth Programme of Law Reform: Criminal Law: Report No 237, HC (1995–96)*. London: HMSO.

Löfstedt, R. (2011) *Reclaiming Health and Safety for All: An Independent Review of Health and Safety Legislation. Cmnd. 8219*. London: HMSO.

Matthewson, K. (2012) 'The Corporate Manslaughter and Corporate Homicide Act 2007 Update', *Expolink*, 28 March [online]. Available at: http://www.expolink.co.uk/2012/03/the-corporate-manslaughter-and-corporate-homicide-act-2007-update/. Accessed 31 January 2013.

O'Neill, R. (2012) 'Give Up. What Can You Do when a Watchdog Just Sucks?' *Hazards Magazine*, 119, July–September [online]. Available at: http://www.hazards.org/votetodie/giveup.htm. Accessed 1 July 2013.

—— (2013) 'Work Rules', *Hazards*, 121, January–March: 8–9.

O'Neill, R., Pickvance, S. and Watterson, A. (2007) 'Burying the Evidence: How Great Britain Is Prolonging the Occupational Cancer Epidemic', *International Journal of Occupational and Environmental Health*, 4: 428–436.

Palmer, H. (2008) 'The Whole Story', *SHP Online*, 10 December [online]. Available at: http://www.shponline.co.uk/features-content/full/the-whole-story. Accessed 15 January 2009.

Robens, L. (1972) *Safety and Health at Work: Report of the Committee 1970–72. Cmnd. 5034*. London: HMSO.

Rogers, S. (2011) 'Mortality Statistics: Every Cause of Death in England and Wales, Visualised', *The Guardian*, 28 October [online]. Available at: http://www.guardian.co.uk/news/datablog/2011/oct/28/mortality-statistics-causes-death-england-wales-2010. Accessed 31 January 2013.

Schmidt, V. and Thatcher, M. (eds) (2013a) *Resilient Liberalism in Europe's Political Economy*. Cambridge: Cambridge University Press.

—— (2013b) 'Theorizing Ideational Continuity: The Resilience of Neo-Liberal Ideas in Europe', in V. Schmidt and M. Thatcher (eds), *Resilient Liberalism in Europe's Political Economy*. Cambridge: Cambridge University Press, 1–50.

Slapper, G. and Tombs, S. (1999) *Corporate Crime*. London: Longman.
Snell, K. and Tombs, S. (2011) 'How Do You Get Your Voice Heard When No-One Will Let You? Victimisation at Work', *Criminology & Criminal Justice*, 11(3): 207–223.
Snider, L. (1991) 'The Regulatory Dance: Understanding Reform Processes in Corporate Crime', *International Journal of the Sociology of Law*, 19: 209–236.
Taylor, J. (2012) *What Löfstedt Means for the People Who Enforce the Law*. Paper to the Institute of Employment Rights Conference: 'Reviewing Löfstedt: What Now for Health and Safety at Work?' 22 May, Liverpool.
Tombs, S. (1996) 'Injury, Death and the Deregulation Fetish: The Politics of Occupational Safety Regulation in UK Manufacturing', *International Journal of Health Services*, 26(2): 327–347.
—— (1999) 'Health and Safety Crimes: (In)Visibility and the Problems of "Knowing"', in P. Davies, P. Francis, and V. Jupp (eds), *Invisible Crimes: Their Victims and Their Regulation*. London: Macmillan, 77–104.
—— (2013) 'Still Killing with Impunity: The Reform of Corporate Criminal Liability in the UK', *Policy and Practice in Health and Safety*, 11(2), 31–48.
Tombs, S. and Whyte, D. (2003) 'Two Steps Forward, One Step Back: Towards Corporate Accountability for Workplace Deaths?', *Policy and Practice in Health and Safety*, 1: 9–30.
—— (2007) *Safety Crimes*. Cullompton: Willan.
—— (2008) *A Crisis of Enforcement: The Decriminalisation of Death and Injury at Work*. London: Centre for Crime and Justice Studies
—— (2010) *Regulatory Surrender: Death, Injury and the Non-enforcement of Law*. London: Institute of Employment Rights.
—— (2013a) 'Transcending the Deregulation Debate? Regulation, Risk and the Enforcement of Health and Safety Law in the UK', *Regulation & Governance*, 7(1), March: 61–79.
—— (2013b) 'The Myths and Realities of Deterrence in Workplace Safety Regulation', *British Journal of Criminology*, 53(5), 746–763.
Vickers, I. (2008) 'Better Regulation and Enterprise: The Case of Environmental Health Risk Regulation in Britain', *Policy Studies*, 29(2): 215–232.
Whyte, D. (2004) 'Regulation and Corporate Crime', in J. Muncie and D. Wilson (eds), *Student Handbook of Criminal Justice and Criminology*. London: Cavendish, 133–152.
Young, D. (2010) *Common Sense, Common Safety*. London: The Cabinet Office.

12
Regulating Fraud Revisited

Michael Levi

Introduction

Many frauds (and other financial crimes such as money-laundering) are partly or wholly invisible to outsiders, being planned and executed in private and/or, even where the harms themselves are evident, being hard to attribute to the criminal fault of individuals, especially when committed in an organisational context. Many frauds – such as payment-card, some 'advance fee' frauds, 'boiler room' stock scams and 'identity crimes' – become visible after a while, though victims may prefer to believe that they are not victims of fraud. Others, such as price-fixing cartels and the manipulation by banks of LIBOR or Foreign Exchange rates, may be wholly invisible to the public unless a whistleblower comes forward or some other event brings it to the notice of the authorities. Changes in legislation – for example the Fraud Act 2006 – have reduced the ambiguity of fraud allegations.

Any analysis needs to decide whether to focus on the offenders and/or on a range of the crimes. Some acts and high-status actors might be fused, where frauds, health and safety offences, pollution, and so forth are committed by large corporations and capitalists (Friedrichs 2013). However, a historical appreciation shows that many fraud cases prosecuted were committed first by 'servants' and then by 'employees' (Styles 1983), then in Victorian times by specialist as well as more situationally driven opportunistic fraudsters (Levi 2008; Wilson 2006, 2014), and in our times by 'blue-collar' payment-card and cheque fraudsters, plus those 'organised crime' gang members who have blackmailed/seduced corporate staff into fraud or who have hacked into bank computers or payment-card databases and re-sold the data on the global marketplace. These socio-economic groups and networks are complementary, not mutually exclusive. Thus a concentration on 'white-collar elites' would miss many of these offences and offenders, while a focus on the more 'organised crime' fraud offences (Levi 2014a) would neglect the often much larger malefactions committed by elites that may go unpunished because the businesses are 'too big to be prosecuted' (other than for 'regulatory offences' that do not attract corporate life-threatening penalties). A look at broadsheet and even tabloid newspapers will conclude that in this century, both frauds and fraudsters are well publicised compared with earlier eras and in this sense are more visible. However the legal ambiguity (as well as corporate interests of publishers) of higher-profile organisational cases instils greater pre-conviction caution in the characterisation of investigations and 'scandals' as 'crimes' than is necessary elsewhere in the criminal justice process.

An alternative focus on social reaction to the *victims* is illuminating (Levi 1992; Button et al. 2013). Contemporary crime surveys show that 'identity frauds' and payment-card frauds have become among the most common property crimes and that they are sources of substantial anxiety about invasion of control over one's life and property by unseen forces outside one's control. At the higher end, if we look at frauds not so much by the number of each type reported but by the amount of money lost and the amount of money at risk in financial markets, we can better appreciate the public protection and reassurance reasons why institutions such as the Serious Fraud Office (SFO) – created by the Criminal Justice Act 1987 – or parallel institutions in other countries exist.

This chapter seeks to review some key themes in the policing and prosecution of fraud, and examines the nature and impact of changes wrought during the decades since the publication of *Regulating Fraud* (Levi 1987, republished 2013b). Unlike many other forms of property crime, some forms of fraud are 'regulated' formally by both criminal justice and administrative/regulatory mechanisms. In England and Wales (Scotland having always had a different system), criminal justice agencies include police, the Department of Business Innovation and Skills (BIS), the Department of Work and Pensions (DWP), HM Revenue and Customs (HMRC), and – for prosecutions – the Crown Prosecution Service, Financial Conduct Authority, the Serious Fraud Office and Trading Standards. Regulatory and administrative justice agencies include the Financial Conduct Authority, the Solicitors Regulatory Authority, HMRC and in a different way – via cutting off benefits to those deemed to have lied to them – the DWP: default controls avoid prosecution except in the most serious and intentional (and prosecutable) cases.[1]

Fraud investigation and prosecution in England and Wales: a brief history

Policing is partly about helping to reduce particular forms of crime and offering emergency service help, but it is also about policing 'the dangerous classes', a phrase capable of diverse interpretations and one that should always be qualified by the context of 'dangerous to whom'? So what sorts of frauds against whom are and should be prioritised for protection? And which sorts of 'risky financial criminals' are and should be targeted for intelligence-led monitoring and intervention?

In the United Kingdom, as in the United States and other advanced industrial nations, neither the nature of offender/victim relationships nor the social-class composition of 'white-collar criminals' – convicted or unconvicted – are simple: those involved in obtaining money by deception and corruption include members of the inner and outer circles of 'the upperworld' and 'the underworld', and comparatively junior employees. Even upmarket-sounding crimes such as insider dealing may be committed by the company chairman (still mostly a male) or the company PA (still mostly a female). There is no formal official breakdown available of the forms of fraud. However, based on observation of cases and reports, the vast majority of frauds by volume (not by value) reported to the police (in the United Kingdom, by phone or Internet, the Action Fraud national fraud and Internet crime-reporting centre) and (perhaps) recorded by them are as follows: first, plastic card and allied credit frauds committed by 'blue-collar' criminals, increasingly following 'identity theft'; second, embezzlements by modest-status staff, such as thefts of incoming or outgoing company cheques and their conversion into cash; and third, deceptions by businesspeople obtaining money in advance for goods or loans that never materialise, or goods on credit for which they never intended to pay. In short, involvement in sophisticated financial swindles is far from being the preserve of a social elite. Nevertheless, it is by definition outside the range of the routine criminal lumpenproletariat who still constitute the majority of prisoners, despite falling crime rates for mainstream property offences in many developed countries, including the United Kingdom, in recent decades.

The focus by government and leading City figures on the legitimacy and transparency of financial markets coincided with increased concern about the ability of the criminal process to deal with major fraud. Before 1985, the traditional method of dealing with any fraud was that some of the (then) 588 British police Fraud Squad officers, the Department of Trade and Industry (DTI, now BIS) or the revenue department (or any combination of those bodies) would carry out an investigation (perhaps over several years), prepare a report for their in-house lawyers or (in major police and DTI cases) for the Director of Public Prosecutions (DPP). Sometimes counsel would observe that most of the police effort had been wasted and that the police should really have focused on issues they did not examine properly; then the case would either be dropped or the police would be told to do some further investigation, though this might be difficult, since the police had no official access to bank account information prior to a suspect being charged, and sometimes such bank information would be needed to justify the institution of proceedings. Obtaining evidence from abroad was difficult, partly for incompatibility of common law with civil law countries and partly because it had a low political priority. Eventually, following the failure of some major prosecutions, the focus came onto the inadequacies of jury trial and then to a broader reform of investigation and prosecution in complex or serious cases – the creation of specialists within the DPP's Office and then the Serious Fraud Office (SFO) in 1987 (Levi 1993, 2013b). The SFO is a narrow apex of the prosecutorial pyramid. Its budget fell from more than £50 million in 2007 to £36 million for 2010–2011, and less than £30 million thereafter, though it can apply for extra funds for particular cases, as it did for example in the LIBOR case in which a range of traders in major banks were accused of manipulating an important global inter-bank lending rate to make profits for their institutions and large bonuses for themselves, invisible to the outside world. Below are some recent performance data (SFO 2013: 6):

Table 12.1 Case-performance data for serious fraud office cases 2010–2013

	2010–2011	2011–2012	2012–2013
Number of trials	16	19	12
Number of civil recovery orders	1	3	2
Number of defendants convicted	22	39	14
Total number of defendants tried	27	54	20
Percentage of defendants convicted	81%	72%	70%
Average length of sentence (month)	30.9	50.6	71.3
Total sums removed or recovered from persons, entities and defendants associated with criminal or unlawful conduct	€42.7	€50.2	€11.4

An important component of the prosecution process is the power to obtain evidence, which is usually held by third parties with whom the target has a confidential or even legally privileged relationship (Middleton 2005). Much data needed to support or test a case is held outside the immediate jurisdiction of the investigator or even of the English courts. In most fraud investigations, the police have no power to require answers to their questions, though with relative ease, prior to arrest or summons, they can obtain Production Orders under the Police and Criminal Evidence Act 1984 from circuit judges for *documents* kept within the jurisdiction that are required in their investigations. The SFO can require answers as well as documentation, but following a European Court of Human Rights ruling, answers given under compulsion can no longer be used against defendants. Much work goes into the reconstruction of financial arrangements and their meaning, to be in a position to prove the mental element in fraud, though this is easier since the passage of the Fraud Act 2006 in England and Wales. There remains much dispute over the meaning of terms like 'honest services' in the United States and 'misconduct in public office' in the United Kingdom.

The prosecution and trial of fraud

Few countries have specialised prosecution agencies for fraud. In continental Europe, investigating judges and prosecutors typically deal with all-comers, though because of geography of financial centres and/or personal preferences, some may specialise in corruption, fraud and money-laundering. In the US federal system, US Attorneys (appointed by the President) for each district take on (or reject) cases, though Wall Street cases are part of the Southern District of New York and there the most important cases are handled unless, like Enron, they are headquartered in Houston, or commodities cases may be based in Chicago. Also important is the (elected) District Attorney for New York County (Manhattan) whose office, because of New York's role in global dollar settlements, claims jurisdiction for the vast number of cases that go through New York clearing – sometimes in competition with the Department of Justice's federal jurisdictional claims. State-level prosecutors and regulators – most notably the New York State Department of Financial Services – also play an important role in financial crime cases. In most countries, the prosecutor or investigative judge leads the investigation. By contrast, investigations are much more police-led in England, Wales and Northern Ireland and even in Scotland, despite the stronger and longer established discretionary role of the Procurator Fiscal (see Moody and Tombs 1982, for a classic study).

The Serious Fraud Office has proven to be an important criminal justice and 'political' (with a small 'p') institution, the first agency in Britain to have a bureaucratic interest in prosecuting fraud and a formal role of directing police investigations. Its title gives a sense of power and prestige: the announcement by the Attorney-General that 'the Serious Fraud Office is investigating company X' is intended to trigger the perception that this case is being taken seriously. Notwithstanding, although many trial verdicts result from judicial and jury decisions that may be unforeseeable, the SFO has taken a severe media and political battering over its competence since the mid-1990s, accompanied by labels such as 'Serious Farce Office' and 'Seriously Flawed Office' in the well-researched City Slicker columns of the satirical magazine *Private Eye*. This is for two reasons: first, the fact that high-profile prosecutions did not end in conviction or led to lenient plea bargains; and second, conversely, the fact that some of the few prosecutions of senior corporations and executives were proceeded with at all, offending the sentiments of some business and media people who considered that there had been an overreach of the criminal law to cover what was either tolerated behaviour or behaviour that could be 'more appropriately' dealt with by regulators (Levi 1993, 2011). This was exacerbated by some serious errors of judgment by the SFO in acting on advice of accountancy and law firms who were later alleged to have had inadequately disclosed or ignored conflicts of interest.

The Crown Prosecution Service deals with most fraud prosecutions – including very serious tax frauds – in Headquarters or local case work units, depending on their complexity. In recent years, the Financial Conduct Authority (before 2013 called the Financial Services Authority) has played an active role in prosecuting insider dealing, though questions remain about the conditions under which the risk of being caught and prosecuted constitutes the 'credible deterrent' regularly referred to in its enforcement speeches.

Perceptions of effectiveness – real and symbolic – appear to vary according to the latest 'results', and embody the assumptions that first, acquittal is only very rarely a correct verdict, and, second, if an acquittal occurs, the SFO could not have done its job efficiently. SFO Directors' statements that their objective is to pass the scrutiny of adequacy imposed by the trial judge are regarded as weak, defensive excuses rather than accurate statements of constitutional due-process principle. This has its political effects in resources for the SFO. In the late 1980s and early 1990s, an average of only four SFO cases per annum involved chief executive officers working for financial institutions situated in London's financial markets or public limited companies (Fooks 2003); this may not have differed greatly subsequently. Fooks considers that this is *disproportionately* small, but this judgement depends on what one considers to be the 'true level' of frauds of different types. In the light of recent findings about elite corporate misconduct, one can deduce that such prosecutions were only scratching the surface. But at the time, who (other than the offenders themselves) knew?

The history of the BAE case is elegantly set out in *R (on the application of Corner House Research and others) v Director of the Serious Fraud Office* [2008] UKHL 60. Suffice it to state that when the SFO investigation got close to obtaining information it needed from Switzerland to mount a prosecution of BAE for transnational bribery in relation to the Saudi Al Yamamah arms contract, the Saudis threatened to withdraw counterterrorist assistance, which – doubtless fortuitously – placed it beyond the 'national economic benefit' issues outlawed by s.5 of the Organisation for Economic Cooperation and Development (OECD) Convention on Transnational Bribery as a reason for not prosecuting. The SFO Director eventually agreed that the threat to UK national security overrode the benefit of continuing that particular case against BAE.

Notwithstanding the legal arguments, this produced an international outcry, stimulated by Cornerhouse and other NGOs, and by the OECD itself which continued to question the UK government's sincerity in its commitment to the OECD Convention and its slowness in passing modern anti-bribery laws (which culminated in the tough Bribery Act 2010 which caused alarm among business elites over the personal liability of directors and over constraints on externally invisible corporate entertainment of existing and potential clients). This was an issue that did not excite the public but continues to raise important questions about the objectivity of decisions to prosecute and not to prosecute (as also in the United States, though the Federal authorities have a Congress-approved Special Prosecutor arrangement that seeks – not always successfully, as in President Clinton and the 'Whitewater' enquiry – to depoliticise prosecution decisions about political elites).

The SFO's financial limitations led the ex-Inland Revenue Director Richard Alderman (2008–2012) to focus less on prosecution and more on the need to leverage its efforts via a more general 'fraud and corruption reduction' strategy. This shift generated much criticism and difficulties in the courts over plea negotiations. David Green, the more traditionalist Director of the SFO, in 2012 publicly stated that he would adopt a more prosecution-focused position, leaving broader preventative efforts to others, but the SFO continues to find it hard to pay for a more active prosecution policy.

Even before Richard Alderman announced the policy of seeking to get corporate bribers to volunteer confessions in return for more lenient treatment (which he was unable to guarantee[2]), there was debate about the role of informants in the criminal justice process. Nevertheless, the principle that the first firm to make a full confession is entitled to escape prosecution is built into price-fixing cartel legislation, and the United Kingdom has now adopted the US system of Deferred Prosecution Agreements (though without its Draconian punishments for offenders who are convicted after pleading not guilty, which provide much of the incentive for 'cooperation').

Police attitudes to fraud in the United Kingdom

Interest in fraud among senior police officers has increased since the mid-1980s, probably due to greater attention to it by television, radio, and in the main crime and news sections of newspapers as well as in the business sections that non-specialist officers are less likely to read. Moreover, as in the United States, the prospect of well-paid post-retirement jobs for police officers makes expertise in financial crime investigation a more desirable attribute than has been the case in the past. (Indeed, increasingly, competent Economic Crime officers are being lured out of the police by banks and consultancy/corporate investigation firms.)

Nevertheless, outside the City of London Police and the Economic Crime Command of the National Crime Agency, there is very little evident appreciation by chief officers of the importance of policing fraud, whether of the elite or blue-collar kind: their practical indifference extends to all crimes with corporate victims, and even to most crimes against investors. In this respect, little has changed since the mid-1980s (Levi 2013a), though the sheer volume of increased complaints and complex enquiries into real-estate frauds and public-sector corruption generated larger Fraud Squads, at least temporarily; as Doig and Levi (2009) noted, there was a significant decline in which fraud investigators were replaced by financial investigators who could bring income into the police via proceeds of crime confiscation, and fraud squads themselves have largely disappeared (Doig and Levi 2013), even if there are substantially more staff if we include civilian and social security fraud investigators. The explanation for this neglect is far from clear, but it may reflect some Victorian conception of prudence whereby everyone who does not take sufficient care of their own property deserves little sympathy. Perhaps more important are pragmatic factors such as little political pressure on them to do more about fraud compared with other areas of policing, despite high anxiety about identity thefts and mass-marketing swindles (and lower crime rates); the low productivity of Fraud Squad staff in relation to standard police performance indicators, fraud being vastly more labour-intensive to investigate; police apprehension about their skill levels to deal with both elite frauds and more everyday eCrimes; and chief officers' failure to appreciate the social and economic impact of fraud losses on the local and national economy. The fact, however, that even crimes committed by non-elite persons against corporations are not prioritised by the police indicates that this is not a simple question of the police pandering to 'elite interests'.

Key problems in the criminal justice process and fraud: British fraud investigation in an international context

In the contemporary era, special white-collar-crime investigative bodies exist for the following reasons: First, the 'new classes' of victim – for example, collectors of early retirement/redundancy pay, and senior citizens with savings facing mass-marketing scams – constitute a political risk that calls for a response to these 'deserving victims'. Second, Britain (even more than other countries) was and is concerned about its reputation in the global marketplace, given its dependence upon income from 'invisible earnings' to the balance of payments. Around 2 million people in the United Kingdom work in financial and professional services, of whom a third work in London (http://www.thecityuk.com/financial-services-in-the-uk/uk-by-region/). In March 2012 there were 1.1 million workforce jobs in the financial and insurance activities industry in the United Kingdom, 3.6 per cent of all workforce jobs. In 2011, financial and insurance services reportedly contributed £125.4 billion in gross value added (GVA) to the UK economy, 9.4 per cent of the UK's total GVA. London accounted for 45.8 per cent of the total financial and insurance sector GVA in the United Kingdom in 2009 (Maer and Broughton 2012). Thus whether or not this is a good thing or constitutes an 'unbalanced economy', the financial and professional (i.e., law and accountancy) services sector is currently a major component of the UK economy, and the government feels that it needs to protect those income and balance of payment flows at the same time as protecting its reputation. Financial services are strategically important in a country in which injuries at work have been reduced substantially by closing down many risky environments in the process of de-industrialisation. Britain is the most dependent of advanced industrial countries on its financial services industry. Third, though the importance of this fluctuates over time and space, there are fears that 'organised crime' may infiltrate 'commerce', whether by fraud or by integration of the proceeds of crime in the money-laundering process (Levi 2008). Whether this concern leads to tough action to clean the Augean Stables or to suppression to avoid frightening the horses (and save public enforcement costs) is a difficult judgement which partly depends on the degree and manifestation of 'moral panic' and the need to legitimate the system (Levi 2009, 2013a).

When we discuss elite fraud and its control in Britain, we must see this against the backdrop of global financial and industrial markets. Let us take, for example, the Boesky/Guinness connection in the 1980s. Shapiro's (1985) excellent review of the prosecution approach of the US authorities to securities fraud suggested that most cases were marginal outsiders involved in parochial affairs, but she did not display sufficient awareness of the historically contingent nature of this judgement. Soon after her work was published, the almost accidental discovery of Dennis Levine's insider-trading network led to his sacrificing American trader Ivan Boesky as part of his plea bargain; Boesky informed not only on star investment banker Mike Milken (who, unfortunately for him, had no one higher to trade in, and therefore got a formal ten years' imprisonment, reduced on appeal) – for a good account, see Rosoff et al. (1997, 2013) – but also on those who had formed an illegal operation with him to support the price of the Guinness shares which were being offered in exchange for Distillers shares in the United Kingdom as part of an aggressive corporate takeover bid. This information was passed by the United States regulatory authorities to their UK counterparts, and thence to the police. Perhaps the British authorities would not have prosecuted if they had not been concerned that competitive leaking by the Americans would have harmed the reputation of the UK financial services industry: former Guinness chief executive Ernest Saunders maintained (personal communication) that he was a victim of Margaret Thatcher's desire to show the world that Britain was tough on white-collar crime and of 'the Scottish (business) Mafia' upset at his refusal to move the Guinness headquarters to Scotland, as he had promised. But, whatever the reason, the consequence was the prosecution of a series of major British entrepreneurs and professionals, and the imprisonment

Table 12.2 Incoming requests to Serious Fraud Office, 2003–2012

	2003–2004	2004–2005	2005–2006	2006–2007	2007–2008	2008–2009	2009–2010	2010–2011	2011–2012
Countries assisted	30	31	23	24	30	41	45	45	30
New requests referred	30	35	41	53	45	55	48	40	45

Source: Serious Fraud Office.

of some high-status businesspeople. We live in a global regulatory village, though some parts are policed more heavily than others, and Western governments were proud of operating 'light-touch regulation' before the financial crash of 2007. Competitive pressures in globalised financial services markets intensify this cross-national competition for scarce business.

The multinational convergence in prosecution arises largely because of the risks that fraud is posing to popular capitalism, to investments on securities markets and to deposits in financial institutions, as well as the fear of 'organised crime' infiltration into business. Most such cases involve information and funds held abroad, and often foreign nationals, as implicit in Table 12.2 above.

Yet when it is proposed that officers might have supranational powers, there is massive resistance, not least because it is hard to see how and to whom such officers are accountable (though similar problems arise in cross-border drug investigations, conducted via Europol and Eurojust). This cultural resistance (and antipathy to the EU) is also illustrated by the hostility in many quarters to the idea of the European Public Prosecutor.

Policing powers are influenced not just by law but, inter alia, by the visibility of particular police actions and the tolerance of the courts. Coping with overseas jurisdictions, the difficulty of informal as well as formal action increases considerably, since the patterns of pressure, friendship, and so forth make for fewer and less powerful trade-offs and for greater uncertainty about responses in different cultures. Secrecy statutes also present legal obstacles to the conveying of information which many police officers in many countries find particularly irksome, though these are diminishing under international pressure for mutual legal assistance and transparency in the anti-money-laundering and anti-corruption movements. Evidentiary rules present major problems.

There are also conflicts of interest between different agencies, both nationally and internationally. The 1991–1992 investigations into the Bank of Commerce and Credit International (BCCI) and into the dead financier and publisher Robert Maxwell produced considerable tensions between British and American (Federal and New York) investigators. Such tensions have also arisen in BAE, Enron, and Siemens bribery and fraud cases, the LIBOR and FOREX manipulation investigations, and several cybercrime cases, with extraordinary public protests about over-mighty American prosecutorial approaches, and the US generalised threat of much longer sentences for those who fail to earn credit from cooperation with the prosecutor.

The emotional contradiction many people experience when reviewing the prosecution of white-collar crime is that however ultra-expensive and often fruitless major criminal cases are, convicting 'the suits' seems like a necessary prerequisite of 'equal justice'. This is brilliantly captured in the novel and movie *Bonfire of the Vanities*, where the prosecutors long to put some rich white guys in jail, instead of the poor blacks whom they feel deep down have little real alternative to crime (Wolfe 1987). Serious fraud and corruption prosecutors might get it wrong either in imagining possible lines of defence or in imputing culpability. On the other hand, the depth of prejudicial publicity that follows a corporate collapse is a powerful impetus to carry people forward to prosecution, fuelled by media suspicions of 'cover up' if they do not do so. The prosecution of white-collar crime, as much as any other, entails the perpetual refrains of 'was he behaving dishonestly?' and 'what did he know and what was he told about this transaction?' The criminal law bifurcates people into the crude binary division of 'guilty' *or* 'innocent', and in the complex world of corporate actions where there are so many people who are potentially indictable, this yields strange and bitter fruit, in which many of the prosecution witnesses are as unattractive and prone to generate disinformation as are the defendants. Furthermore, as Braithwaite and Pettit (1990) argue, there is something pointless about pursuing such cases to conviction and imprisonment, when we should be searching for alternative ways of mediating social harms *for all crimes*. Yet to be constructive only for white-collar crimes sticks in the gut, especially if we are afraid that we are being conned by smooth-talking defendants and their representatives into not giving them their just deserts. The fact is that it would cost a fortune to prosecute a large percentage of even detected frauds, health and safety offences, and so forth, and clog up agencies with the extra case preparation efforts so that without large extra resources in times of austerity, the net result might be less inspection and reform than is currently the case.

In deciding whether to expend more scarce resources reactively on cases or proactively in developing intelligence on serious economic criminals, it might be easier if we could expect that financial crime was something people drifted in and out of after a short period. But economic criminals are quite likely to be late entrants to crime (van Koppen 2013), and their potential longevity as offenders is also important: unlike crimes that require agility and speed, fraud capabilities do not diminish with age, and may even be enhanced to the extent that age brings credibility in face-to-face interactions (Levi 2008). Consequently, the demographic/social-class composition of the category of 'fraudsters' is much wider than that for other 'criminals for gain', even if one restricts oneself to convicted offenders. But this applies even more strongly if we extend our analysis to unprosecuted persons. So although many fraudsters 'drift', lifetime offender management may be needed to keep them under surveillance and control. However, who, outside of those convicted of major crimes, should we target and with what sorts of surveillance, given the routine invisibility of their planning and operations, and the difficulty of differentiating them from the routine of legitimate business activities?

Alternative sanctions for white-collar crime: towards regulatory 'justice'?

Decisions about the relative roles of regulators and criminal courts should and will remain a matter of symbolic as well as pragmatic debate: the argument is about the ethics of not criminalising white-collar 'criminals' while other, lesser crooks go to jail, as well as being about the best way of reducing future misbehaviour. This is partly the problem originally addressed by Braithwaite and Pettit (1990) and by Fisse and Braithwaite (1993) in their rejection of a 'just deserts' approach to dealing with crime and corporate accountability generally. In practice, officials are less receptive to applying such a future-oriented approach to fraudsters than to 'corporate criminals', but whether fraud will be dealt with by persuasive tactics or by retributive prosecution depends on many factors. These are whether the victim considers that there is any point in reporting the offence; how busy the police are and whether they are willing to record it; whether it comes to the attention of the authorities in any other way, for example via proactive audits; whether the 'offender' is a live company that has a regulatable future; how morally bad the offender is perceived to be (with organised crime connections increasing substantially the culpability and crime seriousness scores); and how expensive and how successful an investigation and prosecution is estimated to be.

A complicated, multi-jurisdictional fraud involving people with no prior serious criminal records and untraumatised victims losing less than a million pounds is very unlikely to be treated as a high priority in the United Kingdom or the United States, but it partly depends on the caseload of police and prosecutors and whether the suspect is a target for involvement in other crimes. With many fraud cases arising in the context of 'closed' transactions that are not part of a systematic process of offending by companies, one has to distinguish within the overall category of white-collar crime such 'unpromising' cases from those where multiple victims and multiple offenders can be 'encouraged' to change their ways. In the case of multiple victims – whether private or public sector – a review of business processes may yield preventative insights which can reduce fraud (Audit Commission 2012; Doig 2012), but multiple corporate offenders may be harder to spot, as audit firms usually argue.

How would such a forward-looking approach to fraud be implemented, if regarded as socially acceptable? Prevention mechanisms against company directors at large are much more limited than they are with persons selling financial services, who have to be vetted as 'fit and proper' persons before they can be licensed to operate: there is no bar upon anyone setting up in business, however ill-qualified they may be by competence and/or morality, and no bar upon their trading at the risk of others, provided that those others are willing to offer the businesspeople and/or their corporate vehicle credit. As some creditors of the Ostrich Farming Company (OFC) – a 'scam' in which investors were offered high rates of return on the purchase of birds whose meat was supposedly due to rise in price, and found that many of them owned the same bird! – understandably stated, if one of the grounds for the DTI's wishing to wind up the company was that one of its directors had shown himself to be unfit in the past, why was he allowed to become a director of the OFC at all (*The Times*, 11 May 1996)? (Though it is an offence for bankrupts to obtain credit without informing others of their status.) In the United Kingdom and the United States (though not in many parts of continental Europe), people may come out of jail after conviction for fraud and set up a new business or become a director of an existing one without anything to prevent them looting it. Nor, except in rare circumstances in which an application can be made under the Companies Act to wind up the company 'in the public interest', is there any means to put an end to a company unless it fails to pay its debts. *After* their business has 'failed', people can also be disqualified by criminal courts (following offences committed 'in connection with the management of a company') under section 2 and section 5 of the Company Directors' Disqualification Act 1986 ('CDDA'), and by civil courts under sections 3, 4, 6, 8, 10 and 11 CDDA from taking part in the management of a company *in future*, at least without the permission of the court. (This combines a permissive attitude to entrepreneurialism with regulation of persistently fraudulent and incompetent people who are a danger to others.)

Between April 2012 and April 2013, the Business Innovation and Skills Department successfully prosecuted 198 defendants (165 the previous year) (https://www.gov.uk/fraud-bis-investigations-prosecutions-and-enforcement). Of those:

- 123 received custodial sentences, and most of the remainder received punishment in the community ranging from 300 hours unpaid work, community punishment orders and supervision orders
- 50 were disqualified from being involved in the running of limited companies from between 1 and 12 years
- 11 were ordered to pay compensation to their victims ranging from £250 to £33,514
- 15 were ordered to pay £1,439,264 as a result of confiscation proceedings; in the same period defendants paid £1,176,387 to the court to satisfy the orders
- 112 were ordered to pay contributions towards prosecution costs of £255,827.

No harm or criminal profit data are available against which to assess these enforcement results. Altogether, between the end of 1986 and the end of 1997, 4,800 directors were disqualified, two-thirds of them for more than three years. However, the absence of data broken down by multiple 'failed' directors makes it difficult to demonstrate the extent to which this is the commercial equivalent of the 'three strikes and you're out' incapacitation equivalent of imprisonment policy in the United States.

What the *effects* of such disqualifications are is unknown: in practice, there is nothing to stop banned directors from inventing a new identity and starting a new business under a false name, though they commit a criminal offence by doing so. (At the beginning of 1998, a 'hot line' was established to encourage reporting of this offence, though no statistics are available on how often this happens or what is done about complaints.) Unlike those financial services jobs that require authorisation in almost all Western countries, where vetting tends to be more rigorous (including criminal record and personal indebtedness checks), one cannot be confident that their previous status would be discovered even if their *next* company subsequently went into liquidation. There are also problems about defining what corporate involvement constitutes a violation. In short, even where bans are in force and activities are known to the authorities, commercial incapacitation can be incomplete.

The impact of media publicity and disciplinary sanctions upon *organisations* has been revived by the 'naming and shaming' tactics first developed by HM Treasury during 1997 to 'encourage' life assurance firms to compensate the estimated 1.5 million people who were sold inappropriate private pensions when their company pensions were more beneficial to them. Such shaming was then used alongside regulatory sanctions and the threat of de-authorisation to conduct financial services business in subsequent scandals such as the 'mis-selling' of Personal Protection Insurance. Regulated firms paid out £12.9 billion between January 2011 and October 2013 to people who were sold insurance inappropriate to their circumstances (like protection against unemployment for self-employed and for retired people who could never claim on it). It is implausible that senior management did not know that their employee bonus and target-setting led to these abuses which generated so much of their profits (and their own personal bonuses). Much depends on how profitable the firm itself is: if the reason it has gone into crooked business is that it was not managing to break even by legitimate means, the prospects for reform are poor. But if it was committing or turning a blind eye to employee fraud to maximise corporate profits and/or personal bonuses, the prospects for reform – with cultural change and supervision – are better, since the firm can survive without misconduct.

Deferred Prosecution Agreements (introduced into the United Kingdom in 2013) are increasingly used in contexts where financial organisations such as KPMG and HSBC are what I would term 'too big to be failed' (by the regulators). They are usually accompanied by burdensome and expensive requirements for monitoring and cultural/organisational reform that are intended as rehabilitative sanctions. Regulatory penalties can be very large (at least in money terms if not as a proportion of turnover or profit) and can be accompanied by agreed texts setting out very extensive admissions of wrongdoing. In fiscal year 2012, the Securities and Exchange Commission (SEC) Division of Enforcement brought 734 enforcement actions – the second-highest number of actions filed in a single year. Overall, in connection with the financial crisis, the SEC (2012) has imposed many professional and industry bars on individuals; returned more than $6 billion FY 2009–2012 to harmed investors; obtained more than $11 billion in ordered disgorgements and penalties; and filed actions against 129 individuals and institutions stemming from the financial crisis, including more than 50 CEOs, CFOs and other senior officers (though the standing of the firms from which they came does not all fit into the elite category). Mainly due to large LIBOR rate-fixing cases also being considered for prosecution, the UK Financial Services Authority levied fines of £312 million in the year to end 2012, three times higher than the next highest year, rising to £443 million in 2013.

In addition, in December 2013, the European Commission imposed fines of €1.7 billion for operating a rate-fixing cartel. The Euribor investigation 2005–2008 settlement involved Barclays, Deutsche Bank, RBS and Société Générale. In yen LIBOR, the banks involved were UBS, RBS, Deutsche Bank, Citigroup and JPMorgan. These sharp increases in penalties all reflect the targeting of more prestigious firms, but also the fact that those firms had been allowed by management and by regulatory failures to commit egregious and in some cases endemic misconduct against the public. Altogether it has been calculated that 'conduct costs' for ten international banks in the period 2008–2012 totalled £148.02 billion, including provisions against future costs (£100 bn. without) (McCormick 2013).

Whether regulatory sanctions (or formal monitoring) really deter fraudsters depends on what 'sort of people' they are. Even the most hard-nosed tycoons accused of white-collar crime dislike bad publicity, for they generally want others to think well of them. Part of the 'techniques of delinquency' of those who do offend are beliefs – prevalent among offenders generally – that their acts cause no real harm to anyone. Hence the imagery of seriousness in the media and among those whose opinions they may value is important, though the ingenious can always differentiate their contemplated or past acts as belonging to the lower range of harmful or even harmless actions. But the symbolic and practical messages that are sent out to white-collar offenders have an impact on deterrence as well as retribution: hence the controversy over the Queen Mother shaking hands with Guinness convict Gerald Ronson while on parole (Levi 1991). I return to the moral issue because even if it were no less ineffective to deal with people outside the criminal justice process, would it be ethically right to send a few thousand shoplifters a year to jail while leaving a director who stole more than all of them put together to be disqualified and without a criminal record? It might be very difficult to show that senior executives had sufficient mental awareness to found corporate or individual criminal culpability under English law for mis-selling Personal Protection Insurance, and there is no doubt that victims received compensation earlier by treating it as a regulatory rather than as a criminal matter. So it may have been pragmatic, but was it right to deal with the systematic 'mis-selling' of financial services as a compensation issue rather than as a fraud offence?

Conclusion

In a large range of developed and underdeveloped countries, there has been a populist anger against corruption and fraud, and also a movement for 'equal punishment' of social and political elites engaged in crime, though this has only intermittently filtered through to the prosecution process (see Levi and Nelken 1996). During the 1980s, there was a connection between populist pressure and prosecution of more serious financial criminals in the United States (Calavita and Pontell 1994; Zimring and Hawkins 1993) but this is significantly less true today, at least for corporate elites, despite strong public sentiments against 'greedy bankers' (Pontell et al. 2014; Levi 2009, 2013a), to which the UK/US Uncut movement and NGOs such as the Tax Justice Network gave active voice. In countries where corruption has become a major political and economic problem and is recognised as such, anti-corruption agencies have been established: a process encouraged first by the British (though only in their colonies, not in the United Kingdom itself); later by the 1997 OECD Convention which criminalised corporate bribery overseas; and by the UN Convention Against Corruption 2005. It is also stimulated by local pressures and outrage, forcing even India to create an anti-corruption body in 2014, decades after it was first proposed. This trend and variations within it is too substantial a topic to review here (Lord 2013, 2014a, 2014b).

Everyday corruption and frauds like payment-card fraud are highly visible, but higher level misconduct is less visible except when exposed by whistleblowers, civil society or anti-money-laundering obligations that have become much more prominent in recent decades. Unlike the United Kingdom, in France, Italy, Spain and even Switzerland, high-profile investigating magistrates have gone after political elites at home and abroad, and there have been highly politicised attempts to restrain this vigour by bringing them under more central governmental control. The dividing line between corruption and large party political donations (including alleged 'cash for honours') from businesspeople can be hard to determine, and there have been scandals following revelations about large secret cash gifts in France and elsewhere which are required legally to be disclosed. My research for the Royal Commission on Criminal Justice (Levi 1993) – and longer observations and interviews over the past three decades – did not enable me to disentangle whether the non-prosecution of senior industry or governmental persons in some cases was due to 'influence' or merely to the well-attested fact that remoteness from actual decisions makes it hard to convict people for corporate crime and therefore, consistent with the Code for Crown Prosecutors, arguably improper to prosecute them. A good early illustration is the problem of ascertaining the role played by former Home Secretary Reginald Maudling in the corrupt building scandals of architect John Poulson and in the investment 'scams' of American Jerome Hoffman (Gillard 1974), where a 'professional' judgement of the probability of conviction is hard to separate from a 'political' judgement of the downside risks of acquittal (or, for that matter, of conviction).

Though their overall conviction rate (including guilty pleas) varies between two-thirds and over 90 per cent, the low conviction rate in 'famous name' SFO prosecutions makes the Law Officers of the Crown as well as the case lawyers look bad, and this is something they normally seek to avoid. Bureaucracies need the support of politicians (including the Attorney-General) for resources, and there have been major campaigns against the Serious Fraud Office under the rubric of insufficient courage and cost-effectiveness, whose deeper motivation may lie in the ambivalent feelings of politicians and businesspeople about the *desirability* of the effective prosecution of fraud. What sort of system would plausibly provide the kind of transparency of decision-making that might reassure people that decisions were *not* influenced directly or indirectly by 'political' considerations is too major a task for our existing knowledge, but it seems unlikely that any system, even in theory, would meet all the necessary and sufficient conditions for 'true independence'. My object here has been to try to integrate some themes in 'white-collar-crime control' with the mainstream of literature on crime visibility and on police and prosecutorial accountability, and, in an arena unfamiliar to many criminologists, to raise some issues of major practical as well as ideological importance about the methodology of equal justice and impartiality. How to ensure high levels of motivation, skill and courage among prosecutors while giving them the independence that can mean freedom not to do enough remains an elusive task. So too is the broader challenge of raising the visibility of white-collar misconduct (whether or not prosecuted as fraud) via the 'Publish What You Pay' transparency pressures by NGOs to expose data about income received in developing countries for commodities and contracts, and the G8/G20 initiatives to increase disclosure of 'beneficial owners' of companies even in financial havens (to reveal who really controls these businesses): the hope is that by increasing transparency, this raises the risks of doing illicit business and deters.

It seems appropriate to end this review with a quotation from Lord Justice Brett in the unreported case of Wilson v. Clinch (1879):

> I must confess to such an abhorrence of fraud in business that I am always most reluctant to come to the conclusion that fraud has been committed.

When white-collar crime is committed by strangers, it is relatively easy to accept and to act against, though for pragmatic reasons – getting the money back, lack of confidence in the police and courts, and/or not wishing to waste expensive management time – even frauds by strangers usually go unreported. When 'people like us' are involved, it is harder to believe that the person was really dishonest and, though such persons are sometimes punished severely for 'letting the side down', sentencers often experience empathy at their suffering while spending perhaps years awaiting the verdict and at their Fall from Grace. At one level, this humanity – for it is generally empathy rather than a belief that the fraud was not serious (Wheeler et al. 1988; Levi 2010, 2014b) – is laudable. Is it acceptable, however, that such judicial reflection about the value of punishment tends to be restricted to the small elite of white-collar offenders who are not 'selected out' of the prosecution process, and is so seldom extended to those who have no grace from which to fall?

Notes

1. I have excluded here corporate regulatory bodies like the Health and Safety Executive and the Environment Agency who, though socially important, do not deal with fraud. See, for example, Tombs and Whyte (2013a, 2013b).
2. See the important cases of R v. Dougall [2010] EWCA Crim 1048 and R v. Innospec [2010] EW Misc 7 (EWCC) which represent the determination of the judiciary not to allow the SFO Director to agree to specific sentences with the accused in return for their cooperation.

References

Audit Commission (2012) *Protecting the Public Purse*. Available at: http://www.audit-commission.gov.uk/2012/11/protecting-the-public-purse-2012/. London: The Audit Commission.

Braithwaite, J. and Pettit, P. (1990) *Not Just Deserts*. Oxford: Oxford University Press.

Button, M., Tapley, J. and Lewis, C. (2013) 'The "Fraud Justice Network" and the Infrastructure of Support for Individual Fraud Victims in England and Wales', *Criminology & Criminal Justice*, 13(1): 37–61.

Calavita, K. and Pontell, H. (1994) 'The State and White-Collar Crime: Saving the Savings and Loans', *Law and Society Review*, 28(2): 297–324.

Corker, D. and Levi, M. (1996) 'Pre-trial Publicity and Its Treatment in the English Courts', *Criminal Law Review*, September, 1–12.

Cullen, F., Cavender, G., Maakestad, W. and Benson, M. (2006) *Corporate Crime under Attack: The Fight to Criminalize Business Violence*. Cincinnati: Anderson Publishing.

Davis, A. (2013) 'The City in Myth and Reality', http://www.taxjustice.net/cms/upload/pdf/TJF_8–1_-_City_Myth_-_Aeron_Davis.pdf.

Doig, A. (ed.) (2012) *Fraud: The Counter Fraud Practitioner's Handbook*. Andover: Gower Publishing.

Doig, A. and Levi, M. (2009) 'Inter-agency Work and the UK Public Sector Investigation of Fraud, 1996–2006: Joined Up Rhetoric and Disjointed Reality', *Policing and Society*, 19(3): 199–215.

—— (2013) 'A Case of Arrested Development? Delivering the UK National Fraud Strategy within Competing Policing Policy Priorities', *Public Money and Management*, 33(1), March 2013: 1–8.

Fisse, B. and Braithwaite, J. (1993) *Corporations, Crime, and Accountability*. Cambridge: Cambridge University Press.

Fooks, G. (2003) 'In the Valley of the Blind the One-Eyed Man is King: Corporate Crime and the Myopia of Financial Regulation', in S. Tombs and D. Whyte (eds), *Unmasking the Crimes of The Powerful: Scrutinizing States and Corporations*. New York: Peter Lang.

Friedrichs, D. (2013) *Trusted Criminals*. 4th edn. Belmont, CA: Wadsworth.

Gillard, M. (1974) *A Little Pot of Money: The Story of Reginald Maudling and the Real Estate Fund of America*. London: Deutsch.

Levi, M. (1983) 'Blaming the Jury: Frauds on Trial', *Journal of Law and Society*, 10: 257–269.

—— (1987) *Regulating Fraud: White-Collar Crime and the Criminal Process*. London: Routledge.

—— (1988) 'The Role of the Jury in Complex Cases', in M. Findlay and P. Duff (eds), *The Jury Under Attack*. London: Butterworths.

—— (1991) 'Sentencing White-Collar Crime in the Dark: The Case of the Guinness Four', *Howard Journal of Criminal Justice*, 28(4): 257–279.

—— (1992) 'White-Collar Crime Victimization', in K. Schlegel and D. Weisburd (eds), *White-Collar Crime Reconsidered*. Boston: Northeastern University Press.

—— (1993) *The Investigation, Prosecution and Trial of Serious Fraud*. Royal Commission on Criminal Justice Research Study No 14. London: HMSO.

—— (2008) *The Phantom Capitalists: The Organisation and Control of Long-Firm Fraud*. 2nd edn. Aldershot: Gower.
—— (2009) 'Suite Revenge? The Shaping of Folk Devils and Moral Panics about White-Collar Crimes', *British Journal of Criminology*, 49(1): 48–67.
—— (2010) 'Hitting the Suite Spot: Sentencing Frauds', *Journal of Financial Crime*, 17(1): 116–132.
—— (2011) 'Political Autonomy, Accountability and Efficiency in the Prosecution of Serious White-Collar Crimes', in J. Gobert and A.-M. Pascal (eds), *European Developments in Corporate Criminal Liability*. London: Routledge, 189–205.
—— (2013a) *Regulating Fraud: White-Collar Crime and the Criminal Process*. Routledge Revivals. London: Routledge.
—— (2013b) 'Legitimacy, Crimes, and Compliance in "the City": De Maximis non Curat Lex?' in J. Tankebe and A. Liebling (eds), *Legitimacy and Criminal Justice: An International Exploration*. New York: Oxford University Press, 157–177.
—— (2014a) 'Organized Fraud', in Letizia Paoli (ed.), *Oxford Handbook of Organised Crime*. New York: Oxford University Press.
—— (2014b) 'Sentencing the Respectable Offender: Re-collaring the White-Collar Criminal', in F. Cullen, M. Benson and S. van Slyke (eds), *Oxford Handbook of White-Collar Crime*. New York: Oxford University Press.
Levi, M. and Nelken, D. (eds) (1996) *The Corruption of Politics and the Politics of Corruption*. Oxford: Blackwells and Special Issue of *Journal of Law and Society*.
Lord, N. (2013) 'Regulating Transnational Corporate Bribery: Anti-bribery and Corruption in the UK and Germany', *Crime Law Soc Change*, 60: 127–145.
—— (2014a) 'Responding to Transnational Corporate Bribery using International Frameworks for Enforcement: Anti-bribery and Corruption in the UK and Germany', *Criminology & Criminal Justice*, 14(1): 100–120.
—— (2014b) *Regulating Corporate Bribery and Corruption in International Business*. Andover: Ashgate.
Maer, L. and Broughton, N. (2012) *The Financial Sector's Contribution to the UK Economy*. Available at: http://www.parliament.uk/briefing-papers/SN06193/the-financial-sectors-contribution-to-the-uk-economy.
McCormick, R. (2013) http://blogs.lse.ac.uk/conductcosts/bank-conduct-costs-results/.
Middleton, D. (2005) 'The Legal and Regulatory Response to Solicitors Involved in Serious Fraud: Is Regulatory Action More Effective than Criminal Prosecution?' *British Journal of Criminology*, 45(6): 810–836.
Moody, S. and Tombs, J. (1982) *Prosecution in the Public Interest*. Edinburgh: Scottish Academic Press.
Pontell, H., Black, W. and Geis, G. (2014) 'Too Big to Fail, Too Powerful to Jail? On the Absence of Criminal Prosecutions Following the 2008 Financial Meltdown', *Crime, Law and Social Change*, 61(1): 1–13.
Rosoff, S., Pontell, H., and Tillman, R. (1997) *Profit without Honor*. Upper Saddle River, NJ: Prentice-Hall.
—— (2013) *Profit without Honor*. 6th edn. Upper Saddle River, NJ: Prentice-Hall.
Serious Fraud Office (2013) *Annual Report and Accounts 2012–13*. London: TSO.
Shapiro, S. (1985) 'The Road Not Taken: The Elusive Path to Criminal Prosecution for White-Collar Offenders', *Law and Society Review*, 19(2): 179–218.

Styles, J. (1983) 'Embezzlement, Industry and the Law in England', in M. Berg, P. Hudson, and M. Sonenscher (eds), *Manufacture in Town and Country before the Factory*. Cambridge: Cambridge University Press.

Tombs, S. and Whyte, D. (2013a) 'Transcending the Deregulation Debate? Regulation, Risk and the Enforcement of Health and Safety Law in the UK', *Regulation & Governance*, 7(1): 61–79.

—— (2013b) 'The Myths and Realities of Deterrence in Workplace Safety Regulation', *Br J Criminol*, 53(5): 746–763.

van Koppen, M. (2013) *Pathways into Organized Crime: Criminal Opportunities and Adult-Onset Offending*. Ph.D. thesis. Amsterdam: Vrije Universiteit. http://hdl.handle.net/1871/48030.

Wheeler, S., Mann, K. and Sarat, A. (1988) *Sitting in Judgment*. New Haven: Yale University Press.

Wilson, S. (2006) 'Law, Morality and Regulation: Victorian Experiences of Financial Crime', *British Journal of Criminology*, 46(6): 1073–1090.

—— (2014) *The Origins of Modern Financial Crime: Historical Foundations and Current Problems in Britain*. London: Routledge.

Wolfe, T. (1987) *Bonfire of the Vanities*. New York: Random House.

Zimring, F. and Hawkins, G. (1993) 'Crime, Justice and the Savings and Loans Crisis', in M. Tonry and A. Reiss (eds), *Beyond the Law*. Chicago: University of Chicago Press.

13
Invisible Crime, Social Harm and the Radical Criminological Tradition

Peter Francis, Pamela Davies and Tanya Wyatt

Introduction

In writing this book our ambitions have been threefold. First, to examine contemporary criminological research and scholarship in an area that we have been broadly interested in for some 20 years – what we have elsewhere termed invisible crime (Davies et al. 1999). In putting together this volume, we are in no way suggesting that its contents should be seen as exhaustive of invisible crimes or social harms. Far from it. The examples discussed within the 12 chapters have been chosen to bring illustration of the range, type and nature of crimes and harms involved. In each case their 'relative invisibility' is exposed. A second ambition has been to examine whether the core 'features of invisibility' originally identified by Jupp et al. (1999) remain salient as an organising framework to explain why particular actions and or reactions remain hidden and neglected, despite their harmful impact on the lives of individuals and communities. Our third ambition has been to contribute in some small part to a progressive radical criminological tradition (Currie 2007, 2010; Hudson 2010; Matthews 2009, 2014; Scraton 2007; Taylor et al. [1973] 2013) intent on connecting action and reaction through the dynamic interplay between theory, empirical research and intervention (Matthews 2009), and working towards a better and more just society (Currie 2007).

These ambitions have allowed us to collaborate with contributors sitting at ease within a progressive radical criminological tradition whose research, utilising a range of methods and methodologies examines activities and actions, some of which are criminal, many of which fall into the broader category of social harm, that impact considerably on human suffering and yet whose visibility and/or regulation remains limited and at the margins. Equally, and in lieu of the late Victor Jupp, these ambitions have allowed the three of us to align our own political and criminological approaches – namely feminist, radical green and critical realist – in order to reflect upon and refine and develop the original organising thesis.

In compiling this book we have been mindful of the words of Currie (2010) when he argues that a radical realism offers the best hope of providing the intellectual underpinnings for a genuinely progressive approach to crime, harm and suffering around the world. He outlines a series of 'fundamental principles' that while not in themselves political preferences, 'surely are *political* preferences, and they are supported by research and evidence' (Currie 2010:118). They are, in summary that crime and harm should be taken seriously as a lived reality of real people in real communities; that crime, harm and suffering affect some people, in some kinds of places far more than others – that is, there is an unequal distribution of the risk and experience of harm; that macroeconomic policies that reduce inequalities of class, race and gender, that offer generous support for vulnerable families and individuals, and that counter the dominance of market relationships and imperatives, generally impact positively on levels of victimisation – that is, social democratic imperatives (see Reiner 2006, 2012a, 2012b); that micro-level interventions with families, communities and recipients of criminal justice can and do work; and that critique of repressive criminal justice measures is necessary, but so too is the need to be reflexive about the importance of intervention at all levels of analysis (Currie 2010: 113–118).

For Currie, the role of criminology is to articulate a vision about what might be done in the name of these principles, a vision about how to achieve stable and safe communities, a vision to uncover and identify the real perpetrators of crime and social harm, and a vision to deal with the genuinely troubled and damaged while simultaneously promoting social justice and human rights. We hope that in some small way this book aligns to the vision outlined by Currie in that it brings together a number of contributors whose aim is to challenge existing orthodoxies within criminology, expose and uncover neglected harms and suffering, locate them within a political economy of crime and harm, present various mechanisms for intervention, and work towards a just and better future. This final chapter offers the opportunity for us to collate the main organising themes of the book. In reviewing the application of the seven features outlined in Chapter 1 to a range of acts, events and incidents across 12 chapters, it is possible to identify ten points that we believe help support the task of making visible the invisible. These are discussed in the pages that follow. This final chapter also provides an opportunity to reiterate the importance radical criminology plays in making sense of invisible crimes and social harms through the linkage of critical theory, empirical research, and social intervention.

Making sense of invisible crimes and social harms

The first thematic point we would like to articulate relates to the importance of the term 'social harm' to understanding fully those acts and events that are neglected, hidden or invisible. While *Invisible Crime, Their Victims and Their Regulation* (Davies et al. 1999) did not limit itself to an assessment of crimes as defined by the criminal law, the foregrounding of social harm in recognition of the conceptual problems of the term 'crime' has allowed us to extend the remit and focus of the original thesis. That said, we remain cognisant of Matthews's (2009: 345) view of the importance of the 'soft' version of social constructionism. Our use of the term 'social harm' here is broadly in agreement with the observation of Hillyard et al. (2004) and Hillyard and Tombs (2008: 7–14) that the term 'crime' excludes many actions that impact enormously on the everyday lives of individuals and communities, and that a focus on crime further directs attention away from the more serious and disabling social harms of the twenty-first century. Taking a sociolegal standpoint as a departure point, the term 'social harm' allows for a much wider conceptualisation of the range of acts and experiences that remain hidden and neglected (physical, financial, economic, emotional, psychological, sexual, cultural, etc.). It confirms the failure of the criminal law and state regulation to capture more damaging and pervasive acts and events, it places at the centre of discussion the experiences and lived realities of those involved as victims and survivors and, in doing so, it offers a broader opportunity to understand the issues that are most likely to be affecting people during their lives. Moreover, as Hillyard and Tombs (2008: 17) note, it 'permits a much wider investigation into who or what might be responsible for the harm done, unrestricted by the narrow individualistic notion of responsibility or proxy measures of intent sought by the criminal justice process', and it secures opportunities for thinking afresh about what we mean by and what is possible in the name of intervention, prevention and regulation. Importantly, as the contributors to this book demonstrate, the term social harm helps encourage an iterative refreshing and refocusing of the criminological imagination (Young 2011).

The second theme running throughout the book relates to the *nature and manner* in which we have deconstructed what we mean by invisible crime and social harms. It is important to acknowledge difference as well as commonality when researching invisible crime and social harms. In support of this, we categorised the various invisible crimes and social harms as including the body, the home, the street, the environment, the suite and the state. Moreover, as was the case in the original volume by Davies et al. (1999), it remains important to understand what it is about particular acts and events that make them visible or invisible. This can be done by rehearsing Francis et al.'s (1999) original reflections thus: in some cases while the act is relatively common, perhaps because it violates the criminal law, or has attracted a range of legal sanctions, it is the *location* of it that is in some way responsible for its 'invisibility' (e.g., the home). Often, the act or event is not necessarily 'criminal' given that it does not constitute criminal law violation. In some cases the invisibility *itself* is a consequence of new locations, environs and situations (e.g., the virtual). Moreover invisibility can arise as a consequence of the victims' experiences not being acknowledged either through denial or malpractice (e.g., fraud), or because victims and survivors remain unknowing (e.g., pollution). What is certainly apparent is the limited understanding of much victimisation that takes place 'behind our backs' (Walklate 1989). As Francis et al. (1999: 236) highlight, 'Invisible victimisation often occurs because individuals do not *know* or appreciate when they are being victimised; because *others* do not understand how their actions may victimise others; or because the experiences have not been *defined* as victimisation in the formal sense'. Finally, invisibility can arise as a consequence of the form and operation of intervention, regulation and control. For example, Francis et al. (1999: 237) state that practices may operate invisibly in that 'we do not know the processes involved'(e.g., business, financial regulation); or rather that 'in some cases it can be the *consequences* of such regulation that remain 'invisible', while in other cases the *appropriateness* and/or *effectiveness* of the measures remain hidden'. An in many instances, this mixture of elements combine.

A third thematic running throughout the book is the usefulness of the original seven features of invisibility (Jupp et al. 1999) to exposing, categorising, characterising and explaining why a wide range of acts and events remain invisible in everyday life. We acknowledge, as do Davies et al. (1999) that the template and features in no way exhaust the characteristics of particular acts and events we know little about, but rather are indicative. Indeed, as was stated in the original volume, the reader may be able to detail a range of other characteristics of invisibility. Nevertheless, our confirmation of the seven features – no knowledge, no statistics, no theory, no control, no politics, no research and no panic – arose through our own re-reading of the material on the areas in question and of a desire for simplicity and clarity. Our justification for using them in this volume as an organising thematic is that we believe they are useful in mapping the contours of a particular hidden act or event; understanding their extent and impact; and explaining why they remain hidden/invisible in particular locations and at particular points in time. In noting their usefulness, we also reiterate the necessity to focus upon the seven identifying features both *independently* and *interdependently*. Thus, particular acts or events described as 'invisible' may not necessarily exhibit all seven features, and those that do will probably not do so to the same degree (Jupp et al. 1999). As we argue in Chapter 1, such features constitute a template with which to assess 'relative invisibility'. The elements of this template can be viewed as independent of one another but there is also the potential for interaction and for mutual reinforcement.

A fourth thematic concerns the dynamic interplay among politics, economics and power. Politics, for example is important both for building communities and for state-building. In whose interest the state operates, how and why, are all deeply political questions. What goes on in the name of the state is deeply political, and states have at their resources various opportunities to make acts and events visible or invisible and hidden. Furthermore, each of the contributions in this volume acknowledge the interdependencies between politics and economics. For example, a number of chapters explore the impact the late-modern transformation of the Keynesian mixed economy welfare consensus by a neo-liberal, free-market doctrine has had on our understanding of crime and social harm. (Chambliss 1975; Reiner 2012a, 2012b; Taylor 1997).

Moreover, the book provides clarity as to the ways in which the nature, degree and extent of invisibility is underpinned by different sources of power: what we have defined as the moral and ethical, the institutional and organisational, and the systemic. Each contributor to this book highlights a range of power dynamics and the manner in which various power structures impact upon the nature of invisibility. Whether it surrounds the wish of particular organisations to ensure the 'invisibility' of criminal activity and of victimisation in order to protect their 'image' and stock-market position; the power of organisations to allocate, award and refuse financial grants to organisations and individuals to undertake research; the ability of an industry to generate sufficient concern over particular activities to ensure the purchase of the latest regulatory armoury of equipment; the strength of the media to expose particular acts and events or otherwise; or the power of government to legislate, decriminalise and/or suppress information, the interconnections between power, politics and economics in late-modern society remain key to understanding the invisibility or otherwise of particular acts or events.

The discussion of politics, economics and power leads us to the fifth and interrelated thematic of the book: the historical and global contexts. Here the book recognises that for any analysis of invisible crime or social harm to give rise to a fully social theory, an understanding of the wider historic and spatial conditions that inform and influence the commission and decommission of acts, events and experiences must take place (Ruggiero et al. 1998). It is recognised that forms of crime and social harm change over time, not least as a consequence of wider social, political and economic transformations at national/transnational levels. Globalisation, for example, involving 'the adoption of governments and elites of liberalisation, deregulation and privatisation as well as the ideology and politics of laissez faire' (Chesnais 2005, cited in Lea 2010: 145), combined with changes in the movement of capital and finance, and fundamental shifts in international business (Lea 2010), has created opportunities for new forms of crime and social harm. Certainly the reader should by now be acutely aware of the importance given to space, place and time in constructing the strength and patterning of these particular features. That is, the extent to which the seven features are able to help organise thoughts around action and reaction, and the 'invisibility' of a particular act or event, is dependent upon their historical and comparative social, economic and cultural contexts (Lea 2010).

The sixth theme is methodological. Many of the contributions to this volume note the paucity of empirical evidence on the value, form and extent of the activities under review. This is perhaps not surprising in a collection on the nature and extent of invisible crimes and social harms. However, it is also partly a consequence of an over-reliance in much mainstream criminology on the tools and means of examination and measurement that are unsuitable to the task at hand. As Francis et al. (1999: 241) note, 'The two most frequently cited sources of evidence...are crime statistics (compiled by the police or businesses and organisations) and crime surveys. While official criminal statistics detail some activities..., their inability to map all contours... [of crime and harms]...has been seriously exposed'. Moreover, their construction and reconstruction has led some to view official statistics as maintaining levels of invisibility (Tombs 2000). Similarly, many have detailed the problems of industry-specific statistics (Croall 2007; Tombs 2000), while the inappropriateness of crime surveys to uncover much that is hidden is commonly accepted (see, for example, Bowling 1993; Francis 2007).

To explore much invisible crime and social harm requires in-depth exploration of both the processes and contexts associated with them. We are of the view that there is not just one method to research invisible crime and social harm. Rather, we support a mixed-method approach informed by a critical social-science-theoretical tradition (Hudson 2010), with the methods used dependent upon what is being studied, together with the objectives of the research being carried out (see Jupp et al. 2000; Davies et al. 2010; Matthews 2009). Often, however, qualitative and ethnographic approaches are the most appropriate for the researching of invisible crime and social harm for two reasons: first, they are important as means of discovery (Cosgrove and Francis 2010); second, they allow for the collection of rich data on the lived experiences of people about meanings, motivations and emotions.

A seventh theme of the book concerns the nature, form and appropriateness of intervention, regulation and control. There are three areas of discussion that are important here. The first relates to the efficacy, and effectiveness of current criminal justice and welfare approaches and their role in maintaining and/ or exposing crime and social harm. In part, it seems to us, there is a need to locate and explore policy and practice within broader critiques of the late-modern capitalist state, its institutions and control (e.g., Foucault 1976; Christie 2000; Currie 1986; Garland 2000). Certainly there is a need to explore their consequences – both intended and otherwise – and impact. The second concerns the need to explore what a progressive criminal justice system could look like in response to the uncovering of more acts and events that cause suffering and harm. In our view, it should not be the case that the identification of new or visible acts and events should automatically lead to further criminalisation and punitive sanctioning, although in some instances this may well be the case. Rather, what is required is, as Currie (2007) has suggested, a focus upon what a progressive system could look like, one that is able to respond appropriately and proportionately to all acts and events in a rehabilitative and inclusionary manner. The third area is, we believe, the re-engagement in discussions about the nature and opportunities for social intervention, what Currie (2010: 120) calls 'creating blueprints for social reconstruction'. This is particularly so given that much suffering and harm is caused by wider social, economic and political forces. As Currie (2010: 120) notes, there is a need to focus 'much more intensively on how to achieve what I like to call "deep" prevention, well beyond the pallid concept of crime prevention that dominates "as if" criminology' (Currie 2010: 120).

The term social harm not only offers a departure point from an increasing reliance on the criminal law, but also provides the ideal opportunity for creativity and innovation in developing inclusive and progressive responses to acts and events that cause harm and suffering to individuals and communities. Certainly it takes as a starting point the inefficiency and ineffectiveness of the formal criminal justice system, and moves away from the argument that hitherto invisible acts that cause harm and suffering should automatically be criminalised once visible and processed through a punitive and expensive criminal justice system. Rather, a focus on social harm, we believe, calls for a rethinking of the aims and purpose of both criminal justice and social policy in the context of developing progressive ways to support rehabilitation, peace-making and community reconstruction in the name of social justice.

The eighth theme of the book is theoretical and arises from a reluctance of much mainstream criminology to explore and embrace a fully social theory of deviance (Hall 2012). In contrast radical and critical criminological traditions have highlighted the potential of a fully social theory, and of how social harm poses a considerable challenge to the discipline of criminology (Hillyard et al. 2004). Similarly, Walklate (1989), Mawby and Walklate (1994) and Davies et al. (2007) highlight the need for a radical victimology that embraces more fully an understanding of hidden experiences in a search for a political economy of victimology. In both variations the point is the importance of the radical criminological tradition to 'open up' mainstream criminology and victimology to broader theoretical debates taking place. While we would stress caution in embracing 'fads' from parent disciplines, we are also of the view that the theoretical base of criminology has much to learn from sister discipline areas including sociology, politics, geography and social policy. It would benefit still further from a greater comparative angle also.

For us, theorising crime and social harm involves acknowledgement of the socially constructed nature of crime and harm, and the importance of understanding the nature of social categories and their co-production and co-presentation. We are interested in the way in which crime and social harm are constructed through the interaction of the state, the public, the victim and the offender (Lea 2010), in time, place and space. Crime and social harm are products of action and reaction (Lea and Young [1984] 2004; Scraton 2007; Taylor et al. [1973] 2013). The partial nature of much criminology arises from a reluctance to focus on each of the dimensions of crime and harm within a broader social, political, economic and global context. It is for these reasons that a central defining tenet of the book is that of the contribution a radical and critical realist tradition has made to making visible the invisible. This brings us to our penultimate theme: the radical criminological tradition.

The ninth theme running the length of the book is that of the importance of the radical criminological tradition in connecting theory, empirical research and intervention in making visible the invisible (Carrington and Hogg 2002). For us the purpose of radical criminology has always been to take crime seriously (Young 1997), to explore the hidden and neglected areas of study (Jupp et al. 1999; Hillyard et al. 2004), to examine the actions and activities of the state and its agencies (McLaughlin 2010), to uncover the lived experiences of the marginalised, disaffected and neglected (Davies et al. 2007; Scraton 2007) and, importantly, to deconstruct the relationship between the discipline of criminology and the concept of crime (Dorling et al. 2008, 2005; Matthews 2009). While there are variations within and between the radical criminological traditions – as is noticeable within the pages of this book – each of the chapters adheres to a tradition of exposure, challenge and activism in order to link theory, empirical research and action (see Matthews 2009) in the pursuit of a just society. Throughout we have been keen to move beyond 'so what?' criminology (Matthews 2009, 2010) into the realm of a progressive radical criminology for the future (Reiner 2012a, 2006; Currie 2007, 2010; Matthews 2014). As we have noted above, only a radical criminology with an overarching outlook to a political economy of crime and social harm can acknowledge fully the complex relations between those who do – the offender; those that experience – the victim; the state; and the local community – and deliver environmental, social and political transformation and change.

In support of our approach, each of the contributions to this volume acknowledge the relative centrality of class in understanding the relationship between victimisation, social divisions and inequality; the impact of the state and its changing nature on the definition and form of crime and social harm; the importance of the relational and structural in exposing the social, political and economic power dynamics and their influence; and the connections between the global and the local and of how they impact upon crime and cultural phenomena. Throughout, each of the contributors shares the view that intervention is not about just the implementation of strategies, but involves the operationalisation of theories and hypotheses about what might work (Matthews 2009).

The final theme relates to next steps and the future. In exploring the nature and extent of invisible crime and social harms, our approach has been to provide an organising framework that is informed by a critical social science tradition of challenging and questioning commonly held beliefs and ways of thinking about crime, harm, victimisation, regulation and crime control. While we believe we have made some small contribution to this in this current volume, we are cognisant of the imperative to develop further our understanding of those events and acts that bring considerable harm and suffering to those that experience them. In particular, we are mindful of the particular impact crime and social harm can have on the lives of those communities already experiencing hardship as a result of wider environmental, social, political, cultural and economic change (Reiner 2006, 2012b). In doing so, we would suggest that a research agenda must continue to challenge and develop in equal measure six interconnected areas of study. These are:

1. To challenge the value of legal definitions of crime, and to examine the value of the term social harm in identifying those acts and activities that cause major victimisation and suffering and yet remain relatively hidden, neglected or denied. We would share Currie's (2010: 121) view that this must include a particular focus on crimes against humanity, as well as on the wider destruction of the environment and its resources, and thus communities, through the actions of global corporations, the state and big business.
2. To challenge the crude social constructionism to be found in some versions of critical criminology, and to continue to examine the complex interplay between the offender, the state, the victim and the public in making crime and social harms more or less visible across time, place and space. While for some (Dorling et al. 2008) the focus on social harm may mean the abandonment of criminology altogether, for us it means the construction of a radical criminology able and willing to critically examine the social relations of crime, social harm and their prevention and control (Currie 2010; Lea 2010; Matthews 2010).

3. To challenge the logic and imperatives of the neo-liberal political and economic agenda, and to understand further the way in which free-market governmental projects and policies have interplayed with capital and global finance to both create the conditions for crime, victimisation and social harm, and at the same time mask or obfuscate their nature, form and impact, either deliberately or consequentially.
4. To challenge any attempt to decry the importance of understanding the historical, contemporary and global nature of social categories and their production, interpretation and development in making visible the invisible, and to further examine the intersectionalities of class, race, age and gender in order to develop a fully social theory of crime, social harm and victimisation.
5. To challenge actuarial, managerial, punitive and austere forms of crime control, criminal justice and penal interventions, and move beyond the bifurcation of 'what works' and 'nothing works' standpoints to examine progressive, proportionate and appropriate forms of peacemaking, redress and intervention that are theoretically informed, evidence-based and incorporate social and political change as much as criminal justice transformation.
6. To challenge the dominance of much Western mainstream administrative and liberal criminology, and to pursue further the opportunities a radical criminological tradition provides to making visible the invisible by linking critical theory, empirical research and social policy intervention, and by becoming truly global through a greater internationalisation of the radical tradition and its focus and dialogue.

Throughout this collection such themes have recurred in various guises in different places and in different contexts. They are not exclusive to those areas under exploration here, nor are they particularly new in that they have not been stated before. Nevertheless they remain, and while they do, numerous acts, events and activities continue to remain hidden, neglected or, in our word, 'invisible' – be they crimes and criminal activity, victims and victimisation and/or regulatory mechanisms and practices. It is therefore essential that research into hidden and invisible crime, social harms, victimisation and regulation explores these, and investigates their relations to the broader academy in terms of, for example, who gets research funding, why and in what capacity. Failure to do so, we would argue, fails to come to grips with the central feature of this volume, the relative lack of knowledge of particular acts and events and of the reasons as to why this is.

References

Bowling, B. (1993) 'Racial Harassment and the Process of Victimisation: Conceptual and Methodological Implications for the Local Crime Survey', *British Journal of Criminology*, 33(2): 231–249.

Carrington, K. and Hogg, R. (eds) (2002) *Critical Criminology: Issues, Debates, Challenges*. Cullompton: Willan.

Chambliss, W. (1975) 'Toward a Political Economy of Crime', *Theory and Society*, 2(1): 149–170.

Christie, N. (2000) *Crime Control as Industry: Towards Gulags, Western Style*. 3rd edn. London: Routledge.

Cosgrove, F. and Francis, P. (2010) 'Ethnographic Research in the Context of Policing', in P. Davies, P. Francis, and V. Jupp (eds), *Doing Criminological Research*. London: Sage.

Cowling, M. (2008) *Marxism and Critical Criminology: A Critique and a Toolkit*. London: Macmillan.

Croall, H. (2007) 'Victims of White Collar and Corporate Crime', in P. Davies, P. Francis, C. Greer (eds), *Victims, Crime and Society*. London: Sage.

Currie, E. (1986) *Controlling Crime*. London: Sage.

—— (2007) 'Against Marginality: Arguments for a Public Criminology', *Theoretical Criminology*, 11(2): 175–190.

—— (2010) 'Plain Left Realism: An Appreciation and Some Thoughts for the Future', *Crime, Law and Social Change*, 54: 111–124.

Davies, P. (2008) *Gender, Crime and Victimisation*. London: Sage.

Davies, P., Francis, P. and Greer, C. (eds) (2007) *Victims, Crime and Society*. London: Sage.

Davies, P., Francis, P. and Jupp, V. (eds) (1999) *Invisible Crimes, Their Victims and Their Regulation*. Basingstoke: Palgrave Macmillan.

—— (2010) *Doing Criminological Research* Second Edition London: Sage.

Dorling, D., Gordon, D., Hillyard, P., Pantazis, C. and Tombs, S. (2005) *Criminal Obsessions: Why Harm Matters More Than Crime*. London: Centre for Crime and Justice Studies.

Dorling, D., Gordon, D., Hillyard, P., Pantazis, C., Pemberton, S. and Tombs, S. (2008) *Criminal Obsessions: Why Harm Matters More Than Crime*. Revised edn. London: Centre for Crime and Justice Studies.

Ericson, R. and Carriere, K. (1994) 'The Fragmentation of Criminology', in D. Nelken (ed.), *The Futures of Criminology*. London: Sage, 89–109.

Foucault, M. (1976) *Discipline and Punish*. London: Penguin.

Francis, P. (2007) 'Young People, Victims and Crime', in Davies, P., Francis, P. and Greer, C. (eds), *Victims, Crime and Society*. London: Sage.

Francis, P., Davies, P. and Jupp, V. (1999) 'Making Visible the Invisible', in Davies, P., Francis, P. and Jupp, V. (eds), *Invisible Crimes, Their Victims and Their Regulation*. Basingstoke: Palgrave Macmillan.

Garland, D. (2000) *The Culture of Crime Control*. Oxford: Oxford University Press.

Hall, S. (2012) *Theorizing Crime and Deviance: A New Perspective*. London: Sage.

Hillyard, P., Pantazis, C., Tombs, S. and Gordon, D. (eds) (2004) *Beyond Criminology: Taking Harm Seriously*. London: Pluto Press.

Hillyard, P. and Tombs, P. (2008) 'Beyond Criminology', in D. Dorling, D. Gordon, P. Hillyard, C. Pantazis, S. Pemberton and S. Tombs (eds), *Criminal Obsessions:*

Why Harm Matters More Than Crime. 2nd edn. London: Centre for Crime and Justice Studies, 6–23.

Hudson, B. (2010) 'Critical Reflection as Research Methodology', in P. Davies, P. Francis, V. Jupp (eds), *Doing Criminological Research.* 2nd edn. London: Sage.

Jupp, V., Davies, P. and Francis, P. (1999) 'The Features of Invisible Crimes', in P. Davies, P. Francis and V. Jupp (eds), *Invisible Crimes, Their Victims and Their Regulation.* Basingstoke: Palgrave Macmillan.

Jupp, V., Francis, P. and Davies, P. (eds) (2000) *Doing Criminological Research.* London: Sage.

Lea, J. (2010) 'Left Realism, Community and State Building', *Crime, Law and Social Change,* 54: 141–158.

Lea, J. and Young, J. ([1984] 2004) *What Is to Be Done about Law and Order?.* Harmondsworth: Penguin.

McLaughlin, E. (2010) 'Critical Criminology', in E. McLaughlin and T. Newburn (eds), *The SAGE Handbook of Criminological Theory.* London: Sage.

Matthews, R. (2009) 'Beyond "So What?" Criminology: Rediscovering Realism', *Theoretical Criminology,* 13: 341.

—— (2010) 'Realist Criminology Revisited', in E. McLaughlin and T. Newburn (eds), *The SAGE Handbook of Criminological Theory.* London: Sage.

—— (2014) *Realist Criminology.* Basingstoke: Palgrave Macmillan.

Reiner, R. (2006) 'Neo-liberalism, Crime and Criminal Justice', *Renewal: A Journal of Labour Politics,* 14(3): 0–22.

—— (2007) *Law and Order: An Honest Citizen's Guide to Crime and Control.* London: Polity Press.

—— (2012a) 'What's Left?: The Prospects for Social Democratic Criminology', *Crime, Media, Culture,* 8(2): 135–150.

—— (2012b) 'Casino Capital's Crimes: Political Economy, Crime and Criminal Justice', in M. Maguire, R. Morgan and R. Reiner (eds), *The Oxford Handbook of Criminology,* 5th edn. Oxford: Oxford University Press, 301–335.

Ruggiero, V., South, N. and Taylor, I. (eds) (1998) *The New European Criminology.* London: Routledge.

Scraton, P. (2007) *Power, Conflict and Criminalisation.* London: Taylor and Francis.

Taylor, I. (1997) 'The Political Economy of Crime', in M. Maguire, R. Morgan and R. Reiner (eds), *The Oxford Handbook of Criminology.* 2nd edn. Oxford: Oxford University Press.

Taylor, I., Young, J. and Walton, P. ([1973] 2013) *The New Criminology.* London: Taylor and Francis.

Tombs, S. (2000) 'Official Statistics and Hidden Crime: Researching Safety Crimes', in V. Jupp, P. Francis, and P. Davies (eds), *Doing Criminological Research.* London: Sage.

Walklate, S. (1989) *Victimology: The Victim and the Criminal Justice Process.* London: Sage.

Wall, D. and Williams, M. (2010) 'Using the Internet to Research Crime and Justice', in V. Jupp, P. Francis and P. Davies (eds), *Doing Criminological Research.* London: Sage.

Young, J. (1997) 'Left Realist Criminology: Radical in Its Analysis, Realist in Its Policy', in M. Maguire, R. Morgan and R. Reiner (eds), *The Oxford Handbook of Criminology.* 2nd edn. Oxford: Oxford University.

—— (2011) *The Criminological Imagination.* Cambridge: Polity Press.

Index

abuse, 2, 8, 9, 13, 19–20, 26–27, 29, 30, 34, 37, 81–83, 85–87, 90, 92–94, 97–98, 102–118
   child, 2, 28, 110, 114
   domestic, 2, 28
   elder, 29, 102–118
   historical, 40
   of power, 189
   sexual, 9, 19, 26–41, 114
accidents, 145, 146, *see also* disasters
accountability, 14, 28, 183, 192, 202, 208, 215, 233, 239
activism, 2, 114, 116, 252
adults, *see* vulnerable, adults
agenda setting, 48, 49, 52, 58
air pollution, 14, 142–155
animal rights, 53
animals
   as victims, 53, 55, 145, 170
assault, 17, 28, 40
   child sexual, 35
   sexual, 28
attrition, 27, 31–32
Audit Commission/Office, 207, 234

banks, 8, 15, 221, 224, 228, 237
biodiversity, 62, 63, 144, 161, 165, 167, 172, 174
biopiracy, 161–175
blue-collar
   crime/criminals, 221, 223, 228
body, 13, 19, 20, 62, 81, 83, 86, 87, 89, 95, 98, 123, 126, 129, 134, 135, 137–138, 248
bribery, 227, 232, 238
British Crime Survey, 28, 30
burglary, 36, 112
business, 14, 15, 18, 47, 113, 147, 148, 149, 155, 202–207, 210, 211, 212, 215, 222, 223, 226, 227, 228, 230, 231, 233, 234, 235, 236, 239, 240, 247, 249, 253

carbon, 143
   credit, 147–148, 153
   emissions, 143, 145, 148, 149
care homes, 107–109, 113, 116, 117
CCTV, 10, 127
child
   abuse, 2, 28, 40, 110, 114
   sexual assault, 35
   sexual exploitation, 33, 35, 40
   see also vulnerable, children
choreography
   sexual, 124, 129, 130, 134, 136, 137
class, 15, 27, 29, 54, 57, 88, 89, 90, 114, 134, 192, 223, 229, 233, 245, 252, 254
climate change, 20, 44, 61–76, 142–145, 152, 153, 154, 155, *see also* global warming
compliance, 14, 146–150, 202–203, 207
conflict, 16, 17, 45, 47, 93, 150, 151, 170, 174, 179, 181, 184, 189, 192, 226, 232
conservation, 47, 71, 150, 174
consumption, 57, 66, 68, 75, 125, 127, 130, 132
conventional criminology, 2, 6
corporate
   biopiracy, 161–175
   crime, 7, 8, 15, 111, 113, 199, 213, 216, 239
   criminals, 62, 111, 113, 147, 149–150, 228, 233–234
   manslaughter, 21, 199, 213–215
   power, 145–148, 162, 171, 175
   violence, 145
corporations, 8, 11, 14, 15, 18, 21, 49, 55, 57, 59, 107, 111, 146–152, 155, 161–175, 203, 214, 221, 226, 229, 253
   multinational, 163, 165, 170, 172, 174

corruption, 14, 223, 225, 227, 228, 231, 232, 238–239
crime, *see also* abuse *and* assault
    corporate, 7, 8, 15, 111, 113, 199, 213, 216, 239
    cyber, 1, 123, 232
    definitions of, 3, 5–6, 16, 18, 102, 104, 109, 170, 253
    eco, 151–152, 155
    elder, 29, 102–118
    environmental, 8, 14, 15, 20, 21, 46, 61, 149, 154, 168, *see also* green crime
    financial, 7, 8, 21, 107, 221–240
    global, 17, 18, 250
    green, 3, 61, 143, 148–150, 153, 155, 168, 171, 245
    health, 1, 7, 21, 199–217, 222, 233
    hidden, 1, 2, 8, 9, 12–22, 27–28, 44, 91–95, 113–117, 179, 244, 248, 254
    honour, 20, 81–99
    international, 8, 18
    invisible, 1–22, 27, 29, 32, 39, 40, 44, 45, 57, 59, 64, 81, 92, 123, 126, 129, 134, 136–138, 179, 191, 215, 221, 244–255
    occupational, 7, 106, 111–113, 199–201, *see also* elder abuse *and* health and safety, crime
    organised, 154, 221, 222, 230, 231, 234
    safety, 1, 7, 21, 199–217, 221, 232
    sex, 26–41
    sexual, 9, 19, 26–41, 114
    state, 154
    statistics, 104, 105, 107, 117, 250
    survey, 106, 107, 223, 251
    violent, 19, 28, 29, 38, 83, 112
    war, 16–17, 18, 175–197
    white-collar, 7, 106, 111–112, 222, 223, 229, 230, 232, 233–238, 239–240
    workplace, 21, 39, 111, 199, 201, 206, 212–216
crime control, 2, 240, 253, 254
crimes, types of, *see also* abuse
    air pollution, 14, 142–155
    assault, 17, 28

bribery, 227, 232, 238
burglary, 36, 112
child sexual exploitation, 33, 35, 40
corporate manslaughter, 21, 199, 213–215
credit and cheque, 223
cyber, 1, 123, 232
domestic abuse, 2, 28
domestic homicide, 28
domestic violence, 2, 13, 28, 29, 85, 92, 93, 96, 97, 109–110, 116
elder abuse, 29, 102–118
embezzlement, 111, 223
female genital multilation (FMG), 82
fraud, 1, 7, 21, 107, 111–113, 123, 147, 149, 221–240, 247
homicide, 28, 84
insider dealing, 223, 226
interpersonal, 8, 27, 32, 37
money laundering, 221, 225, 230, 231, 238
pension fraud, 111–112
pillaging, 161–175
of the powerful, 7
rape, 31–32, 33, 82, 116, 192
tax avoidance, 148
tax evasion, 7
tax frauds, 227
terrorism, 20, 44–59
criminalisation, 21, 96, 103, 123, 125, 179, 199, 213, 214, 215, 250
criminals
    blue-collar, 222, 224, 229
    corporate, 62, 111, 113, 147, 149–150, 228, 233–234
    elites, 222, 223
    fraudsters, 231–233, 238
    high status, 221, 230
    paedophile, 26
    powerful, 7
    white-collar, 223
criminology
    conventional, 2, 6
    critical, 1, 2, 102, 103, 113–118, 245, 251, 253

criminology – *continued*
  feminist, 1, 2, 8, 20, 27, 28, 29, 81, 84, 91, 92, 95, 105, 114, 116, 175, 245
  green, 3, 61, 143, 148–150, 153, 155, 245
  mainstream, 1, **6**, 20, 102, 105, 239, 249, 251, 254
  radical, 1, 2, 3, 7, 8, 21, 244–255
  realist, 2, 3, 245, 252
critical criminology, 1, 2, 102, 113, 115–118, 245, 251, 253
Crown Prosecution Service (CPS), 96, 214, 222, 228
culture, 8, 30, 40, 50, 84–85, 90, 97, 127, 134, 138, 146, 154, 163, 165, 166, 171–175, 212, 216, 231
customs, 222, *see also* law enforcement *and* policing
cyber crime, 1, 123, 232

dark figure, 1, 86
deaths, 10, 17, 142–145, 152, 178, 179, 182, 193
  workplace, 199–201, 208, 213, 215–216
Director of Public Prosecutions (DPP), 34, 224
disasters, 9–11, 12, 14, 15, 44, 62, 70, 144, 145, 146, 152
disciplinary, **6**, 21, 22, 103, 171, 251, 252
disease, 142, 144, 152, 190, 200
divisions
  social, 28, 252
'doing-gender', 38
domestic, *see also* abuse
  abuse, 2, 28
  homicide, 28, 84
  violence, 2, 13, 28, 29, 85, 92–93, 96–97, 109–110, 116
drugs, 1, 35, 132, 164–166, 192, 231

ecocentrism, 154
eco-crime, 151–152, 155
ecological justice, 154
economic, 15, 16, 18–19, 21, 33, 57, 67, 75, 85, 88, 90–91, 93, 97, 108, 117, 123, 137, 150–155, 161, 164–165, 169, 171–175, 184, 201, 202, 203, 205, 211, 216, 221, 227–229, 233, 238, 245, 246, 248, 249, 251–254
  recession, 12, 161
eco-terrorism, 44–59
eco-violence, 148, 151–152
elder abuse, 29, 102–118
elites, 8, 17, 165, 172, 179, 186, 222, 223, 227–230, 237, 238, 240, 249
embezzlement, 111, 224
enforcement, 21, 57, 63, 86, 117, 126
environment, 13, 14, 19, 72, 74, 154, 161, 173, 247
  as a victim, 15, 20
Environment Agency, 17, 240
environmental
  crime, 8, 14, 15, 20, 21, 46, 61, 149, 154, 168, *see also* green crime
  degradation, 172
  destruction, 253
  harm, 14, 61, 62, 72–73, 142–143, 145, 146, 148, 152, 153, 172
  health, 15
  law, 153
  pollution, 14, 15, 20–21, 62, 63, 149, 151
  security, 154
  sustainability, 149
  terrorism, 20, 44–59
equality, 3, 20, 253
exclusion, 36, 133–134, 137, 174
exploitation, 33–35, 40, 46, 55, 58, 104, 111, 116, 124, 152, 161, 162, 166, 169
  child sexual, 33, 35, 40

family violence, 114
  see also vulnerable, families
fear, 27, 32, 40, 44, 45, 49, 50, 56–57, 58–59, 84, 88, 90, 93, 94, 106, 118, 230, 231
female genital multilation (FMG), 82
feminist criminology, 1, 2, 8, 20, 27, 28, 29, 81, 84, 91, 92, 95, 105, 114, 116, 175, 245
financial crime, 7, 8, 21, 107, 221–240

Financial Services Authority (FSA), 226, 237
food, 75, 154, 161, 165, *see also* security, food/water
forced marriage, 96
forests, 143, 153, 168
fraud, 1, 7, 21, 107, 111–113, 123, 147, 149, 221–240, 247
  credit and cheque, 223
  pension, 111–112
  tax, 226
fraudsters, 231–233, 238

gender, 2, 20, 26–41, 61, 82–84, 88–94, 97, 105, 106, 110, 112, 124, 135, 138, 170, 245, 254
genetic
  modification, 53, 57
  resources, 172–175
global crime, 17, 18, 249
global warming, 64, 66, 73, 74, 75, 142, *see also* climate change
globalisation, 18, 20, 145, 155, 181, 186, 196, 249
green crime, 3, 61, 143, 148–150, 153, 155, 168, 171, 245, *see also* environmental, crime
green criminology, 3, 61, 143, 148–150, 153, 155, 245
Greenpeace, 47
greenwashing, 15, 150

harm, 30, 32, 35, 37, 39, 40, 44, 45, 46, 47, 49, 52, 55, 56, 57, 59, 62, 82, 91, 94, 103, 104, 106, 110, 114, 117, 126, 143–145, 149, 151, 152, 154, 155, 161–164, 168–175, 181, 186, 188, 194, 196, 199–200, 207, 210, 215–216, 221, 230, 237, 244–254
  environmental, 14, 61, 62, 72–73, 142–143, 145, 146, 148, 152, 153, 172
  social, 1–22, 83, 98, 102, 103, 111, 113, 114, 117, 142, 143, 145–147, 152, 153, 171, 179, 232, 244, 245
health

crime, 1, 7, 21, 199–217, 221, 232
  environmental, 15
  human, 62, 155
health and safety
  crimes, *see also* health, crime *and* safety crime
  executive (HSE), 200, 205–210, 212
  statistics, 208–209
  victims, 7, 199–201
hegemonic masculinity, 38–39
hidden crime, 1, 2, 8, 9, 12–22, 27–28, 44, 91–95, 113–117, 179, 244, 248, 254
hidden victims, 2, 15, 16, 17, 20, 21, 27, 33, 113, 172, 175, 253, 254
high status criminals, 222, 231
Hillsborough, 9–12, 14, 15
historical abuse, 40
homicide, 28, 84
honour crime, 20, 81–99
  based violence, 81–82, 86, 91–95, 97, 98
human
  health, 62, 155
  rights, 82–84, 95, 96, 98, 103–105, 116–118, 166, 180, 225, 245
  trafficking, 9

indigenous
  knowledge, 21, 162–165, 167, 169–170
  people, 21, 161–175
injury, 201, *see also* workplace
injustice, 1, 3, 4, 7, 11, 16, 18–20, 36, 37, 40, 44, 57, 153, 165, 168, 170, 171, 175, 179
insider dealing, 223, 226
institutional power, 13, 14, 15
intellectual property, 162–164, 166, 168, 169–175
international conventions, 76, 167, 180, 227, 238
international crime, 8, 18
interpersonal violence, 8, 27, 32, 37
invisibility, 12, 17, 19–20, 30, 31, 44, 47, 64, 92–94, 105, 138, 142, 169, 172–174, 179, 180, 181, 233, 247–251

invisibility – *continued*
  contours, 4, 124
  degrees of, 3, 4, 5, 7, 13, 126, 248
  features, 4, 5–7, 11, 12, 17, 18, 168, 171, 244, 247
  relative, 2, 5, 18, 27, 124, 125, 138, 244, 248
invisible crimes, 1–22, 27, 29, 32, 39, 40, 44, 45, 57, 59, 64, 81, 92, 123, 126, 129, 134, 136–138, 179, 191, 215, 221, 244–255
  features of, *see* invisibility, features of
  regulation of, 2, 4, 8, 14, 18, 20, 21, 125–126, 132, 146, 147, 149–150, 154, 155, 179, 199, 202–206, 207, 210–212, 214–216, 231, 235, 245, 246, 247, 248, 249, 250, 253, 254
invisible victims, *see* hidden victims
izzat, 81, 87–91

jury, 225, 227
justice
  ecological, 154
  gap, 32, 36, 40
  social, 1, 3, 22, 102, 116, 186, 245, 251

law enforcement, 57, 63, 86, 117
  customs, 223
legislation, 9, 15, 96–97, 102, 114, 211, 215, 221, 228

MacPherson Report, 14
mainstream criminology, 1, 6, 20, 102, 105, 239, 249, 251, 254
Manchester, 123, 126, 137, 139
masculinity, 38–39, 134, 136–137
  hegemonic, 38–39
  structured, 38–39, 41
media, 7, 11, 15, 17, 20, 31, 37, 44–59, 68, 81, 87, 91, 96–97, 107, 134, 142, 145, 168, 170, 180, 182, 187, 196, 199, 226, 232, 236, 237, 249
mislabelling, 57–58

money laundering, 222, 226, 231, 232, 239
multinational corporations, 163, 165, 170, 172, 174

national security, 227
natural resources, 46, 152, 161–163, 165, 172–173
nature, 46, 66, 71, 73, 148, 152, 154, 162, 167, 169, 170, 172–175
news agenda, 48–49, 57
news media, *see* media
newsworthiness, 48, 49, 56, 58
nomos, 178–197
normative visibility, 178–197
NSPCC, 9, 26, 37

occupational
  crime, 7, 106, 111–113, 199–201
  deaths, 199–201
  health and safety, *see* health, crimes
    and safety crimes
offenders, *see* criminals
organised crime, 154, 221, 222, 230, 231, 234

paedophile, 26
pillaging, 161–175
policing, 5–6, 13–15, 17, 20, 31–32, 33–34, 35, 36, 37, 39, 86, 94, 97, 102, 113, 127, 132–134, 142, 154, 181, 201, 222–226, 230–231, 233–234, 239, 240, 249, *see also* law enforcement
  attitudes to fraud, 228–229
political, 11, 13, 15–16, 17, 18, 19, 20–22, 33, 45, 47, 49, 50, 56, 57, 59, 61, 69–71, 81, 85, 88, 89, 90, 93, 98, 114, 118, 142, 143, 145, 146, 153, 155, 184–185, 187, 195, 203, 204, 210, 215–216, 224, 226, 227, 238, 239, 245, 248, 249, 251, 252–254
  agenda, 4, 6, 44, 47, 49, 56, 57, 58, 203
  power, 13, 16, 59, 195
  pressure, 230
  violence, 45, 56

politics, 1, 4, **5–7**, 9, 11, 17, 18, 20, 44–59, 88, 124, 129, 132, 137, 148, 151, 155, 184, 189, 248–249, 251
  of fear, 50
pollution
  air, 14, 142–155
  environmental, 14, 15, 20–21, 62, 63, 149, 151
poverty, 144, 174, 175
power, 5, 6, 12, 13–15, 17–18, 20, 38–39, 44–59, 70, 71, 82, 85, 88–89, 92, 93, 94, 114, 143, 145–148, 152, 153, 155, 161–164, 168–170, 173, 178, 179, 180, 181, 183, 184, 185, 188, 190, 194, 196, 225, 226, 231, 232, 248–249, 253
  abuse of, 189
  corporate, 145–148, 162, 171, 175
  crimes of the, 7
  institutional, 13, 14, 15
  political, 13, 16, 59, 195
  structural, 12
  systemic, 13, 16
predator
  sexual, 26–28, 39, 41
prevention, 9, 26, 96, 97, 104, 115, 127, 154, 234, 246, 251, 254
profit, 56, 147, 150, 163, 164, 166, 167, 172, 174, 203, 204, 224, 235, 236
protest, 15, 46, 47, 50, 54, 55, 57, 70, 153, 171, 232

radical
  criminology, 1, 2, 3, 7, 8, 21, 244–255
  victimology, 251
rape, 31–32, 33, 82, 116, 192
  myths, 31, 33
realist criminology, 2, 3, 245, 252
refuges, 2
regulation, *see* invisible crimes, regulation of self, 14, 149–150, 203
regulatory
  enforcement, 209–210
  practices, 202–206
research agenda, 1, 19, 253
rights, 33, 82–84, 95, 96, 98, 103–105, 116–118, 164, 166–167, 169–171, 173, 174, 180, 188, 225, 245
  animal, 53
  human, 82–84, 95, 96, 98, 103–105, 116–118, 166–167, 180, 225, 245
  victims, 114

risk, 2, 3, 11, 14, 18, 20, 27–29, 33, 44, 49, 50, 56–57, 59, 94, 104–106, 110–113, 143–145, 148, 180, 195, 202–207, 222–223, 226, 229 231, 239–240, 245

sabotage, 54, 58
safety crime, 1, 7, 21, 199–217, 222, 233
Savile Scandal, 9, 11, 12, 26–27, 30, 31, 37–41
scandals, 7, 161, 222, 236, 239
secondary victimisation, 33
security, 17, 47, 50, 57, 188
  devices, 113
  food/water, 154
  national, 227
  social, 16, 228
self-regulation, 14, 149–150, 203
Serious Fraud Office (SFO), 222, 224, 226, 227, 231, 239
sex crime, 26–41
sex work, 13, 20, 123–138
sexual
  abuse, 9, 19–30, 26–41, 114
  assault, 28, 35
  choreography, 124, 129, 130, 134, 136, 137
  crime, 26–41
  exploitation, 33, 35, 40
  predator, 26–28, 39, 41
shame, 20, 27, 32, 40, 82, 84, 85, 86, 88–98
silencing agents, 26, 31–33

social
  divisions, 28, 252
  harm, 1–22, 83, 98, 102, 103, 111, 113, 114, 117, 142, 143, 145, 146, 147, 152, 153, 171, 179, 232, 244, 255
  justice, 1, 3, 22, 102, 116, 186, 245, 251
  security, 16, 229
solicitation, 123–138
state crime, 154
statistics, 1, 4–6, 17, 28, 86, 104–107, 117, 124, 143, 147, 168, 236, 248–250
  crime, 104, 105, 107, 117, 249
  health and safety, 208–209
structured masculinity, 38–39, 41
surveillance, 216, 233
surveys
  British Crime, 28, 30
  crime, 106, 107, 223, 250
  victims, 28–30, 105, 106
sustainability, 149, 154

tax
  avoidance, 148
  evasion, 7
  frauds, 227
terrorism
  eco, 20, 44–59
  environmental, 20, 44–59
trafficking
  human, 9

victimhood, 39, 106, 193
victimisation, 1–22, 26–41, 81, 85–86, 92, 94–95, 98, 102–108, 113–118, 123, 126, 153, 245, 247–248, 252–254
victimology, 2, 102, 114, 145, 153, 251
  radical, 251

victims
  animals as, 53, 55, 145, 170
  child sexual abuse, 28, 33, 114
  environment as, 15, 20
  health and safety, 7, 199–201
  rights, 114
  surveys, 28–30, 105, 106
  vulnerable, 26, 32–37, 40, 104–105, 112
violence, 2, 8, 13, 16, 20, 21, 27–41, 44, 54–56, 58, 81–85, 87, 89, 92–93, 96–98, 105, 108–110, 116, 123, 135, 142–155, 184, 189, 195
  interpersonal, 8, 27, 32, 37
violent conflicts, see conflict
violent crime, 19, 28, 29, 38, 83, 112
vulnerable, 3, 9, 26, 30, 32–37, 38, 40, 41, 55, 104–105, 108, 112–113, 124, 143, 144
  adults, 104
  children, 32, 33
  families, 246
  victims, 26, 30, 32–37, 104–105
  witnesses, 32–37

war crimes, 16–17, 18, 175–197
white-collar crimes, 7, 106, 111–112, 223, 223, 229, 230, 232, 233–238, 239–240
wildlife, 46, 52–53
witnesses, 32–37, see also vulnerable, witnesses
women, 2, 8, 10, 13, 15, 20, 26–41, 81–83, 85, 86, 87, 89–99, 105, 110, 111, 114, 116, 124, 125, 144, 171, 190
workplace, 21, 39, 111, 199, 201, 206, 212–216
  crime, 1, 7
  deaths, 199–201, 208, 213, 215–216
  injury, 201

Printed and bound by CPI Group (UK) Ltd, Croydon, CR0 4YY